D1569972

COYA
COME
HOME

A CONGRESSWOMAN'S
JOURNEY

COYA
COME
HOME

A CONGRESSWOMAN'S
JOURNEY

GRETCHEN URNES BEITO

POMEGRANATE PRESS, LTD.

Library of Congress Catalog Card Number: 88-061061

Hardcover Edition ISBN: 0-938817-02-7

For Pomegranate Press, Ltd:

Editor: Kathryn Leigh Scott
Copy Editor: Smae Spaulding Davis
Book Jacket Design: Tony Gleeson
Book Design and Illustrations Editor: Ben Martin
Ventura Publisher ® Consultant: Leroy Chen
Production Assistant: Kathleen Resch

Notes on the composition of this book.

The text was set in ITC Garamond; and was printed and bound by Arcata Graphics/Fairfield of Fairfield, Pennsylvania.

First Printing 1990.

POMEGRANATE PRESS, LTD.
LOS ANGELES   LONDON

Dedicated to my mothers,

Cora and Anne

TABLE OF CONTENTS

PROLOGUE

December 23, 1958

Room 250, Cannon Office Building

It was quiet for a Tuesday afternoon on Capitol Hill. Congresswoman Coya Knutson stopped work for a moment and stood on the threshold of her cluttered, bustling office suite feeling the silence of the long, empty hallway outside.

Most of her colleagues in the 85th Congress had returned to their home states for the Christmas holidays. Although office doors across and down the hall were open, the usual sounds of urgency—jangling telephones, swiftly scurrying feet—were missing.

But in the Congresswoman's suite there was a sense of hurry: hurry and get it over with, hurry so we can get on to something—someone—else. Her staff worked quickly and efficiently. No one had time to sort anything, but nothing was thrown away. Papers and pictures were spilled into crates, books and mementos tossed into boxes.

Coya moved to her desk and piled the last batch of personal papers into a wooden crate. With hands gritty from packing, she fumbled to remove a single envelope tucked into the corner of the blotter. It was one of the dime store Valu–Pak envelopes Coya herself had bought years ago for the small–town Minnesota hotel she and her husband, Andy, ran. She slid the familiar sheet of lined notepaper out of the envelope and reread Andy's letter insisting that she quit politics and return home.

Coya pictured Andy in his farmer's overalls sitting sideways on a kitchen chair, hunched over and scratching in ink on the tablet at the oilcloth–covered table. She figured there had been a bottle of rye at his elbow, too, with a shot glass next to it. As she had so many times before, Coya tried to refocus her image of the familiar kitchen scene and imagine who else might have been present when Andy wrote that note. Had someone else dictated the letter? Or simply suggested the content?

From the beginning this letter had been more than boozy, late–night sentiments from a lonely husband missing his wife. She had barely glanced at the letter when it first arrived, relieved only that it wasn't another plea for money. Now, eight calamitous months later, Andy's note was not just a pitiful plea to come home. That letter had cost her a humiliating defeat in an election she had been almost certain to win.

Her thoughts were interrupted by sounds of the mail room crew arriving to seal the containers. Each was neatly labeled with a Belgrade, Minnesota address. The boxes were destined for indefinite storage in a friend's garage. The way things were, nothing could be sent to the house in Oklee.

Her eyes slid to one thick file that had been set aside. It contained the applications and progress reports of high school students requesting appointments to Annapolis or West Point. That information would be stored in the mail room, ready for the new Congressman's arrival. Among her last official tasks of the day, she had to help one of the secretaries find a new job. Then, after that...

Her thoughts skipped to her nineteen–year–old son Terry. It had been a difficult time for him, too. Perhaps they could have supper tonight at their old neighborhood haunt, the Dirty Spoon, and discuss their future plans. Coya's secretary, Marjorie Sieber, had offered her a room in her house temporarily. Coya planned to stay there over the Christmas holiday to look for work in Washington.

Coya's eyes fell once more to the letter in her hand, which had irrevocably altered her future and Terry's. Lies. Empty, foolish sentiment. Drunken conceit. Her face burned with anger, and she knew she would live with it the rest of her life.

It was commonly assumed that the 46–year–old Congresswoman had taken her 29–year–old administrative assistant, Bill Kjeldahl, as her lover. Moreover it seemed apparent to many that the bright, aggressive young man had been the power and brains behind the throne. How else, according to the gossip–mongers, could a woman from a small town in Minnesota accomplish so much in so little time? There was no practical way to refute the absurd rumors, and Coya had steadfastly refused to dismiss an assistant recognized as one of the most capable and accomplished on the Hill. Many, even those in her own party who knew the allegations were false, encouraged the rumors because they resented Kjeldahl's influence. Coya was aware of the effect it had had on other women legislators: throughout the Capitol, wary Congresswomen were quietly replacing their male employees with females.

The sounds intruded on her thoughts and she watched the work-men pounding nails into crates. They would soon move on to the last crate, her box of personal papers. On top was a glossy black and white photograph taken at a reception in 1955, her first year in Washington. Laughing and wearing her blue taffeta cocktail dress with the scalloped cap sleeves, Coya was pictured with Speaker of the House Sam Rayburn; the senior Senator from her home state, Hubert Humphrey; and the promising young Senator from Massachu-setts, John Kennedy. Those were heady days, full of excitement, wonder and promise—and no small amount of apprehension, too. Her heart had been in her throat half the time in those days. Mistakes were costly, and she knew the press was always there to remind her of her words and show her a picture of the company she kept. After two full terms in office, she had nothing to be ashamed of.

Today was so different from the day she had moved into the House Office Building four years ago. She had been something of a curios-ity, then—the first woman from the Minnesota elected to Congress for a full term. It had not taken long to prove herself worthy of office. Shortly after she arrived in Washington, she had been appointed to the powerful Agricultural Committee. Among her accomplishments in the House, she acquired a million dollar appropriation to research treatment for cystic fibrosis. She saw her provision of the Title II Bill of the National Defense Education Act signed into law, enabling thousands of students to go to college by borrowing money from the Federal Student Loan Fund. She championed women's rights and had been quick to defend the needs and concerns of the American housewife. And just before the 85th Congress closed its session, the Federal Aid to Education was almost ready to go to committee for

review. She hoped it would be picked up by another Representative—perhaps Congresswoman Edith Green—who could carry it
through the committee process.

With a wrench of bitterness, Coya remembered what Sinclair Lewis
had said would happen when a woman with imagination and knowledge looked beyond Main Street. Like his fictional Carol Kennicott,
Coya had fled from an unhappy marriage to Washington, D.C. Unlike
Carol, Coya gained a position of power and achieved success on her
own. But when rural Minnesota voters had to decide whether Coya's
place was in the House in Washington or in husband Andy's hotel on
Main Street, they agreed with Carol's husband, Will Kennicott. After
Andy's pitiful Coya, Come Home letter was released to the newspapers, colleagues on the Hill had hailed her with enthusiasm and
approval, while her midwestern constituents had turned their backs
on her.

There were many more primaries and campaigns still ahead and
Coya promised herself she would use them to clear her name. Even
if her political career was finished, her life in public service was not
over. It was not over yet.

Coya again became aware of the hammering. Lids slammed down
on the career of a woman politician. Four years of work nailed into
six wooden crates.

Choking on the bitterness and anger she had swallowed too long,
Coya threw a jacket over her shoulders, grabbed her purse and
hurried out of the office.

Alone, and bent on eluding the waves of anguish engulfing her,
Coya rushed out the main door, across the street and over to the
Capitol Building, instinctively following the course she had run so
many times on the way to roll call. Reaching the ground level
entrance under the stairs, she caught her breath, waiting for the
elevator that would take her up to the visitors' level. There, finding
the doors of the House Chambers locked, she walked on down the
hall.

She could have found someone to open the doors to give her a
last look at the place where she had spent so much of her time in the
past four years, but she realized that what she really wanted to do was
to get out and breathe the air of the mild December day. She hurried
along the empty corridor to the main door of the Capitol, and walked
down the first of the hundred steps, slowing her pace and breathing

in the soft moist air. She stopped for a moment to look across the Mall, green even in December. Beyond the base of the Washington Monument her eyes roamed along the reflecting pool to the colonnaded Lincoln Memorial and on to the Potomac River, flowing fast from the northwest. How beautiful, she thought. All of it was so beautiful.

Coya shifted her gaze from the river to the Naval Observatory and looked past Bethesda to the open country that lay far beyond the Potomac. In North Dakota now, where she had spent her childhood, the scanty rays of the late December sun would be sending long slants of light across the snow–covered fields onto a barn. She smiled as she thought of herself as a young girl in that familiar barn, leaning close to the warm, big–bellied cow as she milked it, tilting the pail to catch every last drop. It was always easy to forget the monotony of farmwork in memories. Tomorrow when she had a chance to stop, to think, to plan what might happen next, she could begin to set aside the pain and remember the good times on Capitol Hill. She would start by recalling this peaceful moment and the beauty of Washington, D.C.

She had not lost heart. She would show them. She knew there was more for her to do, she just hadn't yet found what it was. She walked out under the portico and started slowly down the steps when she heard a voice call her name.

A press photographer held up his camera. "Coya!" he called. "Just one more, please."

Coya stopped. Standing on the Capitol steps looking far northwest to the prairie home she had loved and left behind, she posed for the photographer one more time. But without a smile.

Chapter 1

THE VALLEY
WAS HER HOME

The Nonpartisan League is the only star of hope we farm women have. It means to me that we farmers' wives who are always partners will get a more fair portion of the value of the crops we raise.

Mrs Alice M. Whitaker, Missoula, Montana
Nonpartisan Leader: February 4, 1918

It was the beginning of something new, that was certain. Coya looked up at the clear blue sky, then closed her eyes and turned her face to the sun. There was still a bit of chill in the air, but she unbuttoned her wool coat, breathed in the musky sourness of the spring morning and then sighed deeply. Winter was over.

Idly she twirled the mittens dangling loosely on the long string that wound through her coat sleeves and wiggled her toes in her rubber boots. Again she breathed deeply and wiggled her toes. Oh, yes. That last draw of breath confirmed it and certain knowledge flooded into her eight-year-old mind: there was no question that her coat was too small and her boots too tight. There was also a big hole in the thumb of one mitten.

With that same certainty, Coya opened her eyes and sized up her sister who was also standing in a puddle and squishing her boots in the mud. A year younger and that bit smaller, she would be wearing Coya's boots and coat next winter, and Helen knew it. After that, perhaps the coat would be passed on to Eva, now only four years old and wearing a hand-me-down snow suit. But the tricky part, Coya knew, was the future of Crystal's coat.

She closed her eyes and bathed her face in the sunshine. Crystal, who had just turned twelve, was almost four years older than Coya and the oldest of the four Gjesdal (pronounced yes-doll) daughters. She just might be able to wear her coat another year. It all came down to how much she grew this summer. Well, it was something to think about. When the new Sears Roebuck catalog arrived she'd look at the pictures, but it was all more or less idle speculation. If Coya needed a new coat, her parents could afford it, but if Crystal's coat fit, that was that. Her mother was too thrifty to throw money around on things they didn't need. Coya was beginning to see how things worked.

Coya sighed again and another wave of well-being flowed through her. There was an order to the day and, as sure as Monday followed Sunday, there were well established routines that carried them through the weeks and seasons of the year. Coya was beginning to recognize a pattern to life and found it agreeable and secure. There was a time for everything, and things like winter coats and new mittens would be taken care of when the time came. There was also a right and wrong way of doing things—"do it right the first time, and you won't have to do it again." Coya had already learned a sense of duty; if she did her chores first, she could play afterward. All you had to do was follow the pattern and everything would be fine.

Coya opened her eyes to the sun-washed, sparkling clean day and wondered what in the world she was doing thinking about winter coats and chores. Her bed was made, the chickens were fed, the snow had melted and she could be excused for getting dirty because the farmyard was muddy. Carefree and laughing, Coya grabbed Helen's hand and ran toward the barn, splashing through puddles and sliding happily in the slippery mud. It was a day of promise and wonder, definitely the beginning of something new.

While giggling and playing tag in the farmyard, Coya sneaked away and ran into a small building near the barn to hide from Helen. Sheltered from the prairie winds by a stand of trees, the shed was used to store firewood and lumber. Coya looked around at the weather-beaten timber walls and the shafts of dusty sunlight filtering through the cracks. The earthen-floor shed was almost empty at this time of year and she knew her father would not be stacking firewood in there again until the end of summer. The idea struck instantly—a summer house to play in! By the time Helen found her, Coya was already turning her hiding place into a playhouse.

The girls hauled out the debris and salvaged whatever useful pieces they could to furnish their playhouse. They saved the biggest, sturdiest wood chunks for stools and fashioned a table from saw-horses and boards. From the cellar, the sisters scavenged discarded pans and dishes, including a blackened pie tin, some white plates that were chipped and cracked, and mismatched cups and saucers, most of them without handles. From the dump heap behind the barn, Coya retrieved a speckled blue-enameled coffee pot with a small hole in the side and a sugar bowl without handles. They were ready to play house.

The girls went to the summer kitchen to fetch Eva, who was playing on the floor with the pots and pans while their mother baked bread. Crystal, who had to peel potatoes for dinner, wanted to come too, and Helen and Coya begged their mother to let their big sister join them. Soon all four girls were busy making the playhouse cozy.

Every day that summer, the three younger girls played house. They scraped up dust, mixed it with a bit of water, formed it on pans into various textures and shapes, and baked their pancakes, pies, cookies and cakes in the sun. When the tiny red chokecherries and berries were ripe, the girls used them to decorate their mudpies. Crystal, who had to help their mother with the housework and cooking, played with them when she could and helped them make doll mattresses out of cloth and cotton batting.

On very hot afternoons, their mother would sometimes let them make nectar from the brightly colored syrup in the Watkin's bottle, a fruit concentrate sold door-to-door. The girls took turns working the heavy pump handle to draw cold, fresh water for their drink.

The girls did not play store, office, or school. The North Dakota prairie farmhouse was their world and they knew little of life outside their home. In 1918 the Armistice had been signed ending the War to End All Wars. Two years later the Susan B. Anthony Amendment had been ratified allowing American women to vote. Republican isolationist Warren G. Harding, pledging to deal with the nation's domestic issues, replaced the Woodrow Wilson Democratic Administration that had introduced the League of Nations. Closer to home, their father had become an avid supporter of the farmer's Nonpartisan League, a radical grass roots political movement that swept through the midwestern plains like a brush fire.

However, the four young Gjesdal girls paid little heed to their immigrant parents' talk of these events. They went on from day to day, living in their own world that was more Norwegian than American. They spoke Norwegian at home, in school, in church, and in the playhouse. The family read the *Decorah Posten*, a Norwegian language newspaper, and the girls giggled over the "Han Ola og Han Per" cartoon strip. The Gjesdals thought the two immigrant farm hands were so typical: Ola and Per were getting used to the new-world inventions and machinery just as they were.

Although newly arrived immigrants to the midwestern United States faced a flat grassland that required back-breaking labor to cultivate, they wrote glowing accounts back to their countrymen of the vast, new empire they envisioned for their futures. It was fitting that the Great Northern passenger train that brought the newly-landed to their prairie homesteads was named the Empire Builder. Christian Gjesdal, who at the age of fourteen had emigrated from Stavanger, Norway, with his family, dreamed of creating his own empire on the grasslands of North Dakota.

At the turn of the century North Dakota and northwestern Minnesota had some of the last available free land that was also tillable. The roadless prairie had been divided by the government into sections of 640 square acres, with perimeters designated for roads. Under terms of the 1862 Homesteading Act, Christian, as a homesteader and head of family, filed claim on one quarter section—160 acres of public domain near Edmore, North Dakota, on the western edge of the Red River Valley. After living on the claim for five years, making improvements and becoming a U. S. citizen, he could apply for title to the land.

In 1907, the 33-year-old farmer was introduced to 21-year-old Christine Anderson shortly after she arrived from Lillehammer, Norway. Christine supported herself by cooking and waiting on tables in the hotel café in Edmore owned by Christ's older sister Cornelia, a divorcée and the mother of two children.

It was a quiet courtship. The Norwegians' natural trait of reticence is nowhere more evident than when a shy Norwegian bachelor takes a fancy to a shy Norwegian girl. Christian and Christine would not openly look at each other but kept their eyes averted, their glances down. Conversations were halting, with long pauses, and when they spoke it was about the weather or living conditions, not about love or affection. Despite the bashful courtship, Christine married Christ just one year after she arrived in America.

In late winter 1908, the newlyweds moved into their small new home on the prairie. To the Gjesdals, who had grown up in the rock-covered mountainous land of Norway, their homestead was a farming paradise. Nothing stood in the way of a steel plow except the thick, stubborn roots of prairie grass that reached six feet into the black soil. The tall grass had grown for centuries, disturbed only by the hooves of buffalo and the feet of small animals. This was rich, virgin farmland and the Gjesdals' prospects for the future looked secure and promising.

Christ had some savings from his days as a farm laborer which he used to purchase another 160 acres, giving him a half-section of land. Although field work was still done with horsepower, many new farm implements and machines were becoming available that allowed an ambitious farmer to till a larger parcel of land. Harvesters, twine binders and threshing machines benefitted farmers enormously by making grain harvesting easier and more efficient. The farmer could now harvest his wheat quickly if a rainstorm or frost threatened a newly ripened crop. Also, the railroads speeded up the delivery of supplies and transportation of crops to market.

The railroads, however, were a mixed blessing; the monopolies that controlled them fixed grain prices which cheated the farmers. Nevertheless, with farm implements that increased productivity and reduced some of the risk at harvest, farm families were better off than they had ever been. The Gjesdals, with hard work and diligent investments in farm equipment and land, continued to prosper.

On February 16, 1909, exactly one year after their wedding, the Gjesdals' first daughter, Crystal Mabel, was born. When the chubby blue-eyed blonde Cornelia arrived on August 22, 1912, her three-year-old sister couldn't pronounce her name and called the baby "Coya," a nickname adopted by everyone. Helen was born December 23, 1913, and Eva arrived June 1, 1916.

There were striking similarities between Louisa Mae Alcott's *Little Women* and the Gjesdal girls. Like Jo, Coya was spirited, strong-willed, more independent than her other sisters, and protective of her younger sisters. Little Eva, like Beth March, was never as robust as her older sisters.

The Gjesdals lived in a story-and-a-half white frame farmhouse. The four sisters shared two beds in a room warmed by heat rising from a register over the kitchen stove. Their clothes were hung on pegs in the single closet. There was no running water. When it came time to bathe, the galvanized tub was hauled in, placed by the kitchen stove, and water was poured into it from the dipper in the stove reservoir.

Their farm, unlike others around them, did have electric lights. The Gjesdals had the first Delco light plant in the county, a symbol of success in pioneer North Dakota. A gas engine drove the generator, and power was stored in a dozen large batteries. Each day Christ would go to the basement to fire up the gas engine and add water to the batteries. When the lights grew dim, it was a warning to the girls to conserve power by turning off lights around the house. The barn was also equipped with electric lighting, both inside and outside.

There was a bunk house, an old one-room schoolhouse that had been converted into living quarters for hired hands, with the big dinner bell suspended from a rack nearby. Eventually the family acquired two portable cook cars and, in the late 1920s, a large elevator was built with a 3,000-bushel capacity.

Encircled by a dirt road, the farmstead was dominated by the large two-story barn with a huge hay loft and lean-to sheds on either side. One shed was for the cows, the other was used to store supplies of various kinds, and the main barn was the horse stable. Christ was not only dependent on the horses, but so fond of them that he named his daughters Crystal Mabel and Helen Minnie after his two favorites, Mabel and Minnie.

The Gjesdal girls had pets among the farm animals, including an unfriendly rooster and a small mongrel dog, Tootsie. Once Coya stayed in the shed to watch Tootsie whelp seven puppies, and the care the dog gave them made a lasting impression. Nellie was Coya's favorite work horse. One day while her mother was washing clothes, the five-year-old ran out of the house and playfully crawled under Nellie. Coya recalls that the big farm horse remained completely still while she played underneath, as if Nellie sensed the danger. Because of these early experiences, Coya developed a life-long love of animals.

Christine sent money to her parents in Norway for steamship passage, and they soon arrived in Edmore, North Dakota, to make their home with the Gjesdals. Less than two years later, when Coya was seven, her grandmother died. Grandpa Anderson continued to live with the Gjesdals; however, during the summer months, he moved out of the crowded house to sleep in an abandoned chicken coop. A big, burly man, neat and methodical in his habits, Grandpa Anderson seemed to relish being on his own and, in his words, "getting out from under."

It was Grandpa Anderson who managed to grow vegetables and flowers in the kitchen garden. He cultivated, seeded, hoed, harvested and carried water by the bucket, eventually succeeding in providing the quantity of vegetables necessary to feed the Gjesdal family and their farm hands. He also planted a flower garden with pathways among the neat rows of colorful blooms that became a showplace for visitors. Some years later, when he died of a stroke at the age of seventy, the family came to realize how much work he had accomplished. No one had the time or the skill to maintain the gardens after his death. Coya missed Grandpa Anderson very much and the dwindling gardens were a sad reminder of his death.

The playhouse was abandoned when Coya was about ten years old because the girls no longer had time for play. Childhood was over; school and farm work occupied them. Like most farm youngsters, the Gjesdal children were responsible for chores. By the time she was twelve Coya had charge of the pigs, cattle and chickens. They kept enough cows—five or six—to satisfy the family's need for milk and butter. It was up to Coya to herd the cows in from the pasture and milk them morning and evening. If the cows wandered outside the pasture fence, it was Coya who had to find them and herd them back home.

Coya was out of bed every day before dawn in order to milk the cows and finish chores in time to wash up and dress for school. "Barn smell" was something she couldn't stand. Slopping the pigs was her least favorite job. "When I fed them, they would splash smelly stuff on me, and I would hate that, so I would run as fast as I could to the house to change clothes."

The Gjesdals raised pigs for their own use and kept just enough chickens—about one hundred—to keep the family in eggs and poultry meat for supper. Coya's mother detested killing chickens, and one afternoon when she was preparing the evening meal, she offered her daughter ten cents to kill a rooster. Coya had to climb up to the ceiling of the chicken coop and then crawl along the frame before she managed to grab the rooster by a leg. With her mother standing by for encouragement, Coya chopped off his head—and then refused ever to do it again.

Among their household tasks, Crystal was largely responsible for keeping the home clean. When company appeared unexpectedly, she tidied up quickly by throwing things inside a cupboard or behind a door—as Coya says, "the stuff did fly." Helen worked mostly in the kitchen, fetching dairy foods from the milkhouse or the cellar, churning butter, carrying water and doing the washing up. Eva stayed by her mother's side playing with dolls; not as much was expected of the "little one."

Coya's work was mostly outdoors, but the other children also helped with farm work, such as haying. It was a hot and dusty job, so the girls wore hats and long-sleeved shirts for protection against the sun and khaki pants because skirts were too dangerous around farm machinery. A long, tedious procedure, haying occupied most of the summer months from July through September as each crop matured. After the hay was mowed, it was left to dry in the sun for a few days before the hayrake was pulled through the fields to gather it into windrows. The hay loader was then driven over each windrow, piling it onto the hayrack, with the children clambering aboard and stamping down the mound to make more room.

Although the Gjesdals prospered, underneath the daily routine of farm chores and family life, Coya detected a restless tension in her parents, particularly her father. That her parents were searching for a better way of life was evident in their decision to emigrate from Norway and in their early expansion of the farm. But things weren't improving fast enough for Christ, and he channeled some of his considerable energy into the farm protest movement of the time, the Nonpartisan League.

In 1915, when Coya was three years old, a political movement had swept over the plains of North Dakota in a motion so swift, so all-consuming that historian Robert Morlan called it a "political prairie fire." Nonpartisan League (NPL) candidates took control of state offices in 1916. This wresting of power from Big Business was accomplished largely through the brilliant organization of the League's founder, Arthur C. Townley.

Expediency was the watchword of member solicitation; paid organizers and volunteers swept through the prairie from farm to farm signing up new League members. In training organizers, Townley's "applied psychology" was explicit: "Find out the damn fool's hobby and then talk it. If he likes religion, talk Jesus Christ; if he's against the government, damn the Democrats; if he is afraid of whisky, preach prohibition. . .talk, talk, talk until you get his God-damn John Hancock to a check for six dollars."[1] Organizers also labeled local businessmen—the merchant, the banker, the cream buyer—as minions of Big Business.

In 1916, 26,000 League farmers of North Dakota met in township meetings. Change was on the prairie wind. The Gjesdals, along with thousands of other farm families, took up the slogan, "We'll stick." Their sense of unity was reinforced through the *Nonpartisan Leader*, the weekly paper published by the League and an important factor in its success. Every farmer who signed up for the League became a subscriber who was thus apprised every week of developments in the protest movement. Townley's achievement of farmer solidarity was the reason for the League's success.

Prior to the 1930s, the League was the most successful radical political movement in the upper Midwest and, in the tradition of Populist, Progressive and other protest movements, was aimed at eradicating the farmers' dependent, exploited status. Many of the League's membership were recent immigrants who had been attracted to the New World by the promise of economic freedom. They were eager to defend free enterprise from the monopolies that seemed to be crushing it. The wheat farmers of North Dakota saw the Minneapolis Chamber of Commerce, the association of big grain traders and terminal operators, as their primary adversary.

Bulletins of daily wheat prices, determined by the Chamber of Commerce, were sent to all the grain elevators throughout the area, which adhered to the Chamber of Commerce's grading standards. Since there were no terminal markets in North Dakota, farmers there were, in practice, forced to sell through the Minnesota exchanges. When the farmer was ready to sell his crop he had two methods open to him: he could take it to the elevator in the nearest town, or he could ship it—at his own cost—to a commission firm in Minneapolis and take his chances on the grading and pricing there. At the local elevator, invariably under the domination of the grain monopoly, the farmer was at the mercy of the local manager who could falsely grade the grower's wheat and determine the price to be paid.

The farmer had no recourse under this arbitrary system of grading, and price-fixing agreements virtually eliminated any actual competition in the marketplace. The Chamber sold wheat to itself under different names at bottom market prices and would, the farmers claimed, heavily dock loads of grain for "impurities," such as grit. Farmers were angry with the railroad companies and chain banks which supported this system and also made money at the farmers' expense. The League called their competition Big Biz and ridiculed "the big guys" in cartoons and articles in the *Nonpartisan Leader*.

To change the status quo, the North Dakota platform of the League called for state ownership of terminal elevators, flour mills and packing houses. The League also crusaded for a state-owned bank, relief from high freight charges by railroads, state inspection of grain and exemption of farm improvements from taxation. Norwegian farmers like Christ were familiar with public control of production in the old country; it made them receptive to the League's so-called radical solutions. The Gjesdal girls, and particularly Coya, absorbed their father's strong feelings about the importance of farmers sticking together to get better prices by "beating the big guys."

The League's radicalism alarmed many people who feared its socialistic reforms threatened the American ideal of free enterprise. Thus, the Independent Voters' Association (IVA) was organized to engineer a tumultuous campaign against the Nonpartisan League, their appeal especially directed to the newly eligible voters—women. In a newspaper called *The Red Flame*, distributed free by the thousands, they printed scurrilous cartoons of League leaders, lampooning them as being antihome and antifamily.

In North Dakota, Women's Suffrage advocates had worked alongside Leaguers in 1915-1916 to bring about defeat of Republican stalwarts, and in 1917, under League leadership, North Dakota granted women the right to vote for local officials and for state Superintendent of Schools. The latter was the one seat that the NPL lost in its 1918 sweep. The loss of the one state office for which women could vote was a bellwether the League ignored, even though farm women wrote the *Leader* advocating the support of rural women at the polls. On the other hand, the IVA did notice and urged women to get out the vote against the League to "save the family." A comparison of both *The Leader* and *The Red Flame* in these years show a great difference in attitudes toward women. The League did little to encourage or educate women voters, even when women asked for political information.[2] While the *Leader* included recipes and instructions for building birdhouses in its "Farm Woman Page," *The Red Flame* printed articles and cartoons that appealed to women as upholders of the sanctity of the home and telling them—erroneously—that Leaguers were for Free Love. The campaign worked. Even farm women were unsure about voting for the League. IVA's active, vituperative campaign also attacked the League by charging that the leaders were Bolsheviks and referring to the founder as "Comrade Townley."

Yet by 1919 the League had taken control of judicial, legislative and executive branches of state government. In that year's legislative session they enacted their entire program—including the state mill and state bank—and granted North Dakota women the right to vote for all offices. In 1920, the first election in which all women could vote for all offices, the Nonpartisan League, after its five-year meteoric rise, was defeated at many levels—the lack of farm women's votes and the addition of town women's votes had something to do with their defeat. Although Leaguers knew how to motivate farmers who felt powerless against the likes of Big Biz, they did not see that they must actively help farm women overcome a reluctance to go to the polls for the first time and cast their own votes for League candidates.

Although the League's influence diminished, the farm protest movement continued its influence on the Gjesdals through the Farmers Union, an organization established in the late 1920s, with the same goal as the League's: to improve the status of farmers. By 1928 the North Dakota Farmers Union had twenty thousand members.[3] Coya became increasingly aware of how much her father learned through the League and the Farmers Union. He talked frequently about the strategy of common purpose, of presenting a unified front in holding back crops until the market improved. She also heard his lament that farmers were far too independent to stick together long.

Whenever a meeting was called to address farm problems, the Gjesdals were there. The meetings were held in neighborhood homes and, after the serious talk, coffee and doughnuts were served. The get-togethers provided the Gjesdal's with their social life. Occasionally the League would organize all-day family picnics to which guest speakers were invited. In those days the people of the prairie were willing to travel many miles by horse and buggy to hear a speech, and politics was a form of entertainment for the entire family.

In 1920 success was not coming fast enough for Christ Gjesdal. Most grain farmers, like Christ, lost money that year as prices tumbled following World War I. Impatient and discouraged by the economic setbacks, Christ and other local farmers easily fell prey to a Texas land speculator who promised riches to be made in the plains of the Rio Grande River. Enticed by profits and the warm weather, Christ made a $200 deposit on land in the tip of Texas.

When Coya was eight years old, the family moved to Texas for three winter months to live on the land Christ had bought. They left Edmore in December of 1920 for the three-day and three-night train journey. There were no sleepers on the train; they sat up all night. The girls took turns carrying a six-gallon lard pail containing food, mostly sandwiches, that Christine had prepared for the trip. She also packed a glass jar of fig jam in the bucket, and the girls got so tired of eating it that Crystal began calling it "pig" jam.

Coya remembers their new home as "a desert with only a few bits of green along a canal." The vegetation, sparse as it was, was new to them: cactus, mesquite, and ebony. Christ built a one-room cabin and bought Indian blankets for the two beds: three of the girls slept together in one bed, and Eva slept with her parents in the other. Christ also bought a Ford two-seater so they could get around.

It was a time of considerable struggle for the family because they were all accustomed to speaking Norwegian at home and among most of their friends. It was a particularly difficult period for the girls, who were enrolled in the local school. They quickly realized how poor their English was. Their mother could read and write English, and Christ had some rudimentary knowledge of the language, but neither was able to help the girls. Although Coya tried to cope, she had no encouragement from teachers and consistently failed in her schoolwork. She became so frustrated that she began to hate school.

Christ gave up his piece of land in Texas after that winter. He forfeited his investment for the property taxes due on it after deciding that the speculator had sold him "a bill of goods."[4] He figured he could do far better growing wheat back in North Dakota. Christ could not have imagined that one day an irrigation system would transform the barren desert into fertile land and that an influx of Texas settlers would grow orchards with lush fruit.

The Gjesdals returned to Edmore in time for spring planting and worked the North Dakota farm with renewed zeal, buying additional acreage as it became available. Christ managed to get better and better yields, which helped compensate for the low market prices. He also adopted improved farming methods such as rotating crops and fertilizing the soil. The expansion of the farm meant more work, and Coya did her share. In addition to her usual chores with the farm animals, Coya worked in the fields; with no sons to help him, Christ counted on Coya to get the work done.

In 1923 Christ bought three McCormick-Deering tractors at $1,000 each, an expensive touring car—a Reo Flying Cloud—for $1,100, and paid cash for all four vehicles. The Reo was a seven-passenger luxury automobile with side curtains and two jump seats. On the day they took delivery of the vehicles, Coya drove one of the newly-bought tractors in a grand procession from town to farm and, on the way, had to cross a bridge with no guardrail. Christ knew the danger but nevertheless entrusted eleven-year-old Coya, who had never driven a tractor, to manage on her own. She met the challenge and—with pride and considerable relief—delivered the tractor safely to the farm.

After that triumph, Coya was expected to fill in whenever Christ needed an extra driver to haul grain during harvest or deliver a spare part to repair broken machinery. Once Coya had learned to operate a tractor in the fields, she found that driving round after round to cut grain or hay was very boring. She compensated by singing at the top of her voice, claiming later that "if I ever got volume, I got it then." Coya was assigned the task of teaching her sisters to drive, but lost

patience with them, especially Crystal who could only drive in small
circles.

There was always inherent danger in farm labor, and Coya had a
particularly frightening experience when she was twelve. She was
driving a hay mower pulled by a team of horses when a noise startled
them and the team bolted. Very nearly losing her balance on the
awkward machinery, Coya managed to let go of the reins and jump
clear of the mower. It was also a traumatic experience for Christ, who
saw the accident from a distance and was powerless to help.

Christ's management skills and Christine's careful bookkeeping,
together with their combined ambition, accounted for the Gjesdals'
prosperity. Christ didn't work in the fields anymore, and devoted all
his time to the business side of farming. He referred to carefully kept
records of seed prices and daily market quotations to determine when
to sell his grain, and developed excellent relationships with his banker
and elevator manager.

Besides keeping the books, Christine also organized the meals.
During harvest, in late summer and early fall, she and her helpers
cooked three meals a day for twenty to twenty-five hired hands. In
the spring and early summer they employed seven farm hands and
retained one hired man for the winter months. Most of the food was
produced on the farm, but during harvest, the Edmore butcher
delivered meat every few days. Pork, beef and potatoes were the
staples at dinner. For mid-morning, lunch and afternoon breaks, pork
or beef sandwiches, cookies, doughnuts and, of course, coffee were
served. When the farm hands were working in distant fields, the cook
car was sent out, accompanied by the women and girls who would
remain all day preparing and serving food. Coya occasionally helped
her mother with the cooking and cleaning-up, but always preferred
the field work.

In her early teens, Coya took on responsibilities outside the home.
Her Aunt Cornelia had remarried and moved to a farm twenty miles
from the Gjesdals. When her aunt and uncle were away, Coya had
complete responsibility for the farm and shouldered the full load of
work: herding the animals in from pasture twice a day, milking eight
cows by hand, carrying the foamy pails of milk to the summer kitchen
and running the cream separator.

Aside from doing the dishes, which she hated, Coya loved working
on the farm, and especially in the fields where there was always much

socializing among the farm hands. She found the work itself satisfying: to see her father pleased with the day's labors and to look at fields neatly swathed gave her great pleasure. In the long twilight of the northern summer evenings, the entire family would pile into the Reo Flying Cloud and drive out to their fields to see how the crops were doing. Was the wheat up? Did the field need cultivating? Was it time to harvest? They enjoyed these daily drives and, on their return home, would be in better spirits than ever. For Christ, the trips were necessary to oversee the operation, and for the rest of the family it was a chance to be together.

Their hard work paid off. The prairie's boundless sky, the sweep of the giant fields, the perpetual shifting of weather and climate were the continuing backdrop to the dramatic change from subsistence farming in 1908 to the prosperity the Gjesdals enjoyed by the mid-1920s. By the time Christ quit farming in 1936, they cultivated 3,000 acres in different parts of the county, with some of the rented fields as far as fifteen miles from their farmhouse. However, more money and security did not effect material change in their lives while Coya was growing up. The children continued to work alongside their parents and the Gjesdals' increasing prosperity was reflected only in their luxurious automobile, the Reo Flying Cloud, and in a player piano.

Music became an increasingly enjoyable pastime for Coya, and the family encouraged her talent. Her mother had a fine singing voice, and Coya had also inherited musical ability from her father's father ("farfar") who had been a klokker—the church member who led the congregation in singing the liturgy—in his Norwegian village. Coya loved to sing, and she relished the evenings spent grouped around the player piano in the parlor singing hymns and family favorites such as "Red River Valley," "Pretty Red Wing" and "Beautiful Ohio." Dozens of long red boxes with rolls of music were stacked next to the player piano, including many classical selections, and Coya looked forward to her turn at pumping the pedals to play a roll of music. She quickly learned to play piano by ear by picking out the tunes on the rolls of music, and was soon adept at accompanying her sisters during sing-alongs when they weren't using the player.

One link with the Gjesdals' community was local newspapers delivered by mail. Aside from the Nonpartisan League *Leader*, they subscribed to two weeklies, *The Edmore Herald* and the *Devils Lake*

World, and a daily paper, the *Grand Forks Herald.* In the early rising Gjesdal household, with farm chores to do first thing in the morning, the newspapers were put aside to be read after supper.

The family trips to town were few because the farm made them largely self-sufficient. They purchased little besides flour, sugar and baking powder and, because Christine bartered butter and eggs for these staples, the grocery bill was never very big. Before they bought the beloved Reo, a trip to town with horse and buggy took all day no matter what the season. Horses and sleigh were still used in winter because the automobile could not get through the snowdrifts.

The traditional winter sleigh ride to Edmore was at Christmas, and those six miles were a very cold ride indeed. They would buy lingonberries, a fruit similar to cranberries, but smaller and deeper in color and with a more intense flavor. They were expensive and available only at Christmas-time, and therefore a very special treat. *Lutefisk* was imported from Norway for Christmas and arrived in 100-gallon wooden barrels. The storekeeper would plunge his hand into the barrel, let some of the water drip off, and then quickly wrap the fish in oiled paper. For many immigrant families, eating *lutefisk* was a remembrance of life in Norway where, in the hundreds of years before refrigeration, cod fish steaks were dried in the autumn and stored in the rafters of country homes. Then, as needed, the dried fish was soaked in lye, or *lut,* until reconstituted and finally washed in fresh water before being simmered in boiling water.

Home life on the prosperous Gjesdal farm was not all happiness. Coya's world turned dark the day she realized that her dad drank too much. Christ was a solitary drinker. During her early childhood Coya was not aware of the problem, but when she was about fourteen, she watched in horror as her father flew into a drunken rage, making Christine cry with his shouted insults. After that incident, Coya became more aware of Christ's erratic behavior and realized it was because of his drinking. He kept the liquor in the basement near the electricity-producing Delco plant. He made regular trips to the cellar on the pretext of checking the batteries, and each time he took a nip of whisky. Because the bottles were similar, Coya began to worry that he wouldn't be able to distinguish between the liquor and the acid used for the Delco light batteries.

Christ also stashed liquor in several places in the machine shed. When Christ was drunk, he would verbally abuse Christine. He never hit her, but his rantings were loud and hurtful. Christine would ignore his behavior as long as she could, trying not to show emotion or say anything that would prolong his outburst. Finally, when his harangue became too much for her to bear, she would burst into tears. She hoped that as long as she could pretend nothing was wrong, others would not notice. But eventually, as his drinking problem became more apparent, it also became general knowledge in Edmore.

Christine's primary concern was keeping the family together; moreover, during Christ's binges, it was up to Christine to maintain the farm's production. When Coya realized the extent of her father's alcoholism and the effect it had on his family, she vowed to never drink liquor of any kind.

Economically, the Gjesdals continued to fare well. They were frugal with their cash reserves and, when the Great Depression came, they didn't suffer as many other farm families did whose resources were overextended. They talked about the Wall Street crash at home and, although one of the Edmore banks closed, the crash barely affected the family. Drought was a greater concern for Christ during that time, with its attendant heat, dust and plagues of grasshoppers. As Coya noted years later, "When the grasshoppers stopped by for lunch, most of the crops went with them."

Coya attended the township school, a one-room building in the country about a mile-and-a-half from their farm. One teacher taught the nine pupils there who ranged from grades one through eight. Coya had little trouble with reading, geography and history, but arithmetic was very difficult for her. "It was as if blanks were in front of my eyes," she said later. "I must have missed something, and I just didn't know how to get through it. My parents didn't know how to help me, and didn't have time anyway."

Somehow she managed to "get by" in school, but when she reached the seventh-grade a new teacher, Juliet Ivesdahl, made a difference for her. She worked with Coya throughout the seventh and eighth grades, often tutoring her at home, and by the end of her eighth-grade year, Coya was a good student. It was a turning point for the teenager because she was able to pass the state tests, which at that time were of great importance: a student who did not pass the eighth-grade tests, could not go on to high school.

During grade school Coya was a rather serious young girl but without any particular ambition. Her life was disciplined by school, church and her chores on the farm. Coya was always an overweight youngster. Because she worked outdoors and did a great deal of lifting, Coya ate more than her sisters and developed a robust, strong body. Her figure was quite well developed by sixth grade, and because of that the boys teased her on the playground. As she entered her twelfth year, she began to feel uneasy about her weight. During these adolescent years, Coya regarded herself as ugly. Until she was thirteen, she wore her hair in an unbecoming "King Tut" style— cropped short in a straight line from ear tip to ear tip with long straight bangs across her forehead. All four sisters wore their hair chopped in this fashion, patterned after the ancient Egyptian hairstyle, but it was a particularly unflattering haircut for Coya's round face.

Winter posed special problems for pupils and teacher. Normally the girls walked the mile-and-a-half to school, but in the winter the hired man drove them in a cutter drawn by horses. On especially cold mornings, their mother would place heated stones or a heated iron wrapped in paper at their feet. By the time they got to school, their lunches would be frozen. The first thing the girls did when they arrived was to place their lunches on the stove in the center of the schoolroom.

Indoor plumbing was installed in the school during the early 1920s. It was a luxury that many people were unfamiliar with in their own homes, and Coya remembers that the first flush toilet she saw was in the country schoolhouse. Toilet tissue was also provided, replacing the old rural standby, discarded copies of the Sears Roebuck catalogue.

The Norwegian-American culture was a continuing influence on young Coya. She lived partly in the land of her parents because Christ and Christine lived between memory and reality, with the wealth of two cultures and the divided loyalty that it caused. To assuage their homesickness many immigrants, like Coya's father, sought land where other Norwegians had settled. The *bygdelag* and the church were both extensions of the parents' life in Norway.

A *bygdelag* is an organization of emigrants from a particular rural district of Norway who gather to preserve the heritage and strengthen the bonds with their home region. At *lag* meetings, a spirit of fellowship is foremost; in addition, nostalgia for childhood homes, food, celebrations and dialect is expressed in programs of speeches and music. The Gjesdals were active in Christ's *Stavanger-Vest Agder* and Christine's *Gudbrandsdalen bygdelags*. Besides meeting in their villages, groups of *bygdelags* would gather for *stevnes,* or conventions. The first time that Coya was ever paid for singing was at a *stevne* to celebrate *Syttende Mai,* or May 17th, the Norwegian Independence Day. Dressed in *bunad,* the traditional dress from her family's region of Norway, fourteen-year-old Coya sang a song in Norwegian at the *stevne* in Petersburg, North Dakota. She was thrilled to be paid two dollars for her performance.

The Gjesdals were also active members of the Norwegian Lutheran Church in Edmore. Most Sunday mornings the family went to worship services. Christ attended less regularly than Christine and their daughters. Christine was also active in the church-affiliated Mission Society and Ladies Aid.

On Sunday nights Coya and her sisters attended Luther League meetings, the organization for adolescents in the church. The strict Lutheran Church outlawed dancing and drinking; the young people found their fun in getting together for high-spirited games after the program of devotions and hymn singing.

Unlike other churches—such as Catholic or Methodist churches started as missions by European or eastern United States church bodies—midwestern Lutheran churches were begun by the Norwegian pioneers themselves. Norwegian Lutherans were on their own the moment they left home because the clergy in the state-run churches of Norway showed scant interest in the emigrants streaming to the American Midwest. The vigor of the budding Lutheran congregations in the United States and their fervor in adapting to their new country can be explained by the fact that Norwegian immigrants had to fend for themselves in funding and organizing their churches.[5] Once the congregations were formed, their very existence depended upon members taking active roles in governing the church and raising money to support it. Individual congregations had needs they could not meet alone and gradually they banded together in "synods"— councils comprising groups of regional Lutheran churches. There were numerous synods, each expressing subtle differences in religious persuasion, because immigrants tended to bring with them the controversies dividing the high and low churches of Norway, as well as their regional rivalries.[6]

A landmark was the 1917 merger of three of the largest Norwegian synods to form the Norwegian Lutheran Church Synod. As the church parishes merged, their outlook shifted for the sake of the young people to end their isolation as a church exclusive to Norwegians. The chief sign of this Americanization was the change from the use of the Norwegian language to English in the worship services.

After Pastor R. A. Oftedal's arrival in Edmore when Coya was thirteen, she began to accept American ways in place of Norwegian customs. In accordance with the Synod's decision to use English, Pastor Oftedal actively campaigned among the older members to adopt English as the language of the church for liturgy, hymns and sermons, and to inaugurate confirmation classes in English for young people.

The pastor was influential in other ways as well. When Coya and her friends in the confirmation class went to the parsonage to help Mrs Oftedal with church mailings and secretarial work, Pastor Oftedal would often complain about the lack of running water and indoor plumbing in their home. It was hard for the children or their parents to understand the minister's dissatisfaction. They took using an outhouse in 30-degrees-below-zero weather as a matter of course.

During her playhouse years, Coya conducted her make-believe household—and her life—according to the familiar Norwegian customs. By her early teens, although the Norwegian heritage would always be an integral part of her, she also had a strong identity with American ways. The many progressive changes within her family and in her community and church during her youth kindled a glimmer of "the sky is the limit" spirit in her.

Coya, who had been a child capable of assuming responsibility beyond her years, was now a young woman. For farm children around Edmore, graduation from eighth grade and Confirmation at church marked their coming of age.

Chapter 2

THREE SCHOOLS
ON THE PRAIRIE

I want my child to do the greater things his heart prompts him to do, unhampered by ignorance, graft and partisan dealing.

First Place winner of the contest,
"What Does The League Mean To Me?"

Nonpartisan Leader, January 7, 1916.

When Coya and Helen moved into the Edmore Hotel in the late autumn of 1927, Coya was reminded of her childhood when she and Helen had played house together in the woodshed on the farm. But this time the whole family pitched in to help the girls set up living quarters. It wasn't to be a make-believe playhouse for children, but an apartment where 14-year-old Helen and 15-year-old Coya would live during the winter months while they attended Edmore High School.

Helen lugged in an orange crate containing plates, a tray of silverware, glasses and cookware, and unloaded it onto the bed. Then she set the crate on end and, using the middle divider as a shelf, arranged the utensils inside the crate. Coya did the same with the crate full of foodstuffs. When she'd finished arranging them on the two shelves, the array of meatballs and fruit sauce in Mason jars and the loaves of bread wrapped in wax paper looked like the pantry at home.

Eva threaded a string through old flower-sprigged curtains and hung them across the two boxes. Now the drab hotel room not only had kitchen cupboards, but a bright, cheerful corner that reminded the girls of home. Christ set up a three-burner kerosene stove and pounded nails into the wall to hang pots and pans. Christine set a can of milk and butter wrapped in wax paper on the outside window sill and admonished her daughters "to store the food on the inside sill at night or it would freeze." Eva and her mother made up the double bed with fresh sheets and blankets, and Christ lit a roaring fire in the wood-burning stove.

By the time Eva and the girls' parents climbed into the Chrysler to return to the farm, the room was cozy and smelled like home. Every evening the girls would bank the fire, and in the morning Coya and Helen would take turns climbing out of a warm bed into the cold room to start the stove again.

In the 1920s it was not easy for farm children to attend high school. Winter temperatures often plummeted to minus-30 degrees; sleighs and cutters were too slow—and cold—for daily transportation to and from school. Nor could many parents afford to pay room and board for students to live in town. The Gjesdals did have the means and went to great lengths to provide their daughters with a high school education. During the early autumn and late spring months the girls drove the family car on the daily twelve-mile return trip to town. By November, however, when there was a chance the roads would be blocked with snow, the Chrysler was put up on blocks and the radiator drained.

During Coya's freshman year, she had lived with her mother and Crystal, who was a senior, in a one-room abandoned school-house the Gjesdals rented a block from the high school. Beds, a table and a few other pieces brought from the farm created a makeshift home. Clothes were hung on nails and pegs; Coya had one "decent dress," which was among the few garments worthy of a coat hanger. Despite the small entryway designed to reduce icy drafts from the front door, Coya and Crystal found the poorly insulated building "the coldest place on earth." There was a bathroom near the front door and the old cloakroom had been converted into a kitchen where Christine prepared meals—including a hot lunch when her daughters raced home at noon. While the girls were in school, Christine worked on her quilts.

The following year, Christ decided he preferred to have his wife at home. Christine agreed with him that Helen and Coya could look after themselves in town. The girls liked the new arrangement and felt very grown up, although they weren't really on their own. Their Aunt Cornelia and her husband, who owned the hotel, lived upstairs. Two other high school girls lived in another large room on the first floor and, because the walls were thin, the girls sometimes sang together while they did their kitchen chores.

Every week Christine would choose a mild winter day, ask the hired man to hitch up a horse to the cutter and travel into town to bring the girls food. Most days Coya and her sister made cold sandwiches and perhaps would eat an apple from the barrel when they came back to the hotel room for lunch. When they cooked, the girls soon learned not to turn the stove's kerosene burners too high because the fuel smoked and left a dirty residue on the hotel walls. Occasionally they would treat themselves to a hot meal at Strand's Café near the hotel.

The high school was very small; total enrollment for all four grades was 75 pupils. By the time Coya reached the upper grades, she felt she had become a good student, yet she earned only mediocre grades. Coya attributed the poor showing on her report card to her limited reading background and the fact that she hadn't yet discovered how to study and apply what she had learned.

Coya had always looked up to her teachers as role models and friends. Of particular influence in high school was young Miss Schaeffer, who taught music. Since there were always school concerts and other programs to prepare, Coya often spent her after-school hours with Miss Schaeffer, preferring her company to that of girls her own age "who played sports and acted silly." Miss Schaeffer encouraged both Coya and Helen to join singing groups, and one year accompanied them to the State Fair where they performed.

There were no organized social groups: school dances were forbidden, and Coya did not go out with boys. Helen, who Coya thought was the best-looking in the family, did date, but Coya considered herself too plain to attract any attention from boys. While she had girl friends in school, she didn't associate much with them after school hours unless they were all preparing a school program. The Gjesdal sisters' social life centered around Luther League, as it had around Confirmation classes in earlier years.

The one extracurricular area in which Coya did excel was music, and in high school she became a soloist in the choir. The Edmore choir always participated in the state music contest, but generally lost to the choir from Starkweather. Coya tried to conceal her dread of competition, but suffered bouts of stage fright before every performance. She managed to sing her solos successfully even though she felt emotionally unprepared to face an audience. At sixteen, she started piano lessons and found her slow progress discouraging. Learning to read musical notes was as difficult for her as studying arithmetic and, because she had originally learned by ear from the player piano, this transitional phase was especially disheartening.

The girls liked being on their own, and yet they were delighted when someone arrived in town to bring them home for the weekend so they wouldn't miss out on the family fun. On one such excursion home in 1928, the girls found Aunt Cornelia's step-son, Elmer Thompson, visiting the Gjesdal farm. The youngster attended Wahpeton Science School and, because he loved to tinker with things, he had built a little radio, about eight inches square, to present to his Uncle Christ's family. The Gjesdals had never seen such a thing and everyone gathered around close to the young man as he set up his contraption. Elmer screwed an adapter into a ceiling light socket and piled books under the radio so its cord would reach the socket. When he plugged the radio in, the tubes lit up and Elmer put on the headphones. Coya could hear squeaks and squawks as Elmer fiddled with the dials until, at last, he found one station that was clear.

Everyone took turns listening and when Coya was given the headphones, she heard a beautiful soprano voice singing, "When the Moon Comes Over the Mountain." Coya got goosebumps. She could hardly believe that sound was coming all the way from the East Coast to their parlor in North Dakota. Coya was supposed to go upstairs to do her homework, but she forgot all about school and wouldn't budge until the wonderful program signed off.

Later Coya learned that the singer's name was Kate Smith. At eighteen, she was only a few years older than Coya and had her own radio program. Coya thought her chest would burst when Smith's remarkable voice soared into the high notes. She ached to sing along and sometimes did, but very softly, not wanting anyone else in the living room to tease her. Coya learned all she could about her idol, and discovered that the sponsor of her radio show paid her thousands of dollars. To be paid so much money for singing seemed impossible to Coya, especially once she learned that Smith had not even had voice lessons. Miss Schaeffer, who thought Coya had a beautiful singing voice, had been urging her pupil to take lessons.

Coya longed to be like Kate Smith and considered their similarities. Kate Smith looked like a schoolgirl, too, and no one seemed to mind that she was stout; in fact, she was much heavier than Coya. But Coya couldn't even imagine what it must be like to sing on the radio, much less to perform on a nationally broadcast show. Elmer talked about radio as the coming thing, so perhaps one day she would get her chance. It was a daydream she kept to herself.

The biggest event of the year at school was graduation. During her junior year Coya was one of those chosen to wait on tables for the senior banquet, and it was then that she learned some of the rudiments of dining etiquette—for example "serve from the right and remove from the left." For farm kids accustomed to family-style dining habits, this was an introduction to worldly social graces. The following year, her senior class wore their best suits and dresses for dinner and they were served by underclassmen. It was the grandest occasion of her young life; the tables were set in a rectangle in the gymnasium, small nut cups with mints were at each place setting, and someone gave a speech before dinner. The menu included an elegant entreé of "veal birds on a stick."

Coya graduated from Edmore High School in 1930. Although her class of eight voted Coya "Most Likely to Succeed," she wasn't particularly inspired or ambitious. At the time, her school years represented nothing more to her than hard work that had to be gotten through, perhaps an attitude toward life that was acquired doing the year-around, never-ending farm chores throughout her youth.

About the time Coya finished high school, she saw her father's alcoholism getting worse, with her mother, as always, the scapegoat. In addition to tongue-lashings, Christ vented his rage in chilling practical jokes. During one drunken binge he left a slaughtered baby piglet on the table next to the dinner bell where Christine customarily sat. Once when guests were expected for dinner, Christ placed a pen and a piece of rubber that resembled spilled ink on Christine's best white dinner cloth. On another occasion she discovered a pool of blood that was, in fact, another rubber cutout left on the dining table. These cruel pranks reduced Christine to tears, and crying seemed to be the only means to temporarily stop his tirades. Another time Christ's ugly, drunken behavior caused Eva to become hysterical, and the child's reaction subdued him. Those were Prohibition years and his method of acquiring the whisky was a mystery, though the family assumed he had a connection in town. On at least one occasion, Helen remembers seeing a woman drive into the farmyard to deliver a number of bottles to Christ.

Most of the time, Christ had an agreeable relationship with his children, but there was a change in his attitude toward them as they matured. It seemed to the girls that once they started to develop minds of their own and pursue their own goals, he was less tolerant of them.

Neither parent showed much affection toward the children. Coya wondered about "kissing." She had heard about it often enough in songs on the radio. One day Coya said to her mother, "I never see you and Dad kiss each other." Her mother did not answer, but gave Coya a strange look. Then she quickly walked across the room and kissed Christ on the lips. The scene made a strong impression on Coya; it was the only time she saw affection between them. Her parents did not hug or kiss their daughters either.

For many years Christine had longed to return to Norway for a visit. By 1930 the girls were old enough to take over their mother's farm duties for the summer and there was sufficient money available for Christine to realize her dream. In the weeks prior to the transatlantic sailing, a relative stayed at the farmhouse sewing new dresses for Christine's return to her homeland. With her cousin Carrie, Christine sailed on the *Stavangerfjord* for a three-month visit to her brother, a silversmith living in Lillehammer.

Christ had little interest in visiting Norway and, besides, someone had to stay home and work the farm during the summer months. However, in June, shortly after Christine left for Norway, Christ unexpectedly announced that with the crops planted and the hay not yet ready for mowing, he could afford to take a week off. On a day's notice, he packed Crystal, Coya, Helen and Eva in the family's new Chrysler touring car and headed west for Yellowstone Park. It was not an easy trip. Once Christ decided to go, the girls had little time to prepare.

Coya did most of the driving—on dirt or gravel roads—and when another car passed, billows of dust engulfed them. It was hot and dirty in the car, yet Christ was uncomfortable unless the windows were fully open. Moreover, Christ chewed tobacco. The girls considered it a filthy habit, and were appalled when he spit the warm sticky liquid out the car window. Even worse, he kept a covered mason jar in the automobile to use as a spittoon.

When they reached the mountains, the narrow, twisting roads without guard railings were too much for Christ. His face was green with fright and he insisted on riding in the front seat with his hand gripping the emergency brake. He did not drink during the entire week of travel.[1]

The family had long been aware that Christ's drinking bouts coincided with the mechanical breakdown of farm machinery. Worry, tension, and his frustration when things were beyond his control were among the triggers that precipitated binges. He regularly traded in his automobiles for new ones—mostly four-door Chryslers after the Reo Flying Cloud—every year or so, but Christ was so concerned that his new Chrysler might break down on their vacation that he decided to bring one of his mechanics along on the trip. The mechanic and his wife followed closely behind in a second car and they later complained to Christ that "we ate your dirt the whole way."

At night they stayed in tourist cabins and prepared meals on the familiar kerosene stove they had brought from home, eating mostly fried eggs on tin plates. By the time they got to Old Faithful, Christ had seen enough. They turned around and drove back home.

On their return, the girls resumed their farm chores. During the three months Christine was in Norway, Coya taught herself to play the guitar by listening to records and strumming along. She soon learned to play by ear and accompanied herself while singing songs such as the "Missouri Waltz."

By 1930 the Gjesdals could afford not only new cars and a transatlantic voyage but, in the depths of the Great Depression, could also afford to send their daughters to college. Crystal attended Mayville State College and later taught school in Devils Lake. Helen earned a degree at Concordia College and taught at a township school. At that time it was possible to get a teaching post without a four-year degree, and both sisters taught in North Dakota for a few years before returning to school for further training. Eva graduated from Pacific Lutheran College in Tacoma, Washington. While there, she contracted a virus that left her in weakened health for the rest of her life.

At that time only about one-fourth of the high school graduates in North Dakota went on to higher education.[2] The Gjesdal sisters were the only girls who left their small town to attend college. Coya chose Concordia, a four-year liberal-arts college in Moorhead, Minnesota, because it had a good music department. In September 1930, Coya's parents drove her to the depot in Devils Lake where she boarded a train for the 140-mile journey to Moorhead.

Concordia College, owned by Upper Midwest Norwegian Lutheran synod congregations, had an enrollment of 430 students. The school, like other Norwegian Lutheran colleges, was religion oriented, with many of the male students enrolled in pre-seminary courses. It was also an effective channel for preserving Norwegian heritage while introducing the sons and daughters of immigrants to mainstream American life. During the 1930s, Norwegian was spoken on campus, Norwegian plays and programs were produced, and the Edda Society, a club that studied Norwegian culture, was established. Shortly after Coya graduated, the Edda Society was disbanded and Concordia emphasized the American rather than the Norwegian tradition, while preserving its bonds with the Lutheran church.[3]

Coya chose music as her major field of study, and enrolled for private piano and voice lessons with Professor Clara Duea, who became a good friend. Coya paid the additional fees for music lessons and the rental of practice rooms by using the checkbook her father had given her when she left for Moorhead. The Gjesdals' generosity enabled Coya to pursue her music studies without any financial worries. She was one of four freshmen selected to join the prestigious 45-member Concordia College Choir, where she was chosen as a soloist. The choir became the core of her existence; it gave her a sense of pride and accomplishment, and satisfied her emotional need to "belong." She liked the musical director, Herman Monson, who composed some of the choir's music.

Coya continued to suffer from stagefright. During her junior year she was required to give both a piano and a vocal recital and she was petrified on both occasions. Each November and April during her four years in college, Coya toured Minnesota, Wisconsin and North Dakota with the Concordia Choir. Traveling through the Midwest in two squeaky buses, the singers often endured severe weather conditions ranging from frigid temperatures to treacherous dust storms. The Western North Dakota dust bowl produced winds so fierce that the students had to protect their faces with thick scarves, and they often arrived for a concert with parched throats, their clothing stiff with grime. Nevertheless, the hardships of touring were worth it for Coya: "I still remember marching into concert halls as a member of that highly regarded choir."

Coya began fulfilling her student-teaching requirements by working in the afternoons as an apprentice to a Moorhead High School music and English teacher. Jobs were scarce during the Depression, and to improve her chances of finding a teaching position, Coya had chosen English as a second major. At that time English and music were the two most acceptable fields of study for women who wanted to become teachers in secondary schools.

In college, Coya continued to make friends with her teachers rather than her fellow students. She considered college social life "childish and a waste of time." During freshman initiation week, Coya and a young male student were required to scrub dormitory steps with a toothbrush. Both found the experience mortifying. Even worse, as they moved from doorstep to doorstep, Coya realized that she was blushing—"not just a little bit, but like crazy. I wanted to appear self-possessed and above it all, but I couldn't stop blushing."

Coya still did not date. With her strong and independent nature, she figured that "I probably seemed too self-sufficient to appeal to men. I didn't bother trying to imitate what other girls did to make themselves more alluring. I didn't fuss with my hair or rouge my cheeks. Men would have to like me the way I was or it wasn't worth the trouble. The truth is that, like a lot of young people, I was shy and awkward about the whole business of dating."

Her college activities other than choir were limited to women's organizations: she was an officer of the women's governing board and the student council that worked with Dean Frida Nilsen on planning social activities and monitoring dorm violations. The doors of the girls' dorm were locked at 10 p.m. weekdays and 11 p.m. on Saturdays. If a resident was consistently late for these curfews, the women's governing board could "campus" her and curtail her free time. Girls were also disciplined for being too noisy in the dorm. The boys' dorm had no curfews.

Each day Coya attended the required chapel services, held upstairs in Old Main. She went regularly to meetings of the Lutheran Daughters of the Reformation (LDR), a group organized by Frida Nilsen, which attracted members much like Coya: Norwegian girls from small towns and farms who were devout in their faith. Coya was also active in a similar club of sixty members, the Mission Crusaders, a more pious group who demonstrated their dedication by setting regular meetings at 8 o'clock on Sunday mornings.[4]

Coya's college experience was an extension of her church life and Norwegian background at Edmore. She paid little attention to politics, except to note which major office holders were elected. With other students, she listened to the radio in her dormitory living room and heard the election returns that declared Franklin D. Roosevelt President of the United States.

North Dakota politics in the 1930s revolved around William Langer. A popular country song declared that the Thirties belonged to "Wild Bill" Langer because no one else wanted them. In 1932, Langer was elected Governor of North Dakota for a stormy term that involved court battles and charges that he misused the powers of office. In the spring of 1934, he was indicted by a federal grand jury on charges of openly soliciting and collecting money for political purposes from federal employees to buy *Leader* subscriptions. They were asked to pay an amount equal to 5% of their annual salaries, a political "tithing." In spite of his conviction after a six week trial Langer campaigned vigorously in the next election and he and League candidates won easily. When the State Supreme Court removed Langer from office, many of his supporters, including Christ Gjesdal, considered him a martyr for being "tarred and feathered" by the legal system. In December 1935 Langer was found innocent. In 1936 he ran for governor again and won. Langer became a hero to the Gjesdals and thousands of other farmers; however, his daring, aggressive course earned him the enmity of Conservatives and some segments of the old Nonpartisan League. Langer's tribulations were a frequent topic of conversation at the Gjesdals' dinner table.

By the mid-1930s, the League, though diminished, retained some of its influence. The Farmer's Union in North Dakota was still successful, turning over $5 million of business annually, and supplying local cooperatives with feed, fertilizer, twine, fencing, seed and groceries. The Gjesdals continued to be a part of this cooperative, and Christ regularly attended meetings.

When Coya returned home for the Christmas holidays in 1931, there was a surprise awaiting her. Her father made no mention of it when he met her at the train and drove her to the farm, but the first thing Coya saw as they arrived home was a little boy standing on the front steps of their house. The toddler was wearing a hat so big that it fell down over his eyes.

"Whose little boy is that? " she asked.

"Ours, I guess," replied her father, turning to see her reaction.

Coya was astonished. Christ told her that Richard Monroe was the youngest of six children who had been neglected by poverty-stricken parents. When the parents separated, it was discovered that the children had been living in a cold, dark house and been given little to eat. Families in the community volunteered to care for the youngsters—among them the Gjesdals—and each child had been sent to a different home. Christ, 56 years old, and Christine, 44, lavished attention on the fifteen-month old child, showering him with hugs and kisses that they'd never bestowed on their daughters. The boy had been nicknamed Richie, but the Gjesdals soon began calling him Sonny. The entire family doted on the little boy.

During the summer months Coya returned to the usual routine on the farm, working from dawn to dusk driving a tractor, feeding animals, cooking and serving meals to the farm hands and laboring in the fields. However, there was fun to be had as well, and new young people to meet. Often, when the hay was stacked and the harvest finished on their own farms, young men and women would seek work on other farms throughout the grain-growing region of Minnesota and North Dakota. Coya enjoyed their banter and joking, but did not pay special attention to any one worker until she met Andy Knutson.

In the summer after her freshman year in college, Coya, eighteen, and Andy, twenty-one, became more than acquaintances. Andy had been working for Christ during four harvest seasons, but he had been "just one of the bunch" to Coya until that summer.

She had gotten to know Andy when he came around to see his sister, Anna Knutson, who worked with Coya preparing food and cleaning up the cook car. Although Anna was nine years older than Coya, the two women were compatible and often played the card game Whist during the long summer evenings. Sometimes Andy would pull up a chair and sit backwards on it, talking about the local news from the Knutsons' hometown of Oklee, Minnesota. Coya noticed that Andy came around more and more often, both in the evening and during the day when the women were washing up after the noon meal.

Andy was well liked and loved to joke, but he was also surprisingly shy and retiring. Coya would catch him looking at her, and she found herself blushing, the heat stealing up her neck and onto her cheeks. She thought she saw Andy blush, too, but she could not tell for sure because his face and neck were already reddened by the wind and sun.

As they got to know each other, Andy teased Coya mercilessly when she delivered lunches to the men in the fields. When the two worked together hauling hay to the barn, there was much joking and playful banter between them. Coya liked having a young man pay attention to her. Once Andy borrowed a car and they drove to Devils Lake to see a movie and have a soda.

The following evening, Coya and Andy walked from the barn to the cook car after the chores were done. They laughed together about the balky cow that had stuck her foot in the pail and kicked it over while Coya was milking. When Coya looked up at Andy, he bent down and lightly kissed her on the lips. Taken aback, Coya walked briskly to the cook car where they joined Andy's brother and sister for a hand of Whist. Coya was too shy to look at Andy, and she wondered if the others noticed her red face. Nice girls were not supposed to kiss boys, or even hold hands.

When harvest was finished in September, Andy returned to his family's farm in Minnesota and Coya went back to college in Moorhead. She continued to think about Andy, and they began writing to each other.

In the summer of 1933, after her sophomore year, Andy invited Coya to visit his family. When she got off the train in Grand Forks where Andy was supposed to meet her, she did not see him anywhere on the platform. For a moment she wondered if she had taken the wrong train or if he'd forgotten about her. She went inside the station and her heart skipped a beat when she saw Andy near the drinking fountain. He stood on one foot and then the other, too shy to look her in the eye. She was nervous, too, but so relieved to see him.

It was a 70-mile drive to Oklee and they didn't have much to talk about. When they arrived at the Knutson farm, only Andy's mother, Gunhild, was there to greet her. She was a big, strong woman with brown eyes and gray hair, and she was knitting a sock. Gunhild stopped work and poured coffee from a big grey enamel pot into large white cups and the three sat at the kitchen table eating homemade Norwegian wholewheat flatbread slathered with homemade butter. It tasted wonderful to Coya after the five-hour journey, but she couldn't help but think that her own mother would have prepared sauce, fresh bread, and doughnuts or sugar cookies for guests.

Aslak and Ole, Andy's father and brother, came in from chores and washed their faces and hands in the blue enamel basin before joining them at the table. Coya liked Andy's father immediately. He was soft-spoken and looked kind. He was shorter than his wife, had a neat mustache and smoked a pipe. Coya already knew Ole, who had worked for her father, and she liked him a lot. The five spoke in Norwegian and talked about the flax crop, the last rain, which of their neighbors had telephones, and how everyone else in the large Knutson family was getting along. Coya felt at home.

Andy's and Coya's backgrounds were similar. His parents, Aslak and Gunhild Knutson, had emigrated from Setesdalen, Norway and settled in Bygland, Minnesota, near the Red River. When land near Oklee became available for homesteading in 1896, they moved to a 160-acre tract of prairie land in Equality Township, northeast of Oklee. Of the Knutsons' eleven children, only five were still living. Their daughter Mary was married to a neighboring farmer named Gunnulf Brievold, and their son Torkel worked for the highway patrol. Anna, Ole and Andy were still living at home.

Coya liked the Knutsons and sensed that Andy's family liked her in return. They were kind, generous people and Coya thought of them as *folklige*, a Norwegian word meaning homey. Coya observed that Andy's mother was clearly the kind that spoiled her children. If Andy and Ole had "celebrated" the night before, Gunhild indulged her boys by letting them sleep late. It was fine with her if Aslak had to do all the chores without help.

Coya stayed four days and had a wonderful time. Andy borrowed the family car and they went for drives in the country and to Oklee to visit Andy's relatives. His cousin, Gerald Strande, had a radio and they spent an evening with the Strandes listening to Ed Wynne's program. Another evening they went to the Peter Borgan Show, a touring variety show held in a tent erected just outside Oklee. Borgan sang and played the violin and his troupe did a three-act play; however, what everyone waited for was the final act. Borgan put on a red wig and pretended he was "Ole, just arrived from Skratthult, Norway." With a Norwegian accent, he told sad and funny tales of a newly arrived immigrant to America.

Coya had such a fine time with Andy that, back at college when she was supposed to be studying, her thoughts would stray to Andy and the good times they had shared. Andy remained in Coya's thoughts and they exchanged letters.

Having completed a double major in English and music, and a minor in education, Coya earned a Bachelor of Arts degree in May 1934. During her college years, she had taken a giant leap away from being her father's right-hand man. She enjoyed being on her own and she was determined to make a living teaching music. However, Depression and tax delinquency had brought many school districts to insolvency. Few teachers were being hired in the mid-1930s, but Coya was confident that her qualifications would ensure employment.

A teaching position opened in Penn, North Dakota, and Coya was thrilled when her application was accepted. Penn (population 90) was a village forty miles from Edmore and only twelve miles from Devils Lake, where her sister Crystal taught elementary school. Penn's one-block-long Main Street had a bank, blacksmith shop, railroad depot, general store, butcher shop, pharmacy, pool hall, a hotel and the city hall. The two grain elevators produced much of the income that supported the town. Penn, a predominantly German community, had a large number of churches for its size, including Catholic, Presbyterian, and Lutheran churches. Coya did not join the local Lutheran church because it was a member of the Missouri Synod and followed a cultural and doctrinal tradition that was more strict and rigid than was practiced in the Norwegian Synod.

The school was a two-story, white-frame square building that resembled the traditional rural prairie schools more than it did a town school. Elementary school classes were taught in the four rooms on the first floor and the high school, which graduated four to ten students each year, was on the second floor. The Superintendent of Schools, John J. Hogan, taught math and science courses. Coya taught high school grammar, American and English literature, history, psychology and music to both elementary and high school students. She recognized her inadequacies in certain subjects and stayed up late at night in order to learn those lessons she had to teach the following day. It was a demanding schedule and, when she had to prepare both elementary and high school Christmas programs, Coya was so overworked that often she would lose her voice. Yet, she set high academic standards each year when the State Board exams were given and almost all of Penn's pupils passed.

Coya organized a sextet, two trios and a glee club that accepted any student who showed an interest. The sixteen members of the glee club sang in local churches and performed operettas in the town hall. In her estimation, when Coya managed to keep the less talented but ardent members from singing too loudly, the group sounded pretty good. She encouraged her students to participate in regional contests and, with her enthusiastic and sympathetic coaching, they often did well.

Coya became a popular figure in the community. She happily agreed to sing "Because" at local weddings, "O Sole Mio" at community events and hymns as a guest soloist in various village churches. Out of her eighty-five-dollar-a-month salary, she paid twenty dollars for room and board in a local banker's home. When the family moved away, Coya found even more suitable quarters—with Tom Torriers, the depot agent, and his wife Irene—where she had the use of the piano and could give lessons. The Torriers and Coya became good friends and when they confided that they wanted to adopt a child, Coya assisted them by writing to the Fargo Foundling Home on their behalf and later providing character references to the adoption officials. The Torriers were able to adopt one-year-old Vincent, who also worked as a depot agent when he grew up.

The Gjesdal family showed support for Coya by driving to Penn to see the high school play she directed and returning a few weeks later to hear their daughter sing a solo at the commencement exercises. In turn, Coya liked to buy them gifts, such as a vacuum cleaner for her mother. The new appliance had a great deal of use that spring when the hired hands knocked holes through the walls and floors to install pipes for running water.

During the summer months of 1935, after her first year of teaching at Penn, Coya realized a dream she had kept secret since her freshman year at Concordia. In college she had immersed herself in classical music and, encouraged by her professors to fully develop her musical talents, Coya began to entertain the notion of a professional singing career. She knew she had a good voice, but she didn't dare confide her fantasies. The idea of a plain farm girl aspiring to be an opera singer seemed too farfetched. But whenever she listened to Kate Smith on the radio, she was inspired by the glorious voice.

Coya knew that however gifted she herself might be, her terror of performing was a major hurdle she had to overcome before she could seriously consider a career on the concert stage. Yet, when she heard her music teachers talk with awe about the fine musical training available at the Juilliard School of Music in New York City, Coya listened closely. If she wanted to study opera and train her voice to its full potential, she would somehow have to attend Juilliard.

After her first year teaching at Penn, Coya decided it was time to find out if she could "measure up." She had made great strides during that year; on her own in a new environment and in charge of her own affairs, she blossomed with a new-found confidence. If ever she were to take the risk of testing her mettle in New York, this was the time.

Coya had never visited a metropolitan area, not even "The Cities," Minneapolis and St. Paul. The idea of traveling to New York City and attending the most prestigious school of music in the country was overwhelming. Still uncertain about going to New York, she decided to visit Oklee and talk things over with Andy. He had his own farm now, which he bought from earnings as Christ's hired hand. It was a quarter-section of land (about 160 acres) across the road from his parents.

While he drove her home to Edmore in his new Plymouth, Coya discussed her dreams—and her doubts. Andy was a willing listener, but he neither encouraged her to go to New York nor tried to dissuade her. Coya was disappointed. She had no one to turn to for advice and she had hoped Andy could fill that role. Andy was not at all ambitious and he wasn't the sort of young man who made plans or thought ahead beyond the following day. He lived by his favorite expression, "what will be will be," and went along with whatever turned up in his life. It would not have occurred to him that the young woman he fancied might become too sophisticated and "advanced" for him. Someday their paths would cross again and then, he figured, whatever would be would be.

Coya's decision to go to Juilliard was ultimately her own. Christ gave her six hundred dollars tuition, travel and living expenses. In late June of 1935, her father drove her to Moorhead where she boarded a bus for Minneapolis and then transferred to one bound for New York.

After three days and two nights of travel, the bus pulled into mid-town Manhattan in the middle of the night. Tired, and with ankles badly swollen from "sleeping sitting up," Coya picked up her suitcase and made her way to the nearest boardinghouse. She was shown a dreary room and told that the toilet was down the hall. More than a little apprehensive about her surroundings, Coya entered the darkened bathroom, pulled the string attached to a dangling lightbulb and was startled by the sight of an enormous cockroach, the first she had ever seen. The following day she found lodging in a rooming house near Columbia University.

Despite bad beginnings, the country girl fell in love with the big city. She was awed by St. Patrick's Cathedral, dazzled by the Radio City Music Hall Rockettes, and overwhelmed by the view from the top of the Empire State Building. She managed to find her way by subway and ferry to the Staten Island home of her cousin Elmer Thompson and his wife Elsie. Elmer, the young man who had built her family's first radio, was now working for the Philco Corporation, a manufacturer of radios and phonographs. She also had her first view of the Statue of Liberty.

In the city, the variety of luxury goods astonished her, and she splurged on a Bulova watch for Eva. Her sister's reaction was, "Honestly, that kid spends."[5] On another shopping spree Coya bought herself a black sealskin coat, on sale for $45. She liked it not only because it was sleek and warm but because it made her look slender.

Soon after she arrived in New York, Coya found that she could get tickets to a CBS radio broadcast of the "Major Bowes' Original Amateur Hour," a favorite program she had listened to every Sunday night in North Dakota. Although Edward Bowes had started the program only a year before, by 1935 it was voted the most popular in America. The broadcast reached 37 million listeners each week. Bowes, who had already made a fortune in real estate, held auditions for his radio show in the Capitol Building, which he owned.

Coya wanted to sing on the Amateur Hour and, on one of her visits to the studio that summer, she was chosen to perform. Coya found Bowes a striking presence. A grey-haired man with a huge face, a Roman nose and a pompous manner, he sat on stage like a sultan and struck the famous gong when he and his studio audience decided they had had quite enough of a particular performer. Coya had just begun her training at Juilliard and, as one of her teachers there described it, her voice was still a "birdie-in-the-nest" soprano. Though her voice was clear and lyrical, it lacked the volume and theatrical fireworks that Major Bowes' audience demanded. The gong sounded after only four bars of "O Sole Mio" and Coya left the stage feeling drained and humiliated by the ordeal. "I'm too dumpy to be star material anyway," she thought, and comforted herself by recalling the praise she'd received "back home" for singing the same song.

Among the listeners to the broadcast was Andy Knutson, who beamed with pride when he heard Coya's name announced as the next contestant. He later told Coya that "they cut your song off too soon for me to say much about it." His entire family had crowded into the Strandes' house in town to hear Coya sing on Major Bowes' that night. It was common knowledge that the handsome farmer had taken a liking to Coya Gjesdal, although the two saw each other only occasionally.[6]

Juilliard was more personal than she had expected; her classes in harmony and music composition each had fewer than ten students. She took private voice lessons with Professor Bernard, who was very effective in developing the quality of her delicate, high-pitched soprano voice. He told Coya that if she wanted to pursue a professional singing career she would have to quit teaching and devote herself exclusively to music. She was in her early twenties, he reminded her, and her professional training should have begun years earlier.

Coya had gone to Juilliard to learn whether or not her dream of a singing career was realistic. Toward the end of her summer in New York City, Coya came to the conclusion that, while her voice did "measure up," the pursuit of a professional stage career was not to her taste. She had challenged herself to perform on a "live" national radio broadcast and her nerve had not failed her. She could conquer her stagefright.   She'd wondered if her voice was really "good enough," and she had satisfied that doubt.   She'd also proven to herself that she had the discipline and appetite for the hard work that the rigors of a professional singing career demanded, but in weighing her options, Coya decided to return to North Dakota and her teaching work. She missed her family and friends, and she knew she preferred a life in Penn to remaining in New York City. Her two months of voice training and her studies in piano and music composition at Juilliard were well worth the effort, but most of all, she told herself, she would never have to regret not pursuing a dream.

Before the new school term began in Penn, Coya had just enough time for a side trip, and her bus ticket to North Dakota included a one-day stopover in Washington, D.C. She spent the entire day sight-seeing and was struck by the Capital's home-town feeling—an atmosphere she had not felt in New York City.

She was glad to get back to "solid living," as she describes the daily routine of teaching in Penn; her job was her pleasure and fun, and she thrived on the comfortable, familiar structure of her life. Her needs were simple and she was satisfied. During her next two years of teaching at Penn, Coya's confidence grew and she found that she enjoyed teaching more than ever.

Not long after Coya returned to North Dakota, Eva was rushed to the Mayo Clinic in Rochester, Minnesota, where she had surgery to remove gallstones. During the dark days of his daughter's illness, Christ sobered up and, as Eva wrote in her diary, "Dad was just grand."

With Eva recuperating, all the Gjesdals were especially happy to be together for the Christmas holidays in 1935. Christ even joined the family for Christmas church services. Eva, 20, spent all her time at home, embroidering, helping her mother make quilts and doing light housework. She also read Bible stories to Sonny who was now a blue-eyed, rosy-cheeked blond six year old. Sonny was the center of attention during the holidays. Everyone waited for his reaction when he got his gifts, which included a shiny bike and a pair of rabbits. Eva helped Sonny make napkin holders to give to each of his sisters. Christine gave each of her daughters a bottle of perfume, and Coya gave Eva the fanciest dresser set she could find. The girls frolicked with their brother in the new-fallen snow and Crystal took moving pictures of them with her new camera.

The summer of 1936 was the hottest anyone could remember. The heat built up day after day and on July 10th the temperature was 119 degrees. Rain showers began to revive the dying crops, but hailstorms followed that destroyed much of the Gjesdals' wheat.

A pleasant interlude in that hot summer was the wedding of Andy's brother. Torkel Knutson and Orianna Flescher were married in a church ceremony in Twin Valley, Minnesota. Coya, as usual, sang "Because." At the reception she talked with Anna and the other young women who were each saving a portion of their slice of wedding cake to put under their pillows that night in hopes of dreaming about a beau. When they teased Coya about Andy, she was secretly pleased, although she tried not to show it. How handsome he looked in his new suit, she thought. Coya had never before seen him dressed up in a suit, tie and white shirt.

She took home with her a piece of wedding cake, carefully wrapped in paper wedding napkins, and put it under her pillow. She guessed she cared more than she knew for Andy. The following morning she was disappointed not to have had any dreams at all that night. It was Andy she had hoped to dream about.

Chapter 3

THE FARMER'S WIFE

*I am a farmer's wife, if you please, not a "farmerette,"
and I like being one, strange as that may seem to some.*

Mrs James Jessup, McGraw, Nebraska,
Nonpartisan Leader, November 24, 1919.

It was August 22, 1937, Coya's birthday, and she was 25 years old. She lay awake watching the moonlight shining over the barn and silhouetting the grain elevator against the nighttime sky. It was 10 o'clock and still not quite dark. The breeze blowing through the windows brought the smell of freshly-mown hay and she was reminded of past summers on the farm.

Everything was so different this year. Before, she'd always sweltered in the airless bedroom under the eaves, but this year her bedroom was the renovated porch, a godsend. The screened windows on three sides not only caught the slightest breeze, but afforded a magnificent view of the rising constellations and the ever changing moon. The porch was surely one of the best of many improvements her folks had made since the girls had left home. There were also such new labor-saving devices as a cistern that had been dug close to the kitchen door and a pump that carried well water into the house, doing away with the onerous chore of hauling water in buckets. Ironically, the new pump also served the cook car. In earlier years this would have been a blessing, but quantity cooking was no longer necessary because there were no longer any farm hands. Christ had sold the farm.

Her father's decision to sell was abrupt. When Coya came home in the autumn of 1936, she was completely unprepared to find an auction of farm implements in progress. Earlier that year the Gjesdals had invested in their first combine, a machine that did the reaping, threshing and winnowing in one operation. To Coya, it seemed that as soon as new technology made farm machinery more reliable and efficient, Christ lost interest in farming. For all his earlier enthusiasm about buying new farm implements and machinery, Christ missed the backbreaking good old days of the horse and plow. But it was more than that.

During school vacations Coya had always returned home. Now, as a young adult earning her own living, she had a new viewpoint of her parents and their life on the farm. Her father in particular had paid a terrible price. When he couldn't take the constant pressure of running the large farm, he drank, and that happened with increasing frequency. While "under the influence" Christ was mean and belligerent but, in the early days, his drinking bouts seldom interfered with his ability to get the farm work done. However, in the middle of the harvest the previous summer, Christ's drunken hostility caused three hired hands to walk off the job, and others threatened to do so.

Although Christine endured each new crisis with a quiet patience and handled the business affairs with a steady hand, Coya was aware that her parents' relationship had been significantly damaged by the constant strain. On Christine's birthday two years earlier, several of her women friends dropped in to visit and brought refreshments. But the celebration was spoiled when, as Eva wrote in her diary, Christ "carried on." In the end, the pressures brought Christ to the breaking point and the only way he could see to change things was to quit farming.

Coya was pleased that her parents no longer had to work so hard, but it was strange to be back home in summer without having farm chores. She continued to lie awake thinking of all the changes this year had brought. It seemed so strange not to be harvesting; with even a glimmer of light still available at this time of night, everyone would be in the fields. Of course, some things never changed. Christ couldn't shake a farmer's lifetime worry about crops and had been upset that day because the new owners still hadn't started the harvest.

There were other changes in her life as well. She and Eva, who was home from school for the summer, had spent that morning in the kitchen: Eva baking date bread and Coya creating her own birthday cake. Eva had cleaned house, expecting company to "drop by." No one came. The double-chocolate cake with white seven-minute frosting would only add more weight to Coya's already robust frame, so she cheerfully took her decorated cake to the bunkhouse and gave it to the new owner's hired hands. She was glad the cake was appreciated, but she missed the fun of last year when four girl friends had dropped in to wish her happy birthday. They had sat around and talked and sung all evening. But this year her old friends had families of their own and were too busy to visit. It seemed to Coya that she was the only girl in the county who did not have a husband or fiancé.

Coya did not see much of her sisters either. Each had a beau. Even baby sister Eva had not only one, but several boyfriends. Crystal had a special boyfriend who was "serious" about her. And Helen, a year younger than Coya, was leaving the nest first—she was engaged to be married. Helen and her fiancé were usually off by themselves on drives and visits to friends. It was so quiet. And now that the farm was sold, Coya did not feel needed.

Perhaps it was time for her to get married and settle down, but she really didn't want to. She was not sure she ever wanted to be married, and she wasn't sure how Andy felt. Her shy young man liked her, all right, she thought, but he made no signs of wanting to get married. Still, Andy and Coya got along well. She liked the handsome farmer and enjoyed his company. She thought she would like to see him more often. She suspected it was up to her to make that happen.

When the Knutsons told her that a position as English teacher was available in the Oklee High School, Coya immediately applied for it. She wanted the job very much because teaching in Oklee would also give her the chance to see if a serious romance could happen between her and Andy. Oklee, with a population of 494, was five times the size of Penn, and the teacher's pay was better. When the post was awarded to a fellow graduate of Concordia, Coya was disappointed. She decided to look for another job close to Oklee. During a subsequent visit with the Knutson family she heard about a music and

English teaching position in Plummer, a small town fifteen miles from Oklee.

On a hot July day in 1937, Andy's cousin, Anna Strande, accompanied Coya on a drive to Plummer. The town had a population of 310 and was bustling with farmers delivering milk cans to the Land O'Lakes Creamery. The Soo Line Railroad Depot was a center of activity, with horse-drawn carts arriving to pick up freight. Many freight and passenger trains on the Plummer Line—the wheat line from Winnipeg to Duluth—stopped to take on water and coal. Plummer's Main Street included several stores, two cafés, a farm implement dealer, and post office. Many Norwegians had settled in the area, and a thriving Norwegian Lutheran Church was one of several in town.

Coya liked the town and applied for the teaching position at Plummer High School. After an interview with Superintendent Herman Berger, Coya was hired. She had taken a step up the career ladder, too; at Plummer she would be paid $120 a month, a 40% increase over her salary of $85 at Penn. She would also be living closer to Andy.

Coya moved to Plummer in September and began teaching high school music and English as well as grade school music. The music classes presented considerable challenge. The students had had song fests and other informal singing, but because the school had not previously had a full-time music teacher, the students could not read musical notation. The music department provided a Christmas program and presented another concert or operetta in the spring. These extracurricular activities were hard to arrange because it was difficult to get enough students together for practice. Many had to go home to do farm chores and others had no transportation to and from their homes outside of school hours.

While Coya's teaching duties were similar to those in Penn, her lesson plans were provided by the state of Minnesota. Coya preferred this system as it ensured a uniform study program for students throughout the state. Coya had no time off during the day. She taught every hour, with a different preparation for each class.

Coya's mode of dress was casual and neat. For school she chose to wear a blouse and a wool skirt, and comfortable low-heeled shoes. The weather could be severe, as it had been in North Dakota, but clothing standards did not reflect that. Even when the temperature plunged to 40 degrees below zero, Coya wore a sweater and skirt ensemble under her winter coat for her customary walk across a snowy field to the school. At that time no responsible woman school teacher would dream of wearing slacks in public, and certainly not in the classroom.

Coya lived on the outskirts of Plummer with the Haaven family, a retired couple with two sons in high school. Mrs Haaven served breakfast, but Coya was on her own for dinner. She usually joined other single teachers at Mrs McCrady's café. They had fun together in that informal atmosphere. Mrs McCrady worked tirelessly in the tiny, hot back kitchen, cooking her hearty meals on a coal stove. It was a very small place without menus; the waitress would recite the daily bill of fare, mostly fried steaks and chops.

In her spare time she took typing lessons from the business teacher, Miss Albright, but there was too little time for practice and she soon gave it up. Pauline Schoenaur, who played piano accompaniment for Coya's music students, became her closest friend. The two women enjoyed going to town together, and if they wanted to "buy something swell," they would join friends who had a car and drive fifteen miles into Thief River Falls on a Friday night. There they socialized with other friends they met in the cafés and shops. Another of Coya's close friends was the constable's wife, Mrs Hanson, a homespun Norwegian woman who reminded Coya of her mother.

During the three years she taught at Plummer, a quiet courtship continued between Coya and Andy. On weekends, perhaps a couple of times a month, Andy would arrive to take Coya to the Knutson farm. His brother Ole and his sister Anna were usually there and the foursome had good times together.

The friendship blossomed into romance because the couple felt so comfortable in this family atmosphere. Their backgrounds were similar and their work together on the Gjesdal farm made them feel completely natural in each other's company. Marriage began to seem like a good idea to them. Coya liked Andy's personality and he was handsome, fun to be with and easy-going. Andy's family and friends were teasing him about when he was going to get around to marrying that good-looking school teacher from Plummer.

Coya looked forward to her visits to the Knutson farm. When supper was over, she and Andy would go for a drive in his Plymouth. One evening Andy drove to Pine Lake and they sat in the car in the lingering autumn twilight, watching the children swimming. As it began to get dark, Coya thought Andy would put his arm around her and they would watch the stars come out. Instead, Andy mumbled something about getting home before dark and pulled the car back on the road. Coya was disappointed.

She realized that when it came to romance she and Andy were slow to catch on. Neither had dated anyone else, and both were shy about declaring their feelings for each other. Under the watchful eyes of parents, Norwegian courting did not amount to much anyway, but both Coya and Andy were awkward and ill-at-ease in their moments alone together. Coya felt naive and innocent in matters of love, and again resented her parents for not giving her some guidance. Andy, too, was backward in knowing quite how to proceed.

Gradually Coya, 27, and Andy, 30, came to an understanding. Coya let him know that she was ready to settle down and, assured of her acceptance, Andy proposed. In the winter of Coya's third year of teaching in Plummer, the couple set a wedding date just far enough ahead to allow for arrangements to be made. Her friends in Plummer gave her a shower, and among the gifts was a prized Fostoria crystal bowl from Pauline.

That February, Andy and Coya drove to Edmore to visit her parents. Coya was disappointed that Christ and Christine did not approve of her choice of a husband. They felt Coya could have done better, yet they had little idea of what constituted a good match. They had provided no guidelines or insight that might have helped their daughters in choosing mates. It seemed to Coya that they looked only at the dollar signs—if a man was making good money, that was what counted. For the Gjesdals and other immigrants, security was the primary goal. Christ and Christine had left poverty behind in Norway and dedicated themselves to working for a life without want. For their children they wanted an easier life than they had had. They were not impressed with Andy Knutson. He was a small farmer with a poor education whose prospects did not look promising.

It was true that Andy didn't have "prospects" and Coya understood her parents' thinking. However, now that the wedding date had been set Coya was sure that she and Andy were doing the right thing. They liked each other and got along well, and that seemed to Coya to be a good basis for a healthy marriage. Although Andy did not earn much money, she could save pennies by planting a garden, canning vegetables and fruit, and helping out with chores so they wouldn't need a hired man. Andy had made it clear that he did not want to move to Edmore and rent land from Christ to farm. "No one's going to get me out of Oklee," he told Coya. That suited Coya, who knew that her father was more ambitious than Andy and that they would not get along.

When Coya and Andy left Edmore in a flourish of farewells and waving, she could see that her parents had resigned themselves to the wedding. She thought about her parents' marriage and saw little that she wanted to emulate. For the Gjesdals, staying together seemed to be more of a convenience than anything, and it was that way for many couples Coya knew.

On the drive back to Oklee, Coya and Andy talked together more than they ever had. They made plans for the new house they wanted to build on Andy's farm across the road from his parents. They discussed furniture and the household goods they would need to buy. They both hoped to start a family soon and talked about building an extra room for a nursery. Coya felt secure about their future together. She curled up in the front seat of the car and looked carefully at the man she would marry. She loved the twinkle in his eye and his rolling laugh, and thought that they would get along just fine. She told him she loved him and he told her that he loved her, too.

On a cold windy day one week before Easter, Coya and Andy were married at Concordia Lutheran Church in Edmore, North Dakota. The ceremony was held at two o'clock on Sunday afternoon on March 31, 1940 with Coya's three sisters as bridesmaids. Because wedding dresses were not available in local shops, Coya ordered her gown from the Sears Roebuck catalogue. The bridal dress had a white taffeta top with a full-fashioned white net skirt that "stuck out." It cost fifteen dollars. The ensemble was completed with a small veil and she carried a bouquet of red roses and carnations. The light blue dresses that her three sisters wore were also from the catalogue.

Rather than sending invitations, the couple informally asked their friends and family (about 75 guests) to attend the wedding. Afterward they had a party in the church basement where Coya's mother had arranged for the Ladies Aid to cater a luncheon of sandwiches, wedding cake, mints, and coffee. The Ladies Aid charged twenty-five dollars for their food and services, and they were very pleased with their handsome profit. Coya was delighted that everything had gone so well. It was just the wedding she wanted.

After the reception, the newlyweds changed into traveling clothes at the church before leaving on their honeymoon. Christine carefully folded the wedding gown and took it home with her. The Plymouth was packed with the wedding gifts and a few of Coya's things from home. Their destination was Grand Forks, North Dakota where they had reservations at the Ryan Hotel. When they parked in front of the hotel, Coya could see that Andy was nervous. They laughed about registering for the first time as Mr and Mrs, and then walked to the front desk together.

They rose early Tuesday morning for their drive to Oklee. When they returned to Minnesota, Andy remained on their farm to work while Coya went back to Plummer to finish her school year. Even though she enjoyed the work, Coya was prepared to resign at the end of the term. Married women were expected to be full time homemakers and school administrators discouraged them from teaching. Besides, Coya was ready to settle down and start a family.

She looked forward to moving. Coya liked Andy's farm and she was pleased with the small house he had built for them directly across the road from his parents. Andy hired Ted Loylan to build, at a cost of $2,000, a four-room frame house with a living room, kitchen, two bedrooms and a full basement. Andy installed a bathroom, but until they could afford to drill a well to pump water, its fixtures were purely decorative. The kitchen stove used bottled gas and Coya was thrilled with the innovation. "We put one over when we got that," she crowed to her sister Helen. The new stove was quick, clean and, best of all, Coya no longer had to carry wood into the kitchen. Helen was impressed. Cooking with gas was so much easier than trying to adjust a wood fire; with a dial that set the oven temperature, there would be no more guessing.

Coya had figured her life as a housewife would be far better than her mother's had been, but electricity was not yet available in their community, and a Delco light plant was beyond their means. They used a gas lantern as well as several kerosene lamps for lighting. Their Maytag washing machine had a gas motor to drive the agitator and wringer and it made a "putt-putt" sound. In the summertime Coya was happy when Andy could move the washer outside onto the porch. There she would run the hot, newly washed clothes through the wringer, into tubs of rinse waters, and then into a basket near the clotheslines. During the winter she washed and hung the clothes in the basement.

The Knutsons' 160-acre farm was small compared to the Gjesdals' 3000-acre farm, but the crops, animals and farmstead involved a multitude of daily chores for Coya and Andy. The single barn was used both for storing hay and for sheltering the half-dozen cows and 50-to-60 chickens. Because their farm was small, Coya did not have to drive the tractor or do field work. The Knutsons produced cash crops of flax and barley and raised oats and hay to feed their animals.

They also sold cream. Running a dairy required someone to be on hand morning and evening for the milking; Andy was largely responsible for milking the cows, and Coya helped out occasionally. They also had to wash and reassemble the cream separator—all thirty-two discs, two spouts and numerous floats and fillings—each morning. Andy or Coya would then take on the task of turning the separator's hand crank sixty revolutions per minute. The machine whirred until a bell signaled it was ready; then the warm cream would be poured into a can and submerged in cool water to refrigerate it. Coya was in charge of feeding the chickens and gathering the eggs; by 1942, she was selling the eggs for 26 cents a dozen. She also tended the lawn and vegetable garden.

The changing seasons brought variety to their routine tasks. Coya found summers close to perfect. In Oklee there always seemed to be the right amount of sun and rain to produce lush green growth on lawns and trees; in Edmore it had been just a little too dry to sustain greenness once spring had passed. Occasionally, however, there was a heavy summer rainstorm. Coya remembers when five inches of rain fell in a single downpour, and she waded into the farmyard to rescue drowning chickens. Exasperated, she spread newspapers on the floor and brought the chickens into the house

Harvest time was her favorite time of year. It was satisfying to smell the sweet aroma of hay curing in the barn. She enjoyed helping Andy shock the oats and watching him drive off to the co-op elevator, the truck loaded with grain. She and Andy were basking in the warm companionship of newlyweds. One of their favorite times together was milking the cows in the evening, the last chore of the day, when they could talk quietly.

The starlit nights were a special delight. At any time of year, but especially at harvest time, Coya would be surprised by the sudden beauty of northern lights dancing and shimmering across the sky. The broad fields afforded a clear view of the spectacle. She had always enjoyed the beauty and freedom of the open plains. Now, Coya was beginning to prefer the countryside around Oklee to the prairie land where she grew up. There were more wooded areas. She loved to take walks in the autumn; the fallen leaves seemed to warm the earth in a blaze of color. The stands of trees also made her feel protected. As a child, Coya believed the keen winds whipping across the North Dakota plains were strong enough to pick her up and carry her away.

When winter came, their well-built house was kept snug with the aid of a new wood furnace in the basement. In the autumn, neighbors had gathered at farms to split wood and pile it up close to each house. During the months from November to April, wood had to be fed into the stove five or six times a day. As the supply of logs beside the furnace dwindled, the Knutsons replenished it from their stock pile outside. Coya called the stove a "monster waiting to be fed," and it took the efforts of both Knutsons to keep the furnace stoked. But there was nothing cozier than the warmth of the wood-burning furnace.

Winter days brought both pleasure and hardship to the valley. The months spent indoors gave Coya time to think and ponder, a luxury she had never before had in her work-filled life. When temperatures plunged to 20 and 30 degrees below zero and the skies were clear blue, the warm sun penetrated the window glass to cheer and heat the small rooms. On those brilliant winter days, Coya would often see twin bands of the color spectrum glowing in the sky within two ovals of light. Moving across the sky, between these twin lights, called sun dogs, was the sun shining feebly.

In the valley, snow was clean and plentiful, covering any imperfections in the landscape, and the Knutsons insulated their home by banking snow against the foundation of the house. Of course snow brought problems, too. In the late fall of 1940 a fierce blizzard, in which 70 people lost their lives, imprisoned the Knutsons in their house for several days. The icy winds and thick snowfall even prevented the Knutsons from getting to the barn to tend their animals.

During the long winter months especially, Andy and Coya found pleasure in listening to the radio, a battery-operated floor model that took pride of place in the living room. Coya listened to it while she was baking, cooking and cleaning. It was good company; without its voices and cracklings, the house would have been silent when Andy was outside working or across the road visiting his parents.

The radio was also their way of keeping up on world events. On December 7, 1941 Andy and Coya had just come in from milking the cows when they heard the horrifying news that the Japanese had bombed Pearl Harbor. They ran across the road to tell his folks the news and then stayed close to the radio that Sunday listening to the reports of death and destruction. After that Coya and Andy often listened to the radio news to hear what was happening overseas, and never failed to listen to Edward R. Murrow's broadcasts from London. The radio brought the pain home to them.

Soon another radio broadcast became an important catalyst in Coya's life. One June day in 1942, Coya stopped her work at around noon to listen to a speech by the wife of the President of the United States. Eleanor Roosevelt's high-pitched voice, mixed with static, poured into Coya Knutson's airy farm kitchen urging her—and countless other listeners—to become active in the political life of the nation. Mrs Roosevelt said that to provide good government in these extraordinary times, the nation needed astute people—both men and women—to run for political office. The President's wife was expressing her husband's policy.

For first time in its history, a United States President specifically encouraged female participation in politics. Roosevelt made it clear that he was looking for women to work in government, especially in areas of public welfare, by selecting Frances Perkins, a well-known social worker, to serve as Secretary of Labor. Perkins, the first woman member of a Presidential Cabinet, held the post from 1933 to 1945. Also for the first time, Roosevelt instituted regular White House press conferences that included both men and women correspondents.[2]

Eleanor Roosevelt's words struck a responsive chord with the 30-year-old farmwife who admired the First Lady enormously for being one of the few women in public to speak out on social issues. Years later Coya commented: "It was as if the sun burned into me that day. All of a sudden I had an awareness of something I can't explain—but the idea of going into politics popped into my head."

Coya was lost in thought as she continued with her chores after the broadcast. It seemed to her that no one listened to women, not ordinary women who were housewives. Coya's parents had never hesitated to involve themselves in politics, and Christine had attended as many Farmers Union meetings as her husband had. Women, however, seldom spoke at the meetings and the "woman's point of view" was never really taken seriously. Coya was aware that women worked every bit as hard as men on the farm, and they, too, had a stake in the government's agricultural policy and farm legislation, but their voices were not heard. She knew that speaking up in public was a terrifying prospect for her and for most women. Her Aunt Cornelia epitomized the tongue-tied farmwife. She was fearless when it came to plucking chickens out of the hen house, wringing their necks and cooking them up for supper, yet her knees would turn to jelly at the thought of "speaking out in company"—even at her own dinner table.

Coya knew that a highlight in her mother's life was entertaining the Ladies Aid in her home for Bible study and group discussion. Coya and her sisters would help prepare for the gathering and then attend the meeting. Coya noticed how difficult it was for the women to join in the discussion. The minister would try to get the women to take part, but it was painful for them to overcome their bashfulness to read aloud from the Bible. Expressing their thoughts and feelings seemed almost impossible. Coya figured that it was because they knew that in a man's world their opinions and feelings didn't amount to much. There was that natural tendency among the women she knew to shrink back from "standing out" or seeming to be "too forward."

Just for a moment, an image of herself on stage at a podium making a speech flickered across her mind. The idea appealed to her and she smiled at the thought. What would people say if she ended up in Washington—wouldn't that be something? Perhaps one day she would even meet the First Lady in person.

Although Coya's and Mrs Roosevelt's backgrounds could not have been more disparate, Eleanor Roosevelt had set an example for women that inspired Coya. She was a woman who sought out the forgotten, invisible people who were too timid or poorly educated to speak for themselves. She gave them a voice. Coya recognized a parallel in her own community. Many people were too self-conscious or backward to express their needs. As a teacher, she had come across families who were in dire need of public assistance and were ignorant of government programs that could help them. In small ways over the years Coya had found herself stepping in to help out whenever she could be of use. Now she wanted to actively involve herself in local government and the social welfare of her community.

Later that month, Coya plunged into the political life of Oklee by calling a meeting of neighborhood farmers to discuss bringing electricity to their township, an area of 36 square miles. Coya remembered from her childhood how much the Delco Plant that provided electric light in their home enhanced their living conditions. In 1942 Andy and Coya held the first Equality Township Rural Electrification Association (REA) meeting in their home. Afterward, Coya served coffee and cake to the eight neighbors and two county board members. Although all the farmers who attended the meeting signed up for the service, it was eight years before the county board completed the paper work and electrical lines were brought into Equality Township.

That fall Ross Shetterly, who had been among the neighbors attending the REA meeting, was looking for someone to work as a field representative for the Agricultural Adjustment Administration (AAA), a government agency established early in the Roosevelt administration to deal with acreage allotments and support prices for dairy products and crops. Shetterly asked Coya to fill the position, which entailed visiting farm families and making speeches at community gatherings.

It seemed to be the ideal public service work Coya had hoped to find, yet she hesitated about accepting the job. Even though she welcomed the opportunity to work as a liaison between the Agricultural Administration and the farmers, the thought of frequently being called upon to speak at public gatherings left her weak-kneed with apprehension. However, with Ross Shetterly's encouragement, and her own resolve to meet the challenge, Coya went to work.

As a field woman in wartime, it was her responsibility to help step up food production and make farm families aware of the importance of their contribution to the war effort. She encouraged people to continue working their farms rather than to seek defense jobs in factories. The duty she enjoyed most was promoting home vegetable gardens in a program called Food for Freedom. Planting victory gardens was especially appealing because the work seemed such a positive and personal way for people to demonstrate their support for local boys fighting overseas. The food shortages were real enough and tending the backyard vegetable garden was one way everyone could participate in the war effort.

Coya was grateful to be back working. World War II reduced the prejudice against women working outside the home. With men leaving to fight overseas, women were needed to fill the jobs they vacated. Women like Coya were recruited into the labor force through radio broadcasts and newspaper and magazine articles that encouraged them to apply for work, especially in the defense industries.

In the early days of her marriage, Coya had not adjusted easily to having no income of her own. She was accustomed to a regular salary that provided enough money to meet her needs and also to making her own decisions on how to spend it. She could not stretch the household money to cover their living expenses, and the Knutsons were so short on cash that they couldn't even afford postage stamps. Helen enclosed them with her letters so her sister could reply.

Somehow, as poor as they were, Coya had to find the means to buy a car in order to work. During a trip to Minneapolis to see Crystal, Coya enlisted the help of her parents, who were also visiting, in selecting her first automobile. Together they chose a 1929 four-door Model A Ford that cost $75. Coya arranged to pay for it herself in $20 monthly installments. While Christ and Christine headed back to North Dakota, Coya drove her 13-year-old Ford home to Oklee. She was dismayed to discover that the car used four quarts of oil on the 280-mile trip. Fortunately she parked close to the Standard Oil station in Oklee that night because the following morning she found that all four tires were flat. Nels Strande, the station owner, laughed and told her the tires were "patched-up old things and not good for much—you must live right to make it home with tires like that!" Nevertheless, he managed to pump them up so Coya could set off on her first day of work for the government.

She relished the part of her job that required farm visits. However, driving around the county was not an easy matter in any season, particularly in spring when the roads were full of potholes. Before there were paved roads in northern Minnesota some locals used to count five seasons, the fifth being the melting season, occurring between severe winter and the traditional spring of warm sunshine and daffodils. Besides the usual muddy, rutted condition of the roads, there were frost boils that appeared very late in the melting season when the frozen moisture beneath thawed. As the moisture rose to the surface, it expanded the surrounding dirt into "boils," a sticky, messy gumbo that mired car tires and wagon wheels.

Fortunately Coya's Model A chassis had a two-foot clearance and sometimes hers was the only car that could get over the ruts and through the mud. Hot, dusty weather brought a different set of problems, and Coya's Model A was then at a disadvantage. In the dry summer weather, gravel and dirt roads had to be carefully negotiated because a Model A was so high and top-heavy that it easily tipped over if it skidded on loose gravel. None of the roads were paved, except the highway to Brooks. Few women ventured to drive by themselves in the country during bad weather conditions because of mechanical breakdowns and poor road surfaces.

Coya's AAA job required speeches to various groups, most often to organizations such as the 4-H and homemakers clubs. Since she was her own secretary, Coya had to telephone ahead to set up the meetings. Paid on a per diem basis plus ten cents per mile, she worked several days a week and averaged about the same amount she had made teaching full-time in Penn five years earlier. She usually earned about $85 a month, but one month made $150 in salary and mileage charges.

Because of the war, gasoline and tires were rationed; however, both Andy's farming and Coya's job with the AAA were considered vital to the defense effort so they received extra gas ration coupons. Travel was slow. A wartime speed limit of 35 miles per hour was initiated in November 1942.

For her outstanding work with the AAA, Coya was selected as the field woman from northern Minnesota to meet with U.S. Secretary of Agriculture Claude R. Wickard in Chicago in the fall of 1943. With the appointee from southern Minnesota, also a woman, Coya took the train to Chicago. At the meeting, Coya listened to speakers and visited with other field representatives. She was especially pleased when Secretary Wickard sat down and talked to her. Before leaving Chicago, Coya joined other delegates for an evening on the town and her first visit to a nightclub. The show featured a stripper and Coya was so shocked that she never wanted to set foot in a nightclub again.

When she returned to Oklee, she wrote an article about her trip for the *Red Lake Falls Gazette*. Her boss, Roy Shetterly, was impressed and commented, "Coya, you're doing so well that we won't be keeping you long." Coya was thrilled that her efforts were appreciated. She enjoyed her job, and working to her own schedule gave her time to fulfill her roles of wife and homemaker.

World War II brought many changes. Neighbors went off to work for the war effort, some to defense factories, others to battlefronts. The Knutsons mourned those who did not come back from the war and talked glowingly of those who returned with the Bronze Star and battle ribbons. Patriotism was strong in the Oklee community, but because the nation needed people on the home front to raise food, farmers were deferred from the draft and Andy was one of them. Times were improving for farmers. Prices went way up for flax; hay also brought a good price.

There were new ways to earn pocket money during the war years. Andy joined neighbors to cut and gather swamp grass from the marshlands. The cattails and milkweed pods that grew along roadsides and in meadows were harvested for the fluffy material that would be used in stuffing kapok vests for aviators. Oklee volunteers also collected 120,000 pounds of scrap iron and 50,000 pounds of rubber; besides providing strategic materials, these scrap drives served to clean up the countryside.[3]

Andy's parents continued to live just across the road on their farm where they raised cattle and cash crops of grain and hay. Occasionally Coya would walk over to her mother-in-law for coffee and fresh *lefse*, the thin Norwegian pancake made of mashed potatoes, cream and flour. Andy's mother, who was not active in the business end of farming as Coya's mother had been, cooked, cleaned and did such farm chores as gathering eggs. Coya got along fine with Andy's parents who were grateful that their new daughter-in-law could speak to them in Norwegian; Aslak and Gunhild understood spoken English, but could not speak, read or write English.

Coya was so busy that she was seldom able to visit her parents and she was not in Edmore to witness the miraculous change in the Gjesdal home. Her father quit drinking. According to Helen, Christ didn't take a "cure" but used his drinking as a bargaining wedge with Christine. For years Christ had been irritated by his wife's devout religious beliefs, the family's strict church attendance, and Christine's absence from home while participating in church activities. He knew he had to stop drinking and he knew how much his abstinence would mean to Christine. Christ told his wife that if she would quit going to church, he would quit drinking. She quit church; he quit drinking. And from then on he was sober.

But Coya was having trouble with alcohol in her own household. Andy was not happy. He found little pleasure in the monotony of farming and to escape routine chores would join his old buddies for a drink or two in town. Coya didn't mind at first: Andy didn't come home drunk and wasn't abusive as her father had been when he drank. However, about a year after they were married, Andy staggered home, fell on the bed fully clothed and went to sleep without a word. The following morning he was ashamed and promised it would never happen again. Coya believed him. It did not happen again for six months, and when it did, Andy was as contrite as he had been before. It was to become a pattern.

Like her mother, Coya worked hard to make the farm pay. Dairy prices increased during the war and milk wagons began to arrive at the farm to pick up the milk so the Knutsons did not have to haul it into town themselves. The fresh milk was kept cool in a newly built wooden structure that housed a continuously-running natural spring water system. Even with these improvements, times were ripe for a change. It was not long before Coya realized that they were not going to get ahead no matter how hard she or Andy tried.

Coya and Andy wanted a baby and they were very happy to discover in 1942 that she was expecting. Then, without warning, Coya had a miscarriage. The following year she had another miscarriage. During the second miscarriage, Andy stayed at her bedside after Dr. Torgerson left, just as he had after the first miscarriage. However, as soon as she felt strong enough to get out of bed the following day, Andy went to town to drink and play cards with his buddies. Coya was left to milk the cows and do the other chores.

After the second miscarriage Coya was unable to get pregnant again. She knew that she should seek medical help. Perhaps there was treatment available that would help her carry a pregnancy to term. She wanted a child and thought about it frequently, but she let time slip past without consulting a doctor. Andy's drinking and his lack of interest in the farm worried her. Neither of them seemed to find much pleasure in the marriage anymore and, after the second miscarriage, Coya did not know if she really wanted to have a baby with Andy.

Coya began taking on greater responsibility for the management of the farm. She also developed new interests in the community, such as teaching Vacation Bible School at Valle Lutheran Church where the Knutsons were members.

One day she arrived home to discover that the cows had not been milked and that their udders were ready to split. Andy was nowhere in sight. She learned later that he had been in town playing cards. Coya, left on her own to take care of the milking, thought of her father in comparison to her husband. Her Dad had been caught up in the happiness of working to expand his farm, even while that very challenge drove him to drink. He had been a solitary, moody drinker: Andy was a social drinker. Yet, as different as Andy and her father were in their personalities and behavior, the end result was the same: both were alcoholics.

Coya turned to even more hard work as an escape from her problems. However, the more she took on, the less Andy was willing to do. More and more often he would go into town to play cards. Coya was deeply disappointed. She felt there must be something wrong with her that made Andy turn away. She wondered if her life was to be like her mother's, only without children and without financial security. She did not consider divorce—her upbringing would not permit it—but tried to think of some other way out of the hole of despair in which she found herself sinking.

As World War II continued, the manpower crisis intensified; the number of housewives in the labor force doubled. Because many teachers had left for the service or to work in defense plants, the Oklee school board, like others throughout the U. S., was forced to revise drastically its policy of not hiring married women as teachers. There was a reversal in the public's attitude toward employment practices relating to women. In 1936 when George Gallup asked if married women should work, 82% of those polled answered no. But by 1942, 71% said housewives should take jobs.[4] Apparently the people of Oklee agreed with this trend and supported its school board's new policy. Superintendent Quist visited Coya at the farm in the spring of 1944 to recruit her for the very job that she had coveted in 1937.

Coya, however, was no longer eager to accept. She enjoyed being a homemaker; the AAA job fit her schedule nicely, besides enabling her to meet new people on a daily basis. She declined Mr Quist's offer not only once but a second time when he returned in the late summer to ask her to reconsider. By fall he was desperate—they simply could find no one to fill the teaching post—and this time she said Yes. She kept her AAA job and managed to juggle her working activities for about a year. Then, in 1945, Americans rejoiced in victory over Germany and Japan and within a few months, the AAA job, like so many others related to the war, ended.

Coya soon found she was happy working full time at the job she was trained for, teaching. The new junior-senior high school building had been constructed in 1940 with Works Progress Administration (WPA) funds plus $12,000 of local money. Coya had been hired to teach music and English, but because there was such a shortage of teachers, Coya filled in wherever she was needed. Certification requirements were ignored during the last year of the war and Coya was surprised to find herself teaching math, once her nemesis. Often she studied the math books late into the night so she could teach her class the following day. Coya taught with great energy, especially her music classes. A music student remembers that, "she came into the room like a tornado and taught with great enthusiasm—we all wanted to sing for her."[5] The English curriculum was easy to plan because, as in Plummer, a syllabus was provided by the state.

She also liked working in Oklee. The town was given the name in 1910 by the Tri-state Land Company who surveyed the property after purchasing it from settler O. K. Lee. The west half of the county had been settled by French-Canadians who were Catholic and the east half by Norwegians who were Lutheran. In town the two groups worked side by side and enjoyed a mild rivalry. They worshipped and socialized separately, but in the community life of school and business they worked together in a spirit of good-natured competition.

Several teachers made a point of favoring neither ethnic group by meticulously dividing their shopping between Bergeron's, owned by a French Catholic family, and Melby's, owned by a Norwegian Lutheran family. On one occasion Vern Bergeron bragged to Ole Melby that his apples were so good that the women at the school had bought three boxes. Melby expressed surprise because the same teachers had purchased three boxes of apples from him.[6] Melby and Bergeron had a good laugh over the teachers' concerns about maintaining good will between them. However, combining the two groups of children, French and Norwegian, provided lively classes for Coya. Sometimes their differences erupted in taunts, sometimes in good-humored joking; occasionally there was a "bristling" between groups.

Shortly after Coya stopped traveling around the countryside for the AAA, her 1929 Ford gave its last gasp and died. The school district had recently inaugurated a bus service and Coya rode the six miles into town on the school bus with her students until she was able to purchase a used four-door Nash for $600. The car was as an oddity in town: everyone else drove either Fords or Chevrolets. Coya commuted to Oklee unless severe winter conditions made driving difficult. When the roads were blocked with snow or a blizzard was forecast, she stayed in town at the home of her old friend and Andy's cousin, Anne Strande. Anne, 53, was a good-natured housewife married to Nels Strande, the owner/mechanic of the Standard Oil Station.

Coya managed to find a job for Andy in town as a school janitor. During her second year of teaching, Coya and Andy moved from their farm house to an apartment in town for the winter months. With two incomes from the school district, Andy and Coya were earning more cash than they ever had on the farm. But easier money and living in town were mixed blessings for Andy. Although he was not happy being a janitor, his pals were more accessible. According to Coya, every few weeks Andy "went on a toot" and stayed out all night. Coya worried about Andy's on-going drinking problem.

She was also concerned that despite the increase in their incomes, they were still faced with financial problems. She loved farm life, but it was becoming increasingly obvious that they couldn't make a living from their work on the farm. They needed money and Coya kept looking for things she could do to augment their earnings. Besides just supplementing their income, Coya wanted a job that would be as satisfying and challenging as her work with the AAA. Politics appealed to her, and more and more Coya's thoughts turned to Eleanor Roosevelt and her ideals of public service .

Although Coya dreamed of a career in government that would fulfill her own needs and help her neighbors and friends, she neither participated nor kept up on what was happening in state politics. After leaving the Gjesdal home, she had lost touch with the fortunes of her parents' old political party. The Nonpartisan League in Minnesota followed a path that was quite different from that of the League she had known in North Dakota; but it retained the basic philosophy of political protest, that the "fruits of one's labor seemed the passive toys of distant forces."[7]   In the 1920s, the Minnesota Nonpartisan League had joined forces with the Farmer-Labor party, continuing the League tradition of being a third party. At that time the League had attempted to merge with the Democrats, a minority in the state, but that effort had failed. Instead the League had merged with laborers and factory workers in St. Paul and with miners on the Iron Range. These groups formed an uneasy alliance and adopted the name, the Farmer-Labor Party.

The new Farmer-Labor Party at first met with success with Floyd B. Olson at its head, but after Olson's death in 1935 the Farmer-Labor Party began to fade away.   Elmer Benson did not have his predecessor's skill and could not coordinate the radical and conservative elements in the Farmer-Labor party as Olson had.   Some League members fell victim to the Communist line, which used catch phrases—such as "ruthless capitalism"—out of the NPL political heritage.

When the Communist Party made a renewed drive to attain power in the 1930s, Benson capitulated to them by agreeing that Communist sympathisers would hold office in the Farmer-Labor Party in exchange for their support. Voters rejected the Farmer-Labor ideas, and from 1938 on the Republicans were firmly in control of the Minnesota legislature, state offices and congressional seats. Concerned about Minnesota's Presidential ballots, the National Democratic Committee worked for change in Minnesota. In part through the direction of the National Democratic Committee, but also because of the energy and enthusiasm of Hubert H. Humphrey, Orville Freeman, Eugene McCarthy, and Eugenie Anderson, a truly startling achievement was accomplished in 1944.

In an effort to win national as well as state offices in Minnesota, these young leaders negotiated a merger between the Farmer-Labor and the Democratic parties of Minnesota into the Democratic Farmer-Labor party (DFL). The task of merger was not easy. In 1944 Humphrey oversaw more than 250 meetings; some of them took place in the ninth district, which included Oklee. Arthur O. (Spot) Reierson, who was later to champion Coya's political career, was instrumental in bringing the Farmer-Labor members of northwestern Minnesota into the DFL. The DFL party was born in April 1944, amid rumbles of discontent from members of anti-Communist elements who feared that Benson's men representing the Farmer-Labor tradition were being awarded too many influential positions. But the merged Democrat and Farmer Labor parties now had a chance of winning.[8]

Caught up in the everyday life of her first years of marriage, Coya had paid little attention to these changes in Minnesota politics. Yet the same year that the DFL was formed, an incident in Oklee caused Coya to give serious thought to her political aspirations. In October of 1944, Coya was asked to sing at a funeral service in Zion Lutheran Church for John (J. O.) Melby, a 78-year-old Norwegian immigrant who owned a meat market in Oklee.

J. O. Melby, a prominent community leader, first ran for the state legislature in 1926 and was re-elected for eight consecutive terms. While campaigning for re-election in 1944, he died of a stroke. Coya had admired Melby and felt honored to be asked to sing at his funeral. As the service concluded and she watched the pall bearers carry his casket out of the packed church, the thought popped into her head, "I'm going to take your place in the legislature someday, Mr Melby." Coya was stunned that those words had actually passed through her mind, but the notion of running for political office did not seem far-fetched.

Yet how in the world could she someday expect to win the seat held by Melby, a highly-respected Conservative? Coya realized that no matter how much she might want to be a legislator, she was a woman, and she was not sure her neighbors would vote for a woman. And, if she expected to be elected, she would need to develop business and management skills. She would also have to get her personal life in order.

Coya and Andy went on with their routine homelife on the farm during the summer, and tried to make ends meet by working during the winter months at their jobs in town. Both were disillusioned with farming and dissatisfied with the compromises they had to make in order to continue living on the farm. In September, 1944 Andy's 82-year-old father, Aslak Knutson, suffered a heart attack while chopping wood and died shortly afterward. Along with the grief they suffered over his sudden death, Andy and Coya had to deal with the practical considerations of running Aslak's farm. Gunhild and Anna were unable to manage the farm on their own, and Andy and Coya were faced with the prospect of having to take on the additional work.

After considerable discussion, they decided to quit farming altogether rather than expand their operation to include Aslak's acreage. Already living in Oklee during the winter months, Coya and Andy decided to sell both farms and live year-round in town. It was an easy adjustment for Coya, who had long ago left her childhood home to study and work in various towns. For Andy, who had always lived on a farm, the transition was difficult, even though he continued to work both farms during the summer months until the sales were completed.

The move into town meant that Coya would be free to look into various business opportunities that would give them greater financial security. She also knew that if she decided to run for a political office, she would have business experience and a greater visibility within the community.

Step by step, year by year, she was finding her way into politics.

Chapter 4

MAIN STREET

*The grandmother of 2007 will then point to her girlhood
days with pride and longing, as the days when women
were carefree and contented and jolly, when they knew
nothing of the worries of state, when they had no political debts to pay, when all they had to do was mop, and
shop, and get the meals and spank the children.*

"Knitting or Women's Rights"
Nonpartisan Leader, October 4, 1917

It was like that Spring morning when Coya was a girl and she and
her sisters had found the perfect place for a playhouse. The minute
she walked inside the front door, Coya knew the Angleterre Hotel
would be a good place for the family to live and work. The small
lobby with its desk and a few chairs led into a spacious dining room
that contained three booths across the back, six sets of tables and
chairs in the center of the floor and six high stools at a counter. She
smiled to herself as her mind raced ahead with ideas. Coya and Andy
could run the hotel and café, wait on customers and hire Andy's sister
to do the cooking. Once people got a taste of Anna's home cooking,
paying customers would fill the restaurant.

Coya was even more determined that the building should be theirs when she saw the high-ceilinged rooms upstairs. There was plenty of space for the family. The two large corner rooms with double beds at the front of the hotel would accommodate Andy and Coya, the other Gunhild and Anna, leaving six rooms for hotel guests. These smaller rooms each had one sash window and a framed opaque glass transom over the hall door. Their furniture was minimal, but all that was expected in those days: an iron bedstead, a dresser and a wooden chair. A single bathroom would have to be shared by family members and hotel guests.

In October of 1944, Andy and Coya sold their farm for $6,000 on a contract for deed, with payments due in monthly installments, and purchased the Hotel Angleterre for $5,000. The two-story white frame building with a peaked roof looked remarkably like the Edmore hotel that Coya's Aunt Cornelia had once owned in North Dakota. The new living arrangements suited everyone in the Knutson household. They took their meals together in the café and used the small lobby as a living room that they shared with the hotel guests. Eventually Coya bought a piano for the lobby that became a cozy gathering place.

After Gunhild sold her farm, the hotel became her permanent home. She was pleased with the move because she could visit friends whenever she wished instead of having to wait for a ride into town. Anna was glad to have a full-time job; she'd had plenty of experience cooking for farmhands on the Gjesdal farm and it was work she enjoyed doing.

In the autumn of 1944, the Knutsons welcomed Sonny, now known as Richie, into their home. Christine and Christ were unable to transport the fourteen-year-old to high school during the winter months. Besides, while Christ enjoyed his companionship, Christine found it difficult to discipline the teenager. When Richie became restless and uncommunicative, she could not cope with his moodiness. Coya wanted to relieve her mother of the strain. It was decided that Richie would stay with the Knutsons in Oklee during the school year and spend his summers with Helen in Devils Lake.

Eva, who had been working at a church in Fargo, North Dakota, returned to the Gjesdal family home after doctors had diagnosed her ailment as rheumatoid arthritis. She enjoyed Richie's company and was despondent about his move to Oklee, but she helped him pack.

Coya countered Richie's moody behaviour with a brisk cheerfulness, and felt that his presence brought vitality to the family. Andy was pleased to have the youngster living with them, too. Although he did not like school, Richie made friends easily and seemed content. There was one more place at the table now, but otherwise life did not change much within the household. Coya enjoyed the new activity in the house, and helped Richie build a bird house for a school project. She liked hearing the radio broadcasts of Richie's favorite programs, *The Lone Ranger* and *Jack Armstrong*, while she did her housework.

With the school and shops nearby, Main Street was a convenient place for the Knutsons to live. Main Street was a wide, gracious thoroughfare where people parked cars down the center of the street as well as at angles along the curb. The only problem was that until 1955 when they were paved, the streets were impassable in the Spring. Otherwise Coya enjoyed her walk to school and back; she could meet and chat with people on the street and glance into the display windows of stores. There were four grocery stores—one of which was a general store—two hardware stores, four filling stations, a municipal liquor store, two beer parlors, two farm implement dealers, a newspaper office, a bank, a small ready-to-wear shop, a furniture store and a combined barber shop/hairdressing salon. Main Street was prosperous, with only one vacant building in the two-block business section.[1]

Coya, hoping that her husband would take a greater interest in the business, renamed The Angleterre "Andy's Hotel." Hunters and salesmen were the main boarders. Andy took charge of renting the rooms, deposited the daily receipts at the bank, waited on customers in the café and even washed dishes. Andy's Hotel was truly a family business with each one of the Knutsons working there in some capacity. In addition to her full-time teaching job, Coya managed the small café; she planned menus, ordered food, waited on tables, cleaned up, and sometimes cooked. Anna did most of the cooking and baking, and Andy's mother assisted her by peeling potatoes and washing dishes. Business was good. The three grain elevators, the railroad depot, and the creamery brought many people to town, and the cafés and taverns up and down Main Street were usually packed with customers.

After a few months it was apparent that the café was the mainstay of the Knutsons' business. Many of the hunters and members of the railroad crews traveling through Oklee considered Andy's Café the best restaurant between Minneapolis and the Canadian border. Hunters would often bring in their freshly killed ducks and Anna would clean and roast them for dinner. The Knutsons kept their prices reasonable: a T-bone steak cost 75 cents; doughnuts, called "sinkers," were two for 5 cents. It was a "meat and potatoes" restaurant, with pie and cake for dessert. Breakfast, lunch and dinner, as well as morning and afternoon coffee, were served. Because many people came in for afternoon coffee, layer cakes were freshly baked each day, and the specialty-of-the-house was a white-frosted cake decorated with fresh orange slices.[2]

The café had a seating capacity of about 50 people. It was a cozy place and had all the amenities. Electricity was available and Coya was especially proud that they had an ice cream freezer. Because of war-time shortages, people lined up at the candy case whenever a rare shipment of Hershey bars and Wrigley's Spearmint gum arrived.

The Knutsons purchased a washing machine at Seeger Hardware, a modern appliance that could wash, drain, rinse and spin in the same barrel. The Knutsons' other major investment was good linoleum in a maroon-colored brick pattern for the floor of the café. The decor was simple and homey; the wood tabletops were varnished, and no tablecloths were used. The family was too busy serving meals to bother about further redecorating the café. The small restaurant was a warm and inviting place. Coya did much of the daily housekeeping and paid a cleaning woman, Elvina Zimmerman, five dollars to come in every other week to thoroughly scrub the restaurant and polish the counter and tables.

Although there were four cafés in Oklee then—Annie's, Cyr's, Oklee Corner Café and Andy's Café—Andy's was the most popular place in town. "That was where you went to see people," recalled one customer. Andy's was the place for celebrations, too. When Helen and Orlando Chervestad were married on Armistice Day, 1944, the bridal party wound up at the hotel café after the wedding dance. The bride remembers that about fifty people squeezed into the café, but Andy and Coya managed to feed everyone and give good service in the tiny dining room. Coya did most of the cooking, serving and cleaning up while joking and laughing with the patrons. The café was really her domain in the hotel, but Andy always helped her out when they had big groups. Saturday night was the big night in town and Andy's café was the gathering place, especially after dances and other festivities.[3]

The café's daytime business was booming, too, and that was partly because of its location. The Soo Line depot's long wooden platform extended well beyond the station and faced the café side of the hotel. Twice each day a small crowd gathered at the café to await the arrival of the Winnipeg-Duluth train that carried both passengers and freight, including grain bound for the Duluth harbor.

Youngsters never tired of running down the street to greet the old steam train and watch it pull, squealing and shaking, into the station. The black locomotive was quite a sight, puffing smoke and hissing steam as it came to a stop next to the depot. It was a dinosaur from a passing age, with its coal fire in the firebox producing steam to drive the big iron wheels. One of its cars was equipped to carry both passengers and freight; people boarded that car for short shopping or business trips to neighboring towns.

Newspaper carriers, salesmen, delivery men and passengers would drop by the café to wait for the train. Tom Toulouse, the drayman, would back his team of horses to the platform, have his coffee with old friends at the café and then unload packages from the freight car for delivery around town. Once the train pulled out of the depot, the crowd disappeared until the arrival of the next train. Although the café's location, as well as the good food and happy atmosphere, helped make Andy's the most popular café in town, its major source of income was from a game of chance called "punch-boards." In 1947, Governor Luther W. Youngdahl spearheaded an effort that made gambling illegal in Minnesota and the punch-board games were discontinued. Although Coya missed the income, she disapproved of gambling and was in favor of the legislation.

In the spring of 1947, Coya's father died suddenly of a massive heart attack at the age of 72. Coya, Andy and Richie set off immediately for Christ's funeral, but so much new snow had fallen that they couldn't make it to the farm by car. They got as far as Edmore and then had to travel the last six miles by horse and wagon. Coya found her mother in a state of shock over Christ's death. Coya, on the other hand, took his death calmly and tried to help her mother make decisions about her future.

Christine chose to remain living in the farm house. Coya inherited a quarter section of the acreage her parents had leased to neighboring farmers when Christ stopped farming. Following their return to Oklee from the funeral, Coya gave considerable thought to how she might use the inheritance. She was restless. Her mind was open to new business ventures. Because she liked the hotel business, Coya wanted a larger, more profitable hotel. She proposed to Andy that they sell Andy's Hotel and use the proceeds from its sale and the sale of her inherited land to buy the Red Lake Falls Hotel, twenty miles from Oklee. Andy responded with a flat no. There was no discussion. For him, moving twenty miles away was like moving to the moon. He had been born and bred on the farm in Oklee; he had his friends and a way of life he liked. Coya realized that his emotional ties to the town were so strong that there was nothing she could do to persuade him to leave.

Richie had lived with Coya and Andy almost three years, but as he grew older his relationship with his surrogate parents became strained. Coya could no longer get through to him, and he chafed under his big sister's efforts at "parenting." At the age of 17, Richie was uncertain about what he wanted to do with his future, but he did not want to remain in school any longer. He ran away from home and on May 17, 1947, they learned that he had joined the Army. Sometime later Eva heard that he was serving on the island of Guam.

Coya was 35 years old and she and Andy had been married for eight years. It was not a particularly happy marriage and Coya saw that they were growing further apart. There had been little romance in their courtship, and now there was not even a remnant of the playful teasing and easy companionship they had once enjoyed. It had long been apparent to Coya that Andy expected her to take care of him and do all the work just as his mother had.

Coya was juggling the demands of a full-time job with backbreaking labor at home. It seemed that the more Coya was willing to pick up the slack, the happier Andy was to relinquish his responsibility. Andy was well liked in town and was generally regarded as a happy-go-lucky, sweet-natured sort who just wanted to have a good time with his pals. All he asked of life was change in his pocket to buy a few drinks. He was not interested in making improvements on the hotel or working with Coya to secure their future; tomorrow was always a long way off to Andy.

It was hard on Coya whose mind was continuously spinning with new ideas. However strained her parents' marriage had been, they had shared a common drive to succeed and improve their lives. That desire to get ahead had been instilled in Coya, and Andy's lackadaisical attitude was a source of increasing frustration to her.

Coya wondered if adopting a child of their own might be a remedy for the estrangement in their marriage. More and more she longed to have a family, but after her two miscarriages she did not get pregnant again. She was convinced that once they had a child in their home, fatherhood would give Andy a reason to spend more time at home, to work harder and to look to their future. However, when Coya suggested adoption, Andy was lukewarm. Things were fine as they were, he told her. She persisted in talking to Andy about adoption and when he relented somewhat, that was encouragement enough for Coya. After all, she reasoned, Andy had gotten along well with Richie and had shown his best side to the boy.

During Christmas vacation, Coya took the train to visit Crystal in St. Paul. During her stay in the Twin Cities, she visited the Lutheran Welfare Home and asked to meet boys and girl who were available for adoption. She stated a preference in adopting a school-age child rather than an infant who could more easily be placed.

Coya's heart went out to seven-year-old Terence, a skinny little boy with dark hair and blue eyes. He was a lively youngster who was never still for a minute. She learned that his mother had been 20 years old and working as a servant when she became pregnant by the son of her employers. Unable to care for the baby herself, she put him up for adoption. Terry had a long history of being passed from one family to another; something always seemed to happen to prevent his adoption—in one case, there had been a divorce. Terry's mother had come to see him when he was in one of the foster homes, and it had upset the boy terribly that his mother couldn't take him with her. The child had been returned to the orphanage after each "adoption" and had been living there for two-and-a-half years when Coya met him.

She talked with the boy and they found they got on very well. Coya noticed that Terry had several small plants growing in paper cups on his windowsill. He liked to watch the seeds he had planted sprout and grow. Coya told the city boy about the farm land around Oklee, and the youngster grew interested. Terry asked her if he could have a bicycle and a wagon if he came to live with her. Coya told him truthfully that they would have to see about that; they had little money to spare and she did not want to make promises to him that she could not keep.

Coya could see that after so many failed attempts at adoption, Terry wanted to belong somewhere. He was afraid no one would ever adopt him. Coya wanted to take him home immediately, but that was out of the question without Andy's consent.

When Coya returned to Oklee, she talked incessantly about the boy. Gunhild and Anna were all for having a youngster in the house again. They missed Richie and looked forward to having another lively youth in the house. With the women in agreement, Andy decided to give Terry a chance. Coya was thrilled. In a house full of women, she hoped Andy and their young son would develop a bond. The women bought a small teddy bear, a wagon, and readied Richie's little room for Terry. Coya hung a 1948 calendar with a picture of a collie.

She bought him clothes and a suitcase and, during the school Easter vacation of 1948, Coya took the train to St. Paul to adopt their son. Terry was especially happy about the new shoes, his first pair of brand-new shoes from a store. He had always had to wear hand-me-downs that did not quite fit. He seemed a bit scared, but determined to leave the orphanage to live with a family.

Coya brought Terry home to Oklee by Soo Line passenger train. It was his first train ride. During the journey, Coya wondered if what she was doing was best for Terry. The slender little boy desperately needed affection and reassurance and she hoped that she could help him. She stayed awake all night, afraid that Terry—sleeping fitfully—might roll off the seat. As she watched him she wondered what life in Oklee would be like for him.

Bernadette Stromme, a waitress at the hotel, met Coya and Terry at the train station at 4 a.m. and drove them to the Knutsons' hotel. The light was on in the lobby, but the hotel was quiet. Coya was not surprised that at that early hour there was no one to greet them. They tip-toed as quietly as possible up the creaking stairs and made their way to Terry's room. The boy was exhausted from the trip and sleepy because of the hour, but he was excited to see his new bedroom. Coya pushed open the door and switched on the light, eager to see his reaction.

In the sudden glare of light, Coya's heart stopped a beat. Her hand flew to her mouth, but it was too late to hold back the harsh sound of her voice as she called out "Andy, no!"

Coya was stunned. As though it were frozen in a horrifying flashbulb-photograph, she stared at the shocking scene. Her husband was passed out on Terry's bed amid pieces of a broken lamp. The room was torn up and the newly-bought toys strewn about. The teddy bear that Coya had placed on the bed was thrown on the floor and the calendar had been ripped from the wall.

The noise and bright light had roused Andy. He pulled himself up and eyed the child drunkenly. "Go back where you came from—we don't want you around here," he growled.

Terry clung to Coya, hiding his face in the hem of her skirt. Coya gave him a hug and held him close while she told Andy to "get moving!"

As often happened, Andy's drunken bluster faded when Coya spoke to him sharply. Contrite and embarrassed, he got to his feet and shuffled out of Terry's room. Coya felt sick with rage and disappointment, but she tried to behave in a calm, matter-of-fact manner with Terry, hoping her reassuring hugs would soothe him. She helped the boy into his new pajamas and tucked him in before going to bed herself in one of the guest rooms. Terry fell asleep immediately, but Coya lay awake feeling drained and numb.

Over and over she kept asking herself, "Why did he do it?" When she had left for St. Paul, Andy had been fine. He had told her to go ahead with the adoption. There had been no indication then that he would get drunk and behave in this manner. Most of the time he didn't seem to care one way or the other about things and she couldn't even get him to talk to her. "Why," she asked herself, "did he always have to spoil things?"

Terry awoke after only a few hours of sleep. It was a a school day, and Coya decided to enroll Terry that morning hoping it would distract him and erase the ugly memory of Andy's reception . At breakfast the boy was very quiet and spoke only when prompted. Andy was red-faced and quiet, and left the hotel without eating breakfast. Coya and Terry walked to school where the youngster was enrolled in the second grade.

Terry felt numb and sick to his stomach. Instead of slipping into the warmth of a loving family, he had walked into a nightmare. The hotel was not at all the cozy home he had dreamed of. The Knutsons lived among an ever changing mix of strangers, sharing their home with hotel guests. He wondered how long he would be allowed to stay. He knew Andy didn't like him and didn't want him.

He was at an age when he longed for a father who would play ball with him and teach him to fish, but instead Terry had a father who frightened him with his drunken rages. Terry had never before seen anyone drunk. The boy spent much of his first month in Oklee sitting under a cupboard, hiding from trouble and wondering if he wanted to stay after all. He needed to belong somewhere, but it didn't look like it was going to happen here, either. Townspeople introduced him as Coya's and Andy's "adopted boy." That made him feel different and out of place.[4]

Coya could see that Terry was having a difficult time, and she tried to help him. She bought him baby rabbits to raise, and then a dog that Terry named Twinkle. Terry took good care of his new pets. "I knew how hard it was for them to adjust to a new home and new people," he says. She invited his teachers to the café for lunch, hoping that informal visits at home would make him feel more secure and relaxed in the classroom. Coya also encouraged Terry to bring schoolmates to the café for treats. Terry, an active, energetic boy, made friends quickly. His schoolwork was satisfactory despite having had to adjust to a new school toward the end of the term. Jo Quist, the school superintendent's wife, remembers that Terry tried hard to please and to fit in because he felt so insecure after his years in the orphanage. The Quists felt that Coya was anxious to make up for those hard times by being especially patient, fun-loving and generous with him.

In 1948 the Knutsons adopted Terence. It was clear that Andy was not interested in being a father to Terry, but he did not prevent Coya from adopting the boy she had come to love. Andy made the occasional token gesture of kindness toward Terry. Sometimes he would offer the boy "Snaps"—a candy-coated licorice packed in brightly colored boxes—from the café's display case. But Andy seldom, if ever, talked with the boy.

When Andy was offered a job as a school bus driver, he jumped at the chance to abandon his work as school janitor, a position he had always hated. In addition to his hotel duties, he now worked about four hours a day driving students to and from school. He took his new duty seriously and drank only on weekends.

Coya took on the full responsibility for raising Terry. She found pleasure in motherhood and enjoyed the company of her young son and his friends. As Terry grew older, she became more and more involved in his activities. She volunteered to be the leader of his 4-H group, sponsored by the Extension Service of the University of Minnesota. The 4-H's—hand, head, heart and health—emphasized learning by doing. Coya guided the six young club members in various demonstrations, such as grooming an animal and helped them plan hay rides and other excursions. The year's work focused on Achievement Day at the County Fair in Red Lake Falls. Coya's 4-H club members gave cake-making demonstrations, exhibited the animals and vegetables they had raised and displayed crafts such as sewing, quilting and wood-working projects. Terry exhibited his rabbits and Coya entered her apple pie and doughnuts. Each of them won prizes for their entries.

Postwar times were good. By 1948 the farming community of Oklee was prospering with higher prices paid for crops and dairy products. Farm women were getting 39 cents for eggs, a 50% increase over 1942. Farmers were paid $1.67 for barley, a 300% increase; and $7.18 for flax, an increase of 3000%. With extra money to spend, people painted their houses, built additions and planted flowers. Everyone living on farms and in town spruced up.

It seemed to the Knutsons that crop prices started rising about the time they sold their farmland. Neither had second thoughts about their decision; they realized that even with rising crop prices, they could not have made a living wage on their small farm. Andy and Coya preferred the convenience of living in town and they, too, reaped the benefits of postwar prosperity. Farmers and city people alike came into Andy's Café with money jingling in their pockets.

Coya was a popular figure in Oklee. As she had gained self-confidence, her outgoing, friendly nature emerged. She was no longer the awkward, stout farmgirl she had been in college. Coya was often described as "bubbly." She was seen as an attractive woman who kept up a pleasant, neat appearance that conformed to the simple, comfortable dress mode favored by most of the other women in town. She had few clothes and preferred wearing her schoolteacher's wardrobe of sweaters and skirts for all events, whether she was performing at a festive gathering or attending a Ladies Aid supper. Occasionally she used a touch of lipstick. Coya saw herself as an ordinary house-wife, clean and neatly groomed, who dressed for comfort rather than fashion. Like most of the women she knew, she gave herself a home permanent and wore her softly curled hair parted on the side. At five-foot-five-inches, Coya weighed 140 pounds. As long as she remained active, she could maintain that weight.

The women Coya respected, and who admired her in return, valued an ethic of service to home, church and community. Coya embraced this moral code. To her, "getting ahead" and "getting things done" meant an exhausting schedule of serving the needs of others. It was also part of the pattern of achievement through hard work that had been instilled in her as a child.

On most days, Coya would rise at 5:30 a.m. to greet the early-bird customers who started to arrive at the café at 6 a.m. She served breakfast for two hours, cleaned up, and then set off on her two-block walk to school. Coya was obsessive about leaving the hotel in good order before starting her teaching day, but eventually she learned to let some things go. She couldn't be late for school and she couldn't have her mind on the hotel and café while teaching; she had to trust Andy and Anna to take charge in her absence.

After teaching five classes a day, she coached students in music or speech after school. Because she wasn't available to serve afternoon coffee and early supper at the café, Coya hired high school students for 25 cents (and later 50 cents) an hour to help out. Eris Super, a former waitress, recalls that few youngsters could get part-time work and that she felt lucky to have a job at Andy's.

Coya and Andy both enjoyed socializing with the customers. On those days when Coya was free in the late afternoon, she waited on tables and then ate supper with the family in the café. There was church choir practice one night a week and Coya usually had school-work and reading to do in the evenings, but as her last chore at night she tidied up the café. Usually she went to bed at ten, after everyone else in the family had already turned in for the night.

Andy was seen by most people in town as a shy man who accepted things at face value. A conversation with him was nearly impossible; it was not in his nature to probe or exchange ideas. In his quiet, pleasant manner, he offered greetings of the day and an observation about the weather—that was that. Townspeople remember him standing behind the hotel counter, always with a cigar in his mouth and more cigars in his pocket, gently smiling at his friends who teased him about his absent wife. While people knew he went out to drink with his friends and might "have too much" sometimes, he was "one of the boys," one of a group of men who drank and played cards together at Fritz's Tavern, the saloon nearest to Andy's Hotel.[5]

Sundays were devoted to church, family—and more work. On Sunday mornings, Coya, Terry and Gunhild usually attended church while Anna stayed home to cook for the café. Sunday dinners were popular at Andy's and many people came for chicken dinner after church. Coya and Gunhild hurried home to put on aprons and Andy often pitched in to help serve. After the family had eaten, they closed the café around three o'clock. They would then sometimes pay a visit to Andy's sister Mary and her husband Gunnulf Breivold, one of the few outings on which all five Knutsons would go together. The grown-ups spent the afternoon talking, usually in Norwegian, while Terry, who didn't understand the language, sat idly in their company. Gunhild spoke no English and therefore everyone talked in Norwegian whenever she was present. Terry felt excluded from the family circle because not only was he unable to talk with his grandmother, she also unintentionally shut other people away from him. He and Gunhild had no way of communicating; aside from the language barrier, his grandmother was not affectionate.

Anna was the one who spent the most time with Terry and there was always a close bond between them. She looked after Terry while his mother was working and, in her quiet, undemonstrative way she managed to convey that she cared about him. But Terry reserved his greatest love for his mother who was always openly affectionate and tender with him. He was also proud of her because she was different from other children's mothers in her boundless energy and exuberance.

When Terry turned nine, he was free to be on his own more. In Oklee children were allowed to run about or ride their bikes any place in town, stopping in one another's homes without having to ask permission from anyone's parents. Terry was a sensitive youngster who quickly observed the unwritten laws of his new hometown and drew his own conclusions. He became aware that there was an imaginary line drawn down the middle of Main Street, with most Norwegians living on the east side and most French on the west side, each ethnic group residing close to its church. He also saw that people regarded his father as a "good guy" and readily overlooked his frequent binges. Terry knew that if anyone on Main Street were asked "Who is the nicest guy in Oklee?" the answer would be "Andy Knutson." Terry could not understand how people could say that. He was terrified of his father.

Although the café kept her very busy, teaching and the extracurricular activities at school were Coya's major occupation. Parents saw her as a progressive teacher, a characteristic that was not always admired. In health class she taught her students that breast-feeding infants was preferable to bottle-feeding and several parents were outraged that she would discuss such intimate matters with children. The angry parents protested to the school board but their complaints were dismissed.

Coya, who well remembered her own difficulties in school, always made herself available to students who were having problems with their grades. One student was prepared to quit school in frustration, but Coya persuaded her to come to the hotel every night for special tutoring. The student not only made it through high school but went on to college and eventually became a teacher herself. Without Coya's encouragement, she felt she would not have overcome her learning difficulties.[6]

Coya played the piano and sang at school events and led the assemblies in "God Bless America." As adviser to the participants in the annual declamation contest, Coya saw to it that her students produced good essays first, and then coached them in their delivery of the reading. She directed class plays and operettas and helped create programs for the annual school carnival. One year she took charge of the food concession, which earned a good profit on the sale of ice cream, soft drinks and hotdogs.

Superintendent Carl Quist prized Coya as a teacher and remembered that she "was always ready and able to take on extra assignments, and at no extra pay."[7] Coya was pleased that her work was appreciated, but she also believed that teachers *ought* to be paid for these extracurricular activities. Her salary was $400 a month, which was the top of the pay scale, and that meant that she was not eligible for a raise. Still, this was a 300% increase over her earnings at Plummer seven years earlier. In an effort to increase teachers' benefits and raise the pay scale, Coya joined professional organizations such as the Minnesota Education Association and the National Education Association. She was soundly criticized by other teachers who did not think their profession should be subject to unionization. Coya replied, "If we do not organize we won't get anywhere."

Coya was well aware that she could not have participated in all these activities without the practical support of Anna and Gunhild who took on the responsibilities of housework and child care. Coya also found that the day-to-day management of the café became easier with more experience. It seemed to her that everything was settling into place.

One day Coya's Aunt Cornelia saw a photograph of Tor Gjesdal, her nephew and Coya's first cousin, on the front page of the *Dakota Posten.* Christ Gjesdal's brother had stayed in Norway, and his son, Tor, had moved to New York to be the Chief Information Officer for the United Nations. Earlier he had helped set up the U.N. Charter in San Francisco. Coya's aunt was so excited about spotting her nephew in a newspaper that she wrote to him. When she received a warm reply to her letter, Aunt Cornelia proudly spread the word about their famous relative. The American Gjesdals were all proud of Tor's achievements. Coya particularly admired her cousin for devoting himself to government service and international peace.

She kept Eleanor Roosevelt's public service ethic in mind and it inspired her to pioneer new projects in Oklee. She worked with other volunteers to establish a medical clinic, a branch of the Red Cross and a Community Chest Fund. A social group formed at the same time was the Birthday Club. A group of ten women met socially at the home of the honoree and each guest brought a birthday card and a treat for potluck lunch.

Coya told a friend that "once you do some volunteer work well, everybody will hang a job on you." Once a month she took her turn serving at the Ladies Aid community dinners; the women charged 50-cents a plate and still made money. She also worked with the women at church who sponsored an annual fund-raising dinner in the autumn. The church group also regularly catered lunches for funerals and various community events. Everyone was generous about donating food such as sandwiches on homemade buns, a macaroni or rice casserole with ground beef or tuna, a Jell-O salad, or a cake. It was a busman's holiday that Coya thoroughly enjoyed. She'd pack up a hot dish, grab an apron and join the other women in the church basement to laugh and joke while serving huge quantities of food. As it had been for her mother in Edmore, donating time and services to the church was more than just a duty for Coya: it was a highlight of small-town social life as well as an important part of her spiritual heritage.

There were significant indications that the Lutheran church was becoming more American. In 1946 the church synod had dropped "Norwegian" from its name and became The Evangelical Lutheran Church. Although the French and the Norwegians still kept pretty much to themselves, Coya and her family made a point of attending the annual fall dinner at St. Francis Xavier Catholic Church. Not only was it an opportunity to socialize with the French community, it was a chance to enjoy a magnificent meal: roast turkey or chicken served with a special dressing made with bread cubes, meat and herbs.

In addition to her other volunteer work, Coya was a member of the Red Lake County welfare board from 1948 to 1950. She had gained insights and an interest in welfare through her own experiences when she adopted Terry. The three-member board met to examine and evaluate requests for welfare money, and in reviewing these cases Coya was exposed to heartbreaking family dilemmas. People did not know how or where to seek help and when aid finally did reach them, it was often too late to undo the damage of severe deprivation. It was especially painful for Coya to see a family torn apart by problems that had become insurmountable before professional counseling or health and financial assistance were available. Sometimes parents did not know that school meals and free immunization shots were available for their children.

People who had nowhere else to turn began calling Coya at home with their problems. A woman from Red Lake Falls had a ten-year-old son who had threatened his mother with a knife, then climbed to the top of a telephone pole and screamed uncontrollably. The child was a danger to himself, his family, and others, but the parents did not know what to do. Coya wrote to Governor Luther W. Youngdahl asking for his help. The Governor arranged for the boy to be sent immediately to the Brainerd State Hospital where he would get treatment. In many other cases, Coya brought food and clothing to destitute families living near Oklee.

Coya felt strongly that community service did not include the right to pass judgement on other people. She acted on her principle when the funeral of a fellow church member became an issue of contention in town. Osmund Torkelson was imprisoned for the murder of Knute Evje and hanged himself in his jail cell. Because of his crime and suicide, Pastor Lie, the minister of Clearwater Lutheran Church where Torkelson had been a member, refused to preach the funeral sermon or allow the body to lie in state in the church. Pastor J.K. Lerohl of Zion Lutheran Church in Oklee volunteered to officiate at the funeral and Coya offered to play the organ for the service. Coya asked a student of hers, 17-year-old Leona Larson, to sing a solo. The three traveled to the nearby country church where they found the pews full of people. At Pastor Lie's instructions, the closed coffin remained out of view in the vestibule throughout the service. Leona sang *Den Store Hvide Flok,* ("Behold the Host Arrayed in White") an old Norwegian favorite, accompanied by Coya at the pump organ.[8]

With her visibility as a community leader, her teaching and business background and the guise of a good family life, Coya soon attracted the attention of the Red Lake Democratic-Farmer-Labor party (DFL) and was chosen to be their county chairwoman in 1948. Her appointment was proposed by Cliff Longtin, the Red Lake County DFL chairman who was one of the farmers Coya had worked with in her Agricultural Administration job.

Assuming a major office in the local political organization was an important introduction to DFL party politics for Coya, who served as their chairwoman for two years. Red Lake County was small and consisted mostly of farms. The five towns in the county were Plummer, which was largely Norwegian; Oklee, a French and Norwegian community; and Brooks, Terrebonne, and Red Lake Falls, all predominantly French. The populations of these towns ranged from 90 to 1,700, with a total of 6,000 people living in the county.

While Coya was familiar with the county through her AAA job, she was not well informed on state or national politics. With her heavy work load, she rarely had time to listen to the radio or read newspapers, although she did look for Eleanor Roosevelt's daily column, "My Day." She read the *Grand Forks Herald* sporadically and occasionally thumbed through the various periodicals in the magazine concession at the café. Aside from copies of *Time* and *Life*, the newsstand in the restaurant mostly carried movie magazines, comic books and "ladies" periodicals, such as *Ladies' Home Journal* and *Good House-keeping*. As she got more involved in politics, Coya began to check out books at the high school library, particularly biographies of political figures.

With little political awareness beyond that of local affairs in her own county, Coya attended her first Ninth District DFL convention in Detroit Lakes in April and went to the state convention in Brainerd in June 1948. Coya felt "green" and very nervous. Cliff Longtin took her under his wing and introduced her to the Ninth District Chairman, L. J. Lee, and several other established political figures.

She met Arthur O. (Spot) Reierson, a wiry, small man in his 40s, who was described as a "powerful political broker" and "dangerous." He certainly didn't look the part, Coya thought. The farmer from Fosston, Minnesota was quiet, thin, unassuming and chain-smoked Camel cigarettes. She was told he had been called Spot since he was a freckle-faced youngster. She saw nothing in his appearance or demeanor to warrant the reputation, but she did notice that everyone paid attention when he spoke.

She also met 30-year-old Orville Freeman and was impressed by the dark-haired handsome young man whose appearance was made even more interesting by a slightly crooked jaw and mouth, caused by a war injury. A salty ex-marine, and now Secretary of the state DFL Central Committee, Freeman was known as a scrapper. When Coya met him at the convention Freeman was exhausted because he had been up all night with Hubert Humphrey and various other members laying out strategy to oust the leftists who dominated the committee. A key to doing so was to secure seating of the large Hennepin County (Minneapolis) delegation who supported incumbent Harry S. Truman for President. Freeman was chairman of that delegation and he and Humphrey were fighting a rival Hennepin County group that supported Henry A. Wallace for President.

Flanked by "old boys" Longtin and Reierson, who knew everyone, Coya felt like the new girl in town as they made their way through the crowds on the convention floor, turning her this way and that to shake hands and meet people. Her head was swimming with names as first Reierson and then Longtin edged her toward one group after another of delegates: "Say, there, I'd like you to meet Coya Knutson from Oklee." It was Spot Reierson who saw Humphrey enter the room and told Coya it was time for her to meet him.

Her heart thumped and she felt icy chills in her neck as, accompanied by Longtin and Reierson, she made her way toward the knot of people surrounding Hubert H. Humphrey. She was in awe of him. Born and raised in a small South Dakota town, Humphrey had become involved in politics while still a law student at the University of Minnesota. His rise in Democratic politics was meteoric. Already a legend at 37, Humphrey was in his second term as mayor of Minneapolis and running for the Senate.

As Coya approached the retinue gathered around Humphrey, her first impression of him was that his chin stuck out and that he was a non-stop talker. He had the reputation for never being at a loss for words and Coya could see that it was true. Humphrey was medium-height, well-dressed and exploding with energy. He shook her hand, said some nice things about Reierson, and asked her if she liked her new job in the county party. Coya assured him that she did, and she was pleased that he already seemed to know who she was. She had heard that another of Humphrey's characteristics was his remarkable memory. He made it a point to find out about people and then flattered them by remembering things about them. Coya felt light-headed and "sort of shaky" as the three of them moved on to talk with other people.

Coya was not aware of the behind-the-scenes maneuverings going on between the Humphrey-Freeman group and the Communist sympathizers. In 1944 the newly formed DFL had not been dominated by leftists who subscribed to Communist ideas. However, Humphrey had courted Communists in order to bring the Farmer-Labor Party into a merger with Democrats. The Farmer-Labor Party came into the DFL merger with its two distinct wings; in fact, opposition from the Farmer-Labor right was not so much to the merger itself as it was to the continuance of its long battle with the Farmer-Labor left, referred to as Fellow Travelers and Communists. The problem for Humphrey and Freeman was that they did not prevent pro-Soviet radicals from attaining power within the organization. In early August 1946, leftists wrested control of the party away from Humphrey following a roaring dispute at the DFL executive committee meeting. After the fledgling DFL fared poorly in state elections that fall, Humphrey pulled away from his left-wing friends. "If I have to choose between being a Red-baiter and a traitor," he said, "I'll be a Red-baiter."

To reassert leadership, Humphrey ignored the DFL he had organized only three years earlier and formed a separate organization, a state chapter of Americans for Democratic Action (ADA).

The nucleus of the Minnesota ADA was Humphrey, Freeman, and five Humphrey advisers who had worked to bring about the Democratic Farmer-Labor merger in 1944: Arthur Naftalin, a University of Minnesota student, who was Humphrey's secretary; Eugene J. McCarthy, who was running for U. S. Representative to Congress from the 4th Minnesota District; Eugenie Anderson, soon to be named the first woman U. S. Ambassador and posted to Denmark; Evron Kirkpatrick, one of Humphrey's professors at the University of Minnesota; and Max Kampelman, who was Humphrey's close friend.

By the time of the 1948 state convention in Brainerd, the fight between the rightists (ADA) and leftist factions of the DFL had been waged in precinct caucuses and county and district conventions. Control of the party at the state convention hinged on which of Hennepin County's delegations was seated. Freeman's pro-Truman Hennepin County delegation was seated. Freeman was elected state DFL chairman and Humphrey the DFL candidate for Senate. However, leftists refused to give state delegates to the coming National Convention authorization to back Truman.

The fight between rightists and leftists in the DFL continued on into the state Supreme Court, which declared legal the state DFL convention's backing of Truman. Humphrey, the rightist DFLers and the Minnesota ADA finally expelled the Communists from the DFL. In the November 1948 election Hubert H. Humphrey was elected U.S. Senator, ensuring the ascendancy of the DFL party and Humphrey's career.[9]

Despite her lifelong familiarity with the Farmers Nonpartisan League and the Farmers Union, Coya thought of herself as a "greenhorn" in DFL politics. What she did understand was Oklee and her place in it. In any small town a handful of individuals usually keep the social, educational, spiritual and economic wheels turning. In Oklee, Coya was one of those people. It had become Coya's belief that government was everyone's responsibility and that by participating in the political process she could influence public affairs.

Late one night in the early spring of 1950, Coya was sweeping the floor and getting ready to close the café when she looked up to see Cliff Longtin and Elmer Fortier, the grain-elevator manager from Brooks, enter the restaurant. She knew immediately what they wanted and said to herself, "You are going to ask me to run for the legislature."

Six years had gone by since she had sung at J. O. Melby's funeral when the idea of running for the state legislature had first occurred to her. She was aware that Longtin wanted women in the legislature because he thought they would approve of certain education programs. Longtin, a French-Catholic, was in favor of using public funds to transport private-school pupils. Although the Catholic Church he attended in Oklee did not sponsor a school, he felt strongly that the government's policy against disbursement of any tax revenue to private and parochial schools should be changed. Even though it was contrary to the ethics of her mentor, Eleanor Roosevelt, Coya thought it was unfair that children going to private school could not ride public-school buses. Catholic parents paid taxes like everyone else, Coya reasoned, and their children ought to benefit by at least having their transportation to school provided by tax dollars. Coya knew that Longtin was "looking for a live one" who could win the election and she fit the bill. Coya was therefore not surprised when the local DFL leadership asked her to run for J. O. Melby's former seat, currently held by Conservative C. S. McReynolds, as District 65 Representative in the Minnesota Legislature.

The timing could not have been better. The mortgage had been paid in full and the operation of the café and hotel was running smoothly. Her mind was at ease about Terry, who was doing well in school, and Anna was at home to help. The Superintendent of Schools encouraged her to enter politics even though it meant he might lose a hard-working, popular teacher. As a representative Coya would earn $2,500 for the three-month session. It seemed feasible that she could serve in the legislature while continuing her teaching job.

Only one area of her life—her marriage—was not satisfactory. Andy was more withdrawn than ever and avoided any sort of conversation with his wife. When she suggested that they discuss their problems, Andy would turn his back, put on his coat and hat, and walk out the door without a word, sometimes staying away the entire day. Andy refused to take initiative in facing their marital problems, but resented Coya as a "domineering wife" when she broached the subject.

She recognized that, while her high level of activity at work and in the community had become a means of compensating for the lack of companionship she found at home, it only served to exacerbate the discord between them. Coya felt a constant need to prove herself and, because her parents had inculcated their own ambition to succeed, she would always seek opportunities to challenge herself. The reputation she had earned as an outstanding community leader and successful business woman bolstered her own self-esteem, but lowered Andy's. The similarities in their backgrounds, which had at first drawn them together, had become superficial. The differences between them were now pulling them apart.

Some of their problems no doubt grew out of the disparity in their educations. Coya had sixteen years of schooling while Andy had eight. That was not unusual. At that time in Minnesota, women generally had more schooling than men, but it wasn't ordinarily a cause for marital strife.[10] It was the differences in attitude toward expanding their horizons that caused problems. Coya was open to new ideas and was prepared to take chances in life. Andy wanted everything to remain the same. He overcame his reluctance to move off the farm because it meant he would be closer to his friends in town and because it would please Coya. However, once he left the farm, he also relinquished whatever independence and self-determination he felt that he had in their marriage. Coya was now the recognized bread-winner and he worked part-time at whatever jobs she managed to find for him at the school.

Andy did not like it that people in town knew "who wears the pants in the Knutson house." He was resentful of her having usurped the man's traditional role while she was angry at Andy's lack of attention to his family. Society still cherished the idea of "man for the field, woman for the hearth." When his friends teased him about his woman bossing him around, Andy could never come up with a fast, cocky response to save face. Instead, embarrassed and hurt, he would shrug his shoulders and look away.

When Coya was asked to run for the state legislature, she saw it as one of the most gratifying and exciting opportunities of her life. Andy felt that she was going out of her way to make him look foolish and insignificant. Coya wanted to be on her own and Andy wanted to be left alone. By winning the election she could satisfy both their needs. At least for a few months of the year, she'd reside in St. Paul, Minnesota.

No one in Coya's family was excited about her campaign except Andy's brother Torkel, who had been elected sheriff of Polk County in 1942. He had been re-elected several times and enjoyed campaigning. Coya knew she could turn to Torkel and his wife Orianna for encouragement. While family members did not speak disparagingly to Coya about her candidacy, Andy's mother Gunhild protested to Orianna that she did not think it was right for a woman to be in politics.

Even though no women had served in the state Legislature since 1943, Coya felt sure she could beat the three-term Conservative incumbent, C. S. (Clarence Samuel) McReynolds, a respected farmer and beekeeper from Clearwater County who had held the office since J.O. Melby's death. Although the seats were not designated by party at that time, but instead labeled Conservative and Liberal, a candidate's political affiliation was common knowledge. The Conservatives carried a large majority in both the House and Senate, but Coya sensed that the fledgling DFL Party was on the move and that a Liberal could be accepted by voters. In her campaign for the District 65 seat, she would be dealing with a largely rural population and a small-town code of ethics. She had gained an insight into rural politics in the local DFL organization and she had a lifetime's experience of meeting, living and working with these people. She was confident she could gain their support.

Coya had taken stock of her political assets and knew she had much to offer that would appeal to the voters. She felt comfortable speaking in public now, and she'd learned that her musical talents and ebullient personality were crowd-pleasers. Her reputation as a homemaker, teacher, business-woman, church volunteer and community leader with experience in government service would carry her a long way. Through her teaching, the AAA job and her work on the welfare board, she'd met just about everybody in the Oklee and Plummer areas. She had earned high regard for her energetic, nononsense style in helping people through critical family difficulties, and she'd gained a good reputation among farmers for her knowledge of agricultural problems. She had the skills, ambition, drive and sheer physical stamina to run a tough race.

Although it had been seven years since a woman had served in the State Legislature, Coya did not feel she would be handicapped by public sentiment against a woman politician. Her gender had not been an issue in any previous government job or political appointment. Besides, Coya got on well with both men and women. She had always had women friends and enjoyed working among them in school and at church and community functions. She respected the role of the homemaker and was sympathetic to the special needs of women who spent much of their time at home raising children.

Coya felt perfectly comfortable in the company of men talking about reform in agricultural policies, the benefits of rotating crops and the current market price of wheat. She was her father's "son" and there wasn't much about tractors, seed and the effects of Big Biz on farming that she didn't know. She'd never felt squeamish about joining community and political groups dominated by men. As she had for the AAA, she could talk egg and milk prices with the women and hog and barley quotations with the men.

It was up to Cliff Longtin to set up meetings with community leaders and see that she met key people. She planned to begin her campaign in early August, getting her views on education, social welfare and agricultural topics across to all the farm families in her district. The area was sparsely populated and rural; it was up to her to seek out every voter.

In the meantime the one skill she needed to bone up on was typing. She bought a typewriter from the *Oklee Herald* office and sat in a back booth of Andy's Café practicing. She remembered some of what she had learned from the business teacher in Plummer and taught herself how to type. She figured it would come in handy since she did not have a secretary.

Chapter 5

THE LADY
LEGISLATOR

*The legislator lobbyist who wants to make an appeal for
his special interest will have to carry a satchel full of bon-
bon boxes, as well as cigars.*

*Mrs May Wilson, Hurdsfield, North Dakota,
Nonpartisan Leader: October 4, 1917*

*"J*oin the Farmers Union! Join the Farmers Union,"* the people sang.

Coya was in the front row sitting on a folding chair at a monthly
meeting of the Farmers Union in Gully Town Hall. She stole a glance
behind her and saw some fifty people of all ages singing fervently.
After the song she would be called on to say a few words. It wouldn't
be difficult. The crowd was fired up and ready to hear her talk about
the good times ahead.

"Peace and prosperity for all," the song leader shouted at the top
of his voice, raising his right hand toward the ceiling as he yelled, *"for
all."*

Coya joined in with the audience that sang even louder than
before:
*Cultivate your cropland
With the Farmers Union*

Answer the Farmers Union call!

But Coya did not speak at the end of that chorus: the crowd continued to sing and the leader called out the lyrics all over again. The union members were clearly happy with themselves and whatever might be ahead. Coya was glad that she was scheduled to be a speaker because, in keeping with the sentiment of the song, she felt she was answering a call to represent these people in the legislature.

Coya felt at one with these farm families and was glad she had decided to run. In 1950 two representatives were to be elected from the 65th District which comprised three counties: Pennington, Clearwater and Red Lake. All three had agriculture as their single industry and all three were small in both area and population. Clearwater was the largest geographically (1,000 square miles) and Pennington the most populous (13,000 residents). Voters in these three counties were to become Coya's most steadfast supporters throughout her political career.

Four candidates vied for the two available seats: Coya Knutson, Walter E. Day, A. W. Olson and C. S. McReynolds. Walter Day, 70, was from Bagley in Clearwater County. He had been a member of the House since 1919 with the exception of the 1935 session. Active in the cooperative association, he caucused with the Liberal party and was a high vote-getter during his thirty years in the legislature.

A. W. Olson was a dark horse candidate not known to Coya or other DFL members.

C. S. McReynolds, 60, was the incumbent and "the man to beat." McReynolds had several things in common with Coya. Both were natives of North Dakota; he was from Kokomo, and, like Coya, a teacher and a farmer. He had taught for ten years and then entered the honey production business near Clearbrook, twenty-five miles from Oklee. McReynolds operated about 40 bee yards in Minnesota, with about 35 colonies in each yard, and annually transported several hundred of these colonies to Talco, Texas for the winter months. McReynolds served as President of the Minnesota State Beekeepers Association for two years. He was a Baptist and became an ardent worker for the Gideon Society.

McReynolds, a quiet, reserved man, was not inclined to campaign at events like Farmers Union meetings and, because he had already been elected to office three times, he expected to be re-elected again. His newspaper advertisement featured his photograph and the caption *"C. S. McReynolds, the Honeyman; A man who has six years of experience and stands on his past record."[1]*

The DFL endorsed both Coya Knutson and Walter E. Day. Coya's endorsement was part of a team effort by Liberals not afraid to campaign under the DFL banner. McReynolds was not endorsed by the Republican party and his was an individual effort by a Conservative who, like some other Minnesota legislators, did not want to be identified with a party.

Coya campaigned against McReynolds with her usual energy. She was good at entertaining people and, because she emulated the orators at old-time Nonpartisan League picnics of her childhood, she was at her best at events like Farmers Union meetings. She sought out and attended every fair, festival and community event in the district to shake hands and deliver a rousing speech. A woman running for a political office usually held by a man was enough to inspire curiosity and Coya capitalized on that.

Person-to-person campaigning required behavior that was popularly considered "contrary to a feminine nature." But Coya's ebullient personality allowed her to "blow her own horn" and win the approval of both men and women. She sang at Farmers Union meetings in town halls, at Ladies Aid meetings in church basements, and wherever else Cliff Longtin could help her accumulate a gathering of voters. Once she had broken the ice with a song or two, she'd rip into a lively, down-to-earth talk that included several specific issues. She was warm and neighborly and felt entirely at home with people of both Norwegian and French backgrounds. She could speak with authority and disarming directness to housewives, farmers and business people, tailoring her speech to their individual concerns.

The *Thief River Falls Times* reported that at a Business and Professional Women's meeting, Coya gave a "nonpolitical talk," focusing on the woman's place in city, county, state, national and world affairs. She pointed out that women were taking the power of the ballot more seriously than in the past, and concluded that "women voters could carry the nation for the simple reason that there are two million more women voters than men voters."[2]

Once she had addressed the special interests of a particular audience, Coya went on to state the action she proposed taking on three specific programs.

With regard to the Fair Employment Practices Commission (FEPC),

Coya stated "I think we should take the lead in setting up a statewide FEPC to set a good example."[3] The FEPC would protect employment regardless of race, color, creed, religion or national origin. In 1950 no one, Coya included, pressed for protection against discrimination on the basis of sex.

Legislation for fair employment of minorities was a new and controversial issue. In 1941 Eleanor Roosevelt had helped persuade the President to establish a national FEPC to fight racial bias in war industries. In 1947, while mayor of Minneapolis, Hubert Humphrey had first captured national attention when he established the city's Fair Employment Practice Commission. During the late 1940s Republican Governor Luther Youngdahl had campaigned throughout Minnesota for FEPC and had gained support from socially conscious members of divergent religious and political faiths. But many other Republican groups, including the Minnesota Employers Association, opposed fair employment legislation.

In 1950 some DFLers were opposed to it too, but establishment of a FEPC was part of the DFL platform. And Coya brought the idea to northwestern Minnesota while the other district legislative candidates did not mention it. She wanted to open the door to fair employment legislation which would affect her district: there was a sizable Ojibwe Native American population at Red Lake only a few miles from District 65 boundaries. Furthermore, use of Hispanic migrant workers as seasonal labor—such as in cultivating the large potato and sugar beet fields on the far western fringes of the district—was common.

Coya also spoke up on the issue of state aid for education. She explained that "our district needs help to bolster its building program. [Schools are] so overcrowded now, a teacher has trouble getting inside a schoolroom."[4]

The third issue on Coya's agenda was a school health program that would provide school nurses. Coya believed that "we must do something to provide school nurses. We can't get them and can't afford them within the local school budgets."[5] In the various schools in which Coya had taught, care for a sick or injured child had been left in the hands of classroom teachers with no medical training. A sick child should have better care. Public school nurses funded by the state would not only alleviate the problem, but would help to promote good health habits among the students.

Running for the legislature in a small rural district required little cash at that time, although money was needed for newspaper ads and posters. Coya managed her campaign at a total expenditure of $150. The back seat of her car was always piled high with posters and, as she drove back and forth across her district, she'd stop to hand them out at cafés and stores.

Coya added trips to the Clearwater and Pennington County Fairs to her usual visit to the Red Lake County Fair. She searched out crowds wherever they gathered, whether at the livestock parades or at the morning and afternoon 4-H Showmanship Contests and Dress Revues. On Oklee's annual autumn Market Day, Coya was there talking to her neighbors and shaking hands. Coya also used the local radio station KTRF at Thief River Falls.

Throughout the campaign, Cliff Longtin kept his word. Longtin was a father figure to Coya. He took the inexperienced campaigner under his wing and helped her meet people. Wherever the good-natured Longtin went, he was welcome. Wearing his visored cap pulled down over his weather-beaten face, Longtin looked like he had just come out of the field himself. He drove Coya to the farms of key people in the district, and since the weather was fair in late summer and fall, many of these meetings were held in a farmyard or field. Longtin was a highly regarded, important political leader in the district and his personal attention to Coya constituted a major endorsement.

Even though she was an announced candidate, Coya did not directly ask her women friends in Oklee for their votes. One of the social groups in which she was active, the Sew and Save Club, met shortly before the election at the farm home of Mrs Deniston. Six or seven women sat together in the pretty farmhouse knitting baby clothes and embroidering dishtowels while they visited. Coya was filled with the excitement of the campaign and, even though she soon tired of the small talk, she did not bring up the subject because she instinctively knew that the women would be offended by a neighbor and friend going "out in front."

Coya won the election November 7, 1950 and would enter the legislature as a member of the minority Liberals.[6] Years later when constituents were asked how Coya got elected, many answered, "She sang at every wedding and funeral in the county."[7] However, Andy's brother Torkel Knutson did not win re-election as sheriff. His defeat was not unexpected after eight years in office.

Within months of the election, C. S. McReynolds suffered a stroke while tending his bee colonies in Texas. McReynolds was taken to a hospital in nearby Mt. Pleasant, but died the following day, March 21, 1951. Coya was shocked and saddened by his sudden death and wondered whether his disappointment in losing the election had been a contributing factor. Coya knew McReynolds as a kind family man who regarded the sessions in the legislature as a fine job that nicely coincided with the idle months in his apiary. He had not waged a competitive campaign to counter Coya's run for the office because he was occupied in August and September with beekeeping and harvesting honey. Coya sensed that throughout the campaign McReynolds had also been at a loss in dealing with competition from a woman. She recalled the day that he had stopped by Andy's Café and quietly told her, "Coya, you are going to win." Coya knew that his defeat by a woman candidate had been a personal humiliation.

In that same election, Sally Luther , campaigning 280 miles south in Minneapolis, also won a seat in the state legislature. Although eight women had served as Minnesota representatives between 1923 and 1943, the state legislature had been all male since 1943. The Knutson and Luther victories sent women to the legislature for the first time in seven years.

A female legislator in 1950 was so unusual that Coya's election prompted the *Minneapolis Sunday Tribune* to run a feature article by Barbara Flanagan under the headline "Coya Knutson, Woman Legislator, Credits Victory to Baby Talk." Flanagan's article began by explaining that "turning 'Cornelia' into 'Coya' was a fortunate slip of the tongue when two-year-old Cornelia Gjesdal could not pronounce her first name, and instead called herself "Coya." Asked why she used the nickname rather than her given name, she told Flanagan that "Coya and Knutson together give me a good name for politics. I guess Coya has a good American-Indian twang to it or something."[8] The article followed the 1950s editorial style of identifying a woman by her husband's name first and then using her given name: "When Mrs Andrew Knutson set out to campaign for the legislature, the campaign literature read 'Vote for Coya Knutson.'"

While Flanagan wrote about Coya's teaching career and "managing the hotel in summer," she emphasized Andy's role in Coya's life. "When county DFL leaders had asked Coya to run, she thought it over and, more importantly, talked it over with her husband. When she hesitated, her husband 'egged her on,' she said. Andy gave his 100 percent consent, but I don't think he knew what he was getting in for,' Coya said."

Tribune readers were also told about Terry, a fourth grader who played clarinet in the school band and hoped to be a doctor one day. His hobby was trains and he wanted to visit his mother in the legislature so that he could ride a train. Terry was exceptionally interested in politics for a boy of nine, Coya was quoted as saying: "He gets it from his father and from me." Asked to comment on receiving 119 out of 200 votes in Oklee, Coya said, "Terry couldn't understand why I did not get all of them." Flanagan told *Tribune* readers that Mrs Knutson would stay home in Oklee cooking for Christmas until the legislature convened in January. Her holiday specialties were Norwegian pastries called *fatigmand* and *kringler.*

Coya sat at the kitchen table in Oklee and read Barbara Flanagan's article. She smiled at the quote about Terry. Yes, there were a couple of Republicans in Oklee and 11-year-old Terry really could not understand why anyone would vote against his mother. As far as her baking skills were concerned, indeed she did enjoy making Christmas treats. In fact, she wished she had mentioned that she also made *Berlinerkranse* and *lefse,* two of her specialties. All in all it was a good, safe, pleasant little story, Coya thought, and just the sort of Sunday feature folks liked to read. The *Minneapolis Tribune* was the most important and most widely read newspaper in the Upper Midwest. Barbara Flanagan, then a cub reporter on general assignment, would later become the editor of the women's page and a popular columnist.

Flanagan had interviewed Coya by telephone and the questions had come so quickly that Coya barely had time to think. She wanted to put her best foot forward and she was glad that she had had the presence of mind to jot down a few things beforehand. She wanted to convey the image of a traditional and happy homelife, as she had during the campaign.

There were some things about her family that she kept to herself. She did not, for instance, mention the fact that she was the major wage-earner in the household, or that until they bought the small hotel, Andy had been a janitor in the school where Coya taught. When she read the cozy, homey feature story, she got a sick feeling when she thought of the true nature of life in the Knutson household.

As she reread the article, Coya was irritated that it was only after her credentials as a homemaker had been established that Flanagan went on to write about Coya's legislative goals. Issues that were important to Coya—fair employment practices, state aid for education, and a school nurse program—were not mentioned until the closing paragraph. Coya was the only candidate who consistently championed these proposals, which played an important part in her victory.

The "Baby Talk" headline trivialized what she had accomplished. The alliteration helped people remember her name, but was certainly not the reason for her election. She also resented being dubbed Mrs Andrew Knutson. It was inconsistent when the article had made such a fuss about the name Coya winning her the election. It rankled.

But Coya knew that she had contributed to the misconceptions. If it were publicly known that she had problems with her husband, it would have been unthinkable for her to run for office. The fundamental assumptions and attitudes about a woman's role in 1950 dictated that, as the article demonstrated, a wife should follow the lead of her husband and not be "out in front." Coya could not tell Flanagan—or anyone—that there was little left in her marriage. As much as she resented the pretense, Coya realized that her political career would depend upon maintaining the pretty pictures of the happy wife and mother who managed to be both a homemaker and a successful politician in a man's world.

The people of Oklee weren't fooled. Many of them recognized the true nature of the Knutson marriage and accepted Coya and Andy as they were. With Anna to look after Terry and Andy, the Knutsons, as well as Oklee townspeople figured the family could manage for a few months without Mother. The hotel and café, too, could be managed without Coya. Anna would order the food and Andy would be in charge of the till behind the counter. Coya could keep her teaching job because the Minnesota legislature met in a 90-day session every other year beginning in January.

At that time the Minnesota Legislature was considered a citizen's legislature, composed of lawmakers who returned home after the biennial sessions to evaluate the impact of their legislation on themselves and their constituents. Because the legislature met only a few months every other year, it was taken for granted that the members would earn a living in the private sector. Coya had no choice in whether or not to keep her teaching contract. She was the breadwinner and could not have supported the family if school superintendent Quist had not been willing to hire a substitute teacher to replace her during the three-month legislative term. Coya would earn $2,500 as a legislator and $2,400 for the six months of teaching.

When she took the oath of office in the House chambers along with other newly elected members, she was deeply moved. She had walked up the hundred steps and through the gigantic doors of the Minnesota Capitol, a magnificent building designed by Cass Gilbert. Amid all the nervous anticipation and excitement, Coya stopped and stood for a moment looking up at the impressive dome, a scaled-down replica of the national Capitol's, and the realization swept through her that she was beginning to fulfill her dream.

The House chambers of the Minnesota Capitol, a spacious room with alcoves and Grecian columns, located under another dome, is one of the most beautiful legislative halls in the country. Coya gazed around her at the paintings and sculpture and could barely believe that this would be her place of work. Near the Speaker's chair in the front of the room there were young pages sitting in wait for a House member's summons. Coya was intrigued by the electric voting board, a large panel on the wall listing lawmakers' names. When a roll-call vote was moved, the members pressed a button on their desks, indicating red for no and green for yes, and the vote was registered on the board. By the time the clerk closed the roll, the tally on the board already indicated whether or not a bill had passed.

Coya sat in the front row, in the second seat in from the aisle. Alf L. Bergrud, a Republican and the president of Red Owl grocery stores, sat next to her in the aisle seat. Coya respected Bergrud because he took the time to help her understand the legislative process and, although he was from the opposing party, he did not try to influence her vote.

After standing committees had been named and permanent rules adopted, each House notified the other and the Governor announced that the legislative session was open. By observing procedures and by talking with other lawmakers Coya quickly learned the rules. She wasn't skilled in the ins and outs of debate as Sally Luther was and, at times, Coya found the pressure overwhelming. "There were too many new things coming at us—Committee assignments and meetings, and the feeling that everyone was looking at us over their glasses, wondering if we newcomers would make it. My knees would shake at the thought of making a speech."

Coya learned a great deal about politics in those early days from Robert A. Olson, who had been the Federation of Labor president since 1938. Coya saw Olson as a "big, fat, cigar-chomping guy with his hat on." Olson, an experienced lobbyist and politician in his fifties, took Coya under his wing. At day's end, Olson and Coya would sometimes have a hot chocolate in Mickey's diner in back of the Capri Hotel. Coya would just sit and listen. He could talk for hours and not repeat himself, she recalls, giving her the background on people he knew and telling her the history of the Labor Movement. He taught her how to introduce bills and then helped her write them up. Afterward, he showed her how to follow through by buttonholing members to get their support.

Her colleague from the 65th District, Walter Day, was a thorough and methodical person. He was supportive of Coya as a politician and was generous in helping her. Coya respected him as a good man and a solid citizen who was kind to everyone. He did not have a second job and was so frugal that he managed to live at his home in Bagley throughout the year on his meager legislator's salary.

The two education programs that Coya had espoused in her campaign—state aid for education and a state health program to provide school nurses—were funded by the legislature. Cliff Longtin's agenda of allowing parochial students to ride on public school buses was not dealt with by the legislature; a tremendous outcry against the proposal had gone out in America under the banner of "separation of church and state."

FEPC was the topic of fierce debates on the floor and in the press and was brought to a vote in 1951. The legislation promoting fair employment practices did not pass.

As an advocate of health and welfare, Coya worked on a wide range of bills including a proposal to give educational aid to handicapped children, another to provide emergency maternity care for veterans' wives, and a third designed to improve sanitariums. She was a sponsor of Minnesota's first clean-air bill; it prohibited smoking in certain sections of hospitals and public places.

To aid farmers, she authored a bill that would increase the sales of dairy products through a reciprocity agreement that would allow those products to be bought and sold across state lines. In an effort to promote butter consumption in Minnesota, Coya voted against allowing colored margarine to be sold. At that time it was against state law to color the product and only white margarine was available. It was a highly controversial topic because the law stated that margarine could be sold in any color except yellow, the color of butter. Packages of white margarine often contained small packets of food dye that could be combined with the margarine to disguise it as table butter. Coya remembers taking a pouch of dye and pounding it into the margarine. She did it once—and then saw no reason to confuse anybody about what they were eating. Preserving a distinction between margarine and butter by permitting only white margarine to be sold helped the dairy farmers; Coya was happy to give the bill her support. Fourteen years later Minnesota allowed yellow margarine to be sold.

Along with Sally Luther, Coya worked for adoption of the controversial bill to designate parties of lawmakers as DFL or Republican. Although the terms Liberal and Conservative were used, many legislators—most of them Conservative—did not want their party affiliation to be on public record. The party-designation bill was defeated, but the measure was a popular move back home. The editor of the *Red Lake Falls Gazette* wrote "We are pleased that Mrs Knutson voted for the change and made a speech in favor of it. She had the courage to go on record, which few others of the House did."[9] (Twenty years later when Minnesota went to a full-time legislature, legislators began to be designated by party.)

The House members were mainly Conservatives, and many of them were Coya's friends. The House Majority Leader (Conservative) was Roy E. Dunn, an imposing, generous man from Dunvilla, a small town north of Fergus Falls. He was so attentive to the women in the House that on Valentine's Day, Sally Luther and Coya found big boxes of candy on their desks.

When Christine visited the House, Coya introduced her to Roy Dunn who said, "You must be very proud of your daughter." The praise meant a great deal to Coya. She knew that her mother was indeed proud of her but would never be able to say it. "You know how Norwegians are," Coya commented, "they hide their emotions and do not let things open up for them, holding back feelings. I wonder what Dad would have thought."

Coya admired her friend Sally Luther. Bob Olson admitted that he thought Sally Luther talked too much. Coya, on the other hand, envied her colleague's ability to stand up and articulate her views with such clarity and force. Luther was a graduate of Vassar and had had debating experience in the League of Women Voters. Coya thought her friend was more skilled than she was as a freshman legislator. "Sally spoke out and was a real pioneer. She started from step 100, while I started from step one."

Sally Luther did speak out. Remembering her first term as a legislator, Luther observed, "When Prudence Cutright was proposed for the [University of Minnesota] Board of Regents, I had to say something. It took courage. It was something for a freshman, to say nothing of a freshwoman, to speak in that House. When men spoke nobody listened, but as soon as they heard the timbre of a woman's voice it was different—utter silence. You suddenly had the attention of absolutely everybody... I said what a terrible thing it was that once again they were about to elect all men to the board of regents. I nearly fainted with fright—and I was a strong person, I thought."[10]

While Luther supported her party, she was unwilling to be intimidated by it or swayed from her convictions. It was a political stand that Coya wanted to emulate.

The majority party in the House had the pick of the best committees. The Speaker made the committee appointments on the basis of the percentage of elected members; for example, if 70% of House members were Conservative, 70% of a committee would be Conservative. Because she was in the minority on a committee or on a vote, Coya was frustrated that she had so little influence. She was appointed to the committees on Co-operatives, Public Institutions, Reapportionment, Elections, and the University; but she held no chairmanships.

Coya was pleased with the work procedures and happy to have secretarial help. A Representative did not have an office of his or her own at that time, and Coya, like the others, would work at her desk in chambers. Her desk was not big, and by the time the ledger for Senate bills and the ledger for House bills had been placed on it, there was little space left to write and work. But this crowded, cramped work space provided pleasing camaraderie.

Coya had promised that if elected she would keep in touch with her constituents. She began to write a column for the six newspapers in her district. It was called "Coya's Capital Chat" and was patterned after Eleanor Roosevelt's daily syndicated column, "My Day." In Coya's first column she told her readers that people do not want to be hungry anymore so "they will turn from one political reform to another just to overcome scarcity. The production of commodities in our country excels any other in the history of the world. Our distribution of those commodities to the needful places and people in the world is far from satisfactory. We have hung the sack of oats out in front of the horse, but he can't run fast enough to catch it." She recommended that the U.S. ship tools, machinery and trained personnel to help bring about the agricultural revolution: "Being 'our brother's keeper' is not an idle phrase."[11]

Coya enjoyed writing the column, but it entailed a great deal of work. She wasn't permitted to use a pool secretary for this type of project. Most of the columns were written on the typewriter at the hotel—weekly when the legislature was in session and occasionally during the recess. There was no way of duplicating the pages in Oklee except to use the mimeograph machine at school "where you had to monkey with purple ink." Coya usually typed and mailed an original to each of the six newspapers.

During her three months at the Capitol, Coya lived in what she called "the darkest dungeon, a two-by-four" room at the Capri Hotel next to the World Theatre in St. Paul. The room was so small that she could barely walk around the bed; a dresser was the only other furniture. Coya did not have much money and this was the cheapest decent room with a bath that she could get. Because she did not have a car, she would catch a ride "with the guys" to the Capitol, or take the bus.

Coya saw little of her family during the session. Although she would have liked to go home for a weekend now and then, there wasn't time or money to make a 560-mile round trip. Andy did not care to visit the Twin Cities, but Terry made the trip several times. When there was money to spare, Coya was eager to give the eleven-year-old a chance to ride the train and sit with her in the legislative chambers. She did not often allow him to miss school, but occasionally made an exception for important events. While Coya was occupied in the legislature, Terry was free to roam the Capitol Building and go to the lunch counter whenever he wished. He enjoyed the train trip and being with his mother, but St. Paul brought back unhappy memories of being an unwanted child at the orphanage. Coya tried to replace those recollections with new experiences and show him a good time.

Sometimes they would have Chinese food, a change from the meat-and-potatoes fare at home. They went to the three-ring Shrine circus and Terry loved the daredevil trapeze artists and the wild tigers roaring at their trainer. Staying in the hotel was fascinating for him because there was an elevator, a new experience. And it never failed to amuse the boy that each time the car stopped at a floor, the jolt made the elevator operator's toupeé move.

Twenty-five-hundred dollars, and reimbursement for one round-trip fare between St. Paul and the representative's home, was the total payment for legislators. There were no provisions for health insurance, pension or benefits of any kind. Although Coya would have appreciated additional funds for weekend trips to Oklee, she managed to live comfortably on the salary.

Coya was happy to return home that spring of 1951. She had missed Terry, her friends and teaching. Anna, in her gentle and generous manner, had taken good care of Terry in Coya's absence. Anna's only complaint was that Terry would strip the refrigerator of food and have a feast with his friends.

However, it was apparent that Coya's marriage was over. When Coya went to their bedroom the night she returned home from St. Paul, she found that Andy had locked the door. Coya moved into one of the small guest rooms. Any pretence of intimacy was over and she and Andy never slept together again. Andy and Coya did not quarrel; they simply no longer paid any attention to each other. Coya considered divorcing Andy, but divorce was so frowned upon that she couldn't muster the nerve to go through with it.

Terry, Anna and Gunhild were glad to have Coya back. Terry was a part of the "gang" around Oklee. The children pulled one another in their wagons up and down the streets and their dogs ran with them. Terry's little black Spaniel, Twinkle, would get rides in Terry's wagon. Once Joe Dufault opened the Oak Theatre on Main Street the children could also go to movies. When Terry wanted to be by himself, he would stay in his room and play with his model train, its line of cars speeding around the figure-eight tracks that were equipped with switches and semaphores.

Coya noticed that when she returned after her first legislative session, her friends and neighbors in Oklee seemed to look at her with a new attitude of respect. Now that she had won the election and served her first term, even her women friends—with whom she had avoided discussing her political aspirations—admired her gumption. The townspeople took pride in having someone from their own school and community in the legislature.

Back home Coya's routine returned to what it had been. She continued to contribute time to her community and to participate in the organization of emigrants from the Setesdals District in Norway where Andy's parents had been born. The *Setesdals Lag* (association), had its three day *stevne* (rally) in Oklee every year, and people attended from as far away as Wisconsin and North Dakota. The *stevne* featured programs that included folk dancing, Norwegian films and fiddle music. Coya helped out by organizing Norwegian song fests.

With so many visitors expected, the *Oklee Herald* ran an announcement June 10, 1952 that "persons having rooms to rent should call Mrs Andy Knutson, (Telephone 17) who was arranging accommodations."[12] It was not easy to find enough places for visitors to stay. Some homeowners hesitated to rent for fear a guest would come home drunk. Celebrating would go on into the wee hours after the dancing on any or all of the nights of the *stevne*, and Coya helped more than one reveler back to his lodgings. The three Knutson women were tee-totalers, and it was hard for Anna to accept the fact that some of "her people"—including her own brothers—drank. On one occasion the *Telemarken lag* (from another district in Norway) was held simultaneously in Oklee, and one morning Anna complained about "all that hollering and carrying on last night. Wasn't it awful? They must have been Telemarkens."

In mid-July 1952, Coya and L. J. Lee, the Ninth District chairman, took the train to Chicago where they were delegates to the National Democratic Convention. The large television screen in Chicago's Convention Hall impressed Coya. The only television sets she had seen before were in the store windows in St. Paul.

The convention nominated Adlai E. Stevenson for President and Coya was not pleased. He might be a fine intellectual, she thought, but he knew nothing about farming. Tennessee Senator Estes C. Kefauver was her choice, and she was disappointed when he deferred to Stevenson. However, delegates were told that Kefauver could wait and have his chance in 1956. Coya kept to herself after convention hours, only occasionally joining other Minnesotans for a meal and some political talk.

Later that year Coya ran for a second term in the legislature. Even though no strong challenger appeared, Coya campaigned hard. Walter E. Day, her colleague in the legislature, campaigned with her and Coya remembers that "Walter saw that I was more popular than he was, so he hung on to me. But I also picked up pointers from him."

"Vote for Two" advertisements were placed in area newspapers by the DFL. The photographs of Knutson and Day were captioned with the slogan, "Promise to serve the state faithfully and fairly to the best of our ability." In addition, an advertisement endorsing state and local Democratic candidates appeared in local papers.[13]

Coya was re-elected in 1952. She carried all three counties and received the highest number of votes that the district had ever given a candidate—7,953 votes. Day and Olson received 7,516 and 4,442 votes, respectively.[14]

In January 1953 Coya returned to St. Paul with high hopes and the advantage of now knowing her way around the legislature. She hired a secretary to help send "Coya's Capital Chat" to weekly newspapers. During this session, she chose to sit in the back row of the House where she could see everyone and "feel the space." Again she sat second from the aisle, next to Tom Letnes, a Liberal from Nielsville.

Fair Employment Practices Commission legislation was an issue again, and it came close to passage with 87% of Liberal votes and 48% of Conservative votes in favor of the program. The Conservatives won the day again. (Not until the 1955 session, after Coya had left the Minnesota House, was this sensitive issue passed by 97% of the Liberals and 51% of the Conservatives. But Coya continued to work for the program she had espoused in her campaigns.)

Another resolution she actively supported was aimed at better living conditions for migrant workers in Minnesota. Some migrants slept in their trucks without facilities for water, toilets or electricity. Although the legislature did not pass the bill, the publicity generated sympathy for the workers. Some area churches initiated classes for the children of migrants. While working on the measure Coya clashed with her friend and fellow Liberal, Tom Letnes, who employed migrants from Mexico to hoe his crop of sugar beets.

In addition to the Elections and University Committees on which she had served in the previous session, she joined both the Town and

County Committee and the Health and Welfare Committee. The Town and County Committee worked with city councils and county commissioners to assess local needs and present solutions to the problems through the legislative process.

Among the responsibilities of the Health and Welfare committee was visiting and monitoring various agencies on the county or town level. The first institution the committee visited was the Fergus Falls Mental Hospital where all the rooms had recently been repainted, presumably for the legislators' benefit. The patients were made to stand in line as if for inspection while the St. Paul visitors were shown through the wards. Coya was incensed by the procedure because it was degrading to the patients. The committee also toured a University of Minnesota laboratory where a doctor talked to them about experiments on animals. He used "a dog, asleep on a frame in his laboratory, to demonstrate that the animals did not feel pain or suffer." As a lover of animals since her childhood days on the farm, Coya was not impressed with the doctor's presentation.

In one of Coya's weekly columns she reported that Eleanor Roosevelt had come to the House Chambers to visit a friend. Coya was thrilled to be among the legislators introduced to the former First Lady, who had recently completed her term as U.S. delegate to the United Nations. Their meeting was brief, but Mrs Roosevelt was so warm and gracious that Coya wrote in her column that they had talked together as one housewife to another.[15]

Coya's usual buoyant spirits were dampened in the spring of 1953 when her 37-year-old sister Eva became gravely ill. Since graduating from college in Washington, Eva had been taking cortisone to relieve the pain of rheumatoid arthritis. Twice Coya traveled to Colorado to nurse her sister who was in great pain. In her classroom one day, Coya received a telegram from her mother: Eva had taken a turn for the worse. Coya dropped everything and took the train to Colorado. At her sister's bedside she found that Eva was in a semi-conscious state. Her husband was devastated by the thought of losing his young wife. Eva died a few days later when her kidneys failed. Her mother and sisters consoled one another as best they could, and a very sad Coya returned to Oklee.

She arrived home in time to help Jo Quist prepare the annual luncheon for graduating seniors. There was a record number of graduates that spring and, although she was in mourning, Coya pitched in to make the day easier for Jo.[16]

Coya's interests were changing. The enthusiasm and creativity she'd once lavished on the café she now focused on her legislative work. Besides being a drain on her time, the café, although still popular, was not making a profit. Coya began subsidizing its operation from her teaching and her legislative paychecks. Andy's main contribution to the workload was managing the family's money— each day he walked to the bank to deposit the receipts, and went around town paying their bills.

But Coya disapproved of the way Andy did business. An Oklee man, who was a drinking buddy of Andy's, cashed a $5 check, which bounced. Because it had happened before, Andy called the sheriff, who put the man in jail. His distraught wife appealed to Coya. Coya arranged the man's release, but it rankled that Andy had resorted to that measure rather than simply cutting off his friend's credit.

In the summer of 1953 the "closed" sign went up permanently and the Knutsons began to use the café and kitchen space as part of their living quarters. The hotel still had occasional roomers; once or twice a week Andy would rent someone a room, giving him something to do. Anna did the laundry and room-cleaning. Closing the café meant that the five had also lost the camaraderie that came from running the family business. Working together, more than anything else, had connected Andy and Coya since they had first met on her parents' farm. Now it seemed that rather than sharing a home that happened to be a hotel, each family member was merely a guest in the hotel. Personal relationships became even more distant. Ironically, the people of Oklee continued to view the Knutsons as a "solid" family.[17]

Coya was also beset by problems outside the family. What should have been a minor incident ended a close friendship. For many years Coya had valued the companionship of a woman in Oklee who was "always there when you needed her." The two women visited together frequently and talked over all kinds of things. If she happened to drop in to the café when it was crowded, the woman would pitch in to help out—refusing to take a penny for her labor. One afternoon Coya mentioned that soon they would begin serving a larger doughnut and charge five-cents for one instead of two doughnuts for a nickel. The friend told her she should not do that. The ensuing discussion quickly turned into a fierce argument and the woman stormed out of the café. The rift between them was never mended.

Coya realized that their quarrel had essentially erupted out of the envy her friend felt about the many other changes she was making in her life. Coya was getting out of her rut while her friend was not.

Coya encountered another form of jealousy that would plague her throughout her political career. A seasoned politician who had regarded Coya as a protegé confided to her that his wife had become suspicious and envious of their relationship. There had been no hint of impropriety and Coya was shocked to learn that an important and platonic friendship had been misinterpreted. She was hurt and angry. However, she also realized that the wives of politicians spent much of their time sitting at home waiting for their husbands. It wasn't surprising that one of those wives would resent Coya for usurping the husband's time to further her political career. Thereafter, she became very circumspect in her dealings with male associates.

Coya knew everyone in town, but her best friends in Oklee were Anna Knutson and Elvina Zimmerman. Anna was a wonderfully goodhearted person and always pleasant and cheerful. She was happy to stay close to home and didn't like venturing far from the security of family. In her younger years Anna had been a pretty woman who had attracted the attention of a well-to-do bachelor farmer in the district. However, once her suitor's romantic interest became public knowledge, Anna was mortified by the teasing questions of family and friends. She abruptly rejected his courtship. Soon afterward she began indulging her taste for candy bars and doughnuts and gained an enormous amount of weight, eventually tipping the scales at close to 300 pounds. After the café closed, Anna continued to cook for the family and to care for Terry and her mother who, although not bedridden, needed constant attention. Coya sensed Anna's underlying discontent, but there was little she could do to help.

Elvina Zimmerman, the wife of the depot agent and the former cleaning lady for the café, lived next door to the hotel. She often dropped in for a visit, and Coya and Elvina traded confidences and cheered each other up when one or the other was feeling low. Elvina, an attractive, slender woman, had been nicknamed "Wiener" by her brother who said she was shaped like one. The name stuck and everyone, Coya included, called her Wiener.

After closing the café Coya had more free time to consider new political challenges. Serving a larger constituency as the representative from the Ninth Congressional District in the U. S. House of

Representatives appealed to her. Although this would ensure much more time to herself—away from Andy—Coya's primary concern was to move on in her career.

Sally Luther was the inadvertent catalyst in expanding Coya's political opportunities. A *Minneapolis Star* cartoonist had depicted the two women as opposites: Sally svelte and trim, Coya slightly overweight and wearing a housedress; Sally in high heels and Coya in flat shoes. But appearances aside, the two had much in common. They were the only female lawmakers in the legislature and both had 13-year-old sons. Both women were also unhappily married—Sally's husband, Charles H. Luther, later divorced her. Sally invited Coya to her home in Minneapolis for dinner and the women became such good friends that they decided to take a vacation together with their youngsters. It was a two-week busman's holiday driving around the Ninth District to visit political acquaintances.

In August of 1953, Coya and Terry drove to Detroit Lakes where they met the Luthers at the train station. The four stayed at the Greystone Hotel for several days before setting out on their tour of the countryside. Coya found her legislator friend to be a good companion on the trip: "She was fun, and she was also astute and interested in anything that had to do with politics—and that's what I wanted to talk about, too." Sally, who had lived all her life in the city, was interested in learning about Coya's country way of life. The drive through wheat fields and the small towns with grain elevators presented a different world for her. The boys got on well, too, and it was a lark for all four. The women enjoyed visits with political stalwarts such as Barney Allen, the Democratic national committeeman.

It was on this trip with Sally Luther that Coya decided it was time to become a national candidate. She did not discuss her decision with Sally because she knew that her colleague felt that Coya could not win the seat. However, as Coya talked with other political leaders in the district, she became convinced that there would be strong support for her candidacy.

As she traveled through the countryside talking to people, she remembered what farmers had told her when she was working for the AAA. She recalled the struggle she and Andy had had on their farm, and she considered what had happened to farm prices in the aftermath of the postwar bonanza. With an abiding faith in the ideals of the old Nonpartisan League, she knew that she could represent farmers and use the political power their sheer numbers demanded. She would appeal to former Leaguers in her district and felt confident she could garner enough votes to send her to Washington. If she succeeded, she wanted to work for better health, education, and farm incomes in the Ninth District.

It was a difficult decision to leave her place in the state legislature behind; her four years of achievements virtually assured Coya of re-election and area politicians regarded her as unbeatable.[18] However, it wasn't in her nature to seek comfort and security. She felt a tremendous longing to meet a new challenge. She set her sights on Congress.

During her last state legislature campaign she had taken her measure of the Republican incumbent, U. S. Congressman Harold C. Hagen of Crookston, when he spoke in Oklee on Market Day. He was wearing a homburg, which set him apart from the casually dressed locals. Coya regarded his choice of headgear as a visible indication that the congressman was out of touch with his constituents in rural northwestern Minnesota. She figured she could beat him.

She consulted with her lobbyist friend in the legislature, Bob Olson, and he discouraged her from running for the U. S. House of Representatives. He told her she could not possibly win the seat and that he wanted her to stay in the state legislature because he "could run a lot of bills through her." Coya was even more disappointed when she went to Bagley to ask Ninth District Democratic-Farmer-Labor Chairman L. J. Lee for backing to become the endorsed DFL congressional candidate. He flatly refused her, saying "No. The party cannot afford to lose your state legislature spot."[19]

Coya wondered if winning the election might be less difficult than gaining the nomination from her own party to run for Congress. She was disgusted and frustrated that she was being held back for no better reason than that her party did not want to risk losing her seat in the state legislature. They could find someone else. She was ready to move on. Years later Coya recalled, "I had to do it on my own—I found I could not depend on the party. I knew what I had to do, and I had a goal."

In the spring of 1954, when Coya told Andy about her political plans, he flippantly replied that if she thought she could pull off something like that she ought to go ahead. Anna and Terry were lukewarm and Gunhild did not like the idea at all, although she would not tell Coya directly. Only Torkel and Orianna, who operated a variety store 55 miles south of Oklee in Twin Valley, supported Coya's candidacy. In her own family, her mother and two sisters were also cool toward her political ambitions. "Family," Coya thought. "There's nothing like family." She wondered what her cousin Tor Gjesdal would think of her plans.

One Sunday evening she pulled a chair up to the stand with the "candlestick" telephone that stood between the kitchen and dining room. Her heart was in her throat as she dialed "O" and asked the operator to connect her with a New York telephone number. Her fingers gripped the receiver tightly as she waited to hear Tor's deep, pleasant voice. When he answered, she quickly told him about her plans and waited breathlessly for his response. To her relief, Tor was sympathetic and encouraging. Before too many expensive telephone minutes ticked away, the two cousins were making plans for Tor to visit her in Minnesota.

She replaced the receiver on its hook and nodded thoughtfully. She knew she could pull it off and make her dreams come true. She would show them all.

Chapter 6

THE HAPPY
WANDERER

*But the League would be a failure if it accomplished
nothing for the wives, mothers and daughters. It is a
farm woman's movement as fully as a farmer's movement.*

> *"Big Cash Contest for Farm Women—What
> Does the League Mean to YOU?"*
>
> *Nonpartisan Leader: October 23, 1917*

Coya was so happy she could burst. She was sitting on the platform
in the gymnasium at her alma mater where several hundred students
were gathered to listen to her distinguished cousin, Tor Gjesdal,
deliver a speech. It really was something, she thought, to be invited
back as an honored guest and to be introduced by President Joseph
L. Knutson (no relation) as a prominent Concordia alumna. The
reception she had received here and the interest shown in her
legislative career, encouraged her to pursue her idea of running for
U. S. Congress.

With determination she left her thoughts and focused on what Tor was saying: "Peace is something more than the absence of war, and requires that the sense of justice of the nations overcome their passions. To stop the fighting does not stop the problem."[1]

Tor was intelligent and articulate. And his political position mirrored her own. She wanted to be like him. In 1939 Tor, who had been a foreign correspondent in Europe and Asia, became the Norwegian Red Cross representative in China. After Nazi Germany invaded Norway in April 1940, Gjesdal managed to get to Sweden with the help of the Norwegian Underground, and from there to London to join the staff of King Haakon and the Norwegian-government-in-exile. From his London base he operated the information services for the Norwegian resistance movement from 1941 to 1945.

In 1954 Tor Gjesdal became the principal director of the United Nations' Public Information Department, leading the activities of the U.N. information centers in all the major countries in the world, including Soviet Russia. His agency was commonly referred to as "the eyes and ears of the U.N.".[2]

Without anyone except Tor realizing it, Coya was beginning to campaign for Congress. Although the two cousins had not yet met, Tor readily agreed to come to Minnesota in February 1954 to help her launch her campaign. Coya arranged a speaking tour for him which would include three of the Ninth District's largest towns. Tor would speak about the United Nations at a lyceum at the Fergus Falls High School, at the Red River Valley Winter Shows at Crookston, and at the Concordia College chapel service at Moorhead. With Tor's credentials—and her own—it was easy to attract speaking engagements. At each of the three events, Coya was scheduled to introduce him.

While Coya and Terry awaited Tor's arrival at the Grand Forks airport on a frigid day in late February, she felt apprehensive, wondering whether she had asked too much of Tor. He was not only taking time from his work, but he had also come at his own expense.

As the stairs were let down from the DC-3, she wondered whether she would recognize Tor. But when the tall, handsome man bounded down the steps, his trench coat flapping in the icy wind, there was no mistaking his identity. She thought he looked a little like her dad had when he was young.

At last Coya met the cousin she so greatly admired. Tor spoke five languages and she was entranced when he spoke English with a

French accent. Coya was pleased to learn that despite Tor's sophistication they liked to talk about the same things and that—in addition to the other five—"he talked my language." Nevertheless, she "felt like a country bumpkin compared with Tor" because he had that element she felt she lacked: "class."

Tor's first speaking engagement was at Crookston, and Coya arranged a Gjesdal reunion to welcome him. Coya's mother, her sister Helen and her family, and her uncle and his wife all arrived to meet their renowned kinsman. Coya arranged to have the family group photographed for the local newspaper.

Crookston was the home of the incumbent Congressman Harold C. Hagen, and Coya was eager to make an impression there. Gjesdal's speech, "The Accomplishments and the Future of the United Nations," made headlines in the *Crookston Daily Times*, and the accompanying article mentioned that his cousin, Coya Knutson, was a possible Democratic candidate for U.S. Congressional office.[3]

Everywhere they went, the two cousins received good press. The *Fergus Falls Journal* reported that Gjesdal explained in detail the purposes of the U.N. charter that had been formulated in San Francisco.[4] Because the Concordia chapel service was broadcast daily, Tor's speech was heard by radio listeners throughout the area. The tour was a success in every way, especially as a political move for Coya. She was venturing into counties where she was not known, and the personal appearances with Gjesdal provided her with an impressive introduction. She thought voters would remember the woman legislator who stood on the podium with her cousin, the distinguished dignitary from the homeland of the area's largest ethnic group.[5]

On their drives between cities, the cousins discussed a number of social and political topics having to do with Norway and America. Tor told her that in the postwar years the *Storting* [legislature] had passed new labor laws as well as a comprehensive student-loan bill. Coya found their discussions fascinating, and she also realized that through her cousin she was finding the courage she needed to change her life. Gjesdal's visit stirred her, she said, "and gave me the emotional jolt I needed to get started." After he left, she "cried for two days" thinking how much she had missed by not having known him sooner, and wishing she had someone like him to turn to in her daily life. Her emotional reaction to his departure surprised her because she was a woman who seldom cried.

Although now fully committed to making a try for Congress, Coya knew she had to proceed carefully. Few women ran for Congress, and even fewer were elected. After the war, public sentiment had reverted to the tradition of "man for the field and woman for the hearth." However, the reality was that some women, like Coya, worked at jobs that provided the only steady, reliable incomes for their families. In 1950, 31% of the American women worked full time outside their homes—the same as the percentage of working women in Pennington County which Coya represented.[6] Although a substantial number of married women who had entered the work force during the war returned to full time homemaking, others enjoyed the extra income and found self-fulfillment working outside the home.

Always a realist, Coya knew she must overcome the prevailing myth that a woman belonged in her kitchen rather than on Capitol Hill. Never before had midwestern voters elected a woman to the U. S. Congress for a full term.

Coya had plenty of time to plan. The September 1954 primary was months away. The state legislature was not in session that year, and she could begin campaigning in late winter knowing that the school board could hire a substitute teacher if she had to be absent. Because district DFL leaders did not favor her candidacy, Coya did not plan to attend the DFL Ninth District convention in April when a candidate would be endorsed. She knew what she needed to do to set up her campaign and, without declaring her candidacy, she began putting her plans in effect.

Not long after Coya returned to Oklee from the tour with Tor Gjesdal, she met 25-year-old William O. Kjeldahl, a senior in political science at the University of Minnesota who was planning to attend law school. Kjeldahl was a veteran of the Korean War and was traveling throughout the state delivering talks on his wartime experiences. On a cold March day he presented a slide lecture on Korea to the Oklee School student body. Afterwards he and Coya sat down and "talked politics and dreams."

Kjeldahl told Coya that his family was of the old Nonpartisan League tradition and that his grandfather had been on the staff of Farmer-Laborite Henrik Shipstead in his successful bid for the U.S. Senate in 1922. William, like his grandfather, was fascinated with politics and wanted to get experience by running a campaign. He also told her of an undergraduate project in which he had examined and analyzed voting records of his home county, Otter Tail. His evaluations could be helpful to Coya in planning campaign strategy in that area. Impressed by the young man's knowledge and expertise, she asked him to check out the voting record of Harold Hagen, the Republican incumbent. Kjeldahl found that Hagen's position was one that Coya could effectively attack.

In April 1954 Coya asked Bill to become her campaign manager and he readily agreed. Their first press release began by stating the obvious: that "if public support keeps building up" Coya would file June sixteenth as a candidate for the DFL nomination and would attend the June DFL state convention in Albert Lea. She alleged that the Administration's agricultural committees were dominated by Eastern interests and that "we need a permanent agricultural economy which can buy the products of our industries, which give more consumers jobs, who, in turn, buy our agricultural products." Her statement also reflected Coya's concern with another national issue: "We should raise the caliber of our Congressional hearings—indiscriminate, poorly-prepared investigations dishonor social justice and smear innocent people..."[7]

The "smears" to which Coya referred were those of the anti-Communist crusade of Wisconsin Senator Joseph R. McCarthy conducted through the well publicized Senate investigative hearings. James Forrestal, the U.S. Secretary of the Navy during the war, had committed suicide in 1949, almost certainly because of McCarthy's charges. Tor Gjesdal, a friend of Forrestal, shared with Coya his anger at what both of them saw as unfair accusations and unjustified attacks.

Coya also looked to influential women for support in her campaign. She met Marge Michels for the first time when Coya was invited to Moorhead as the main speaker at the 1954 northwestern Minnesota district of the General Federated Women's Clubs (GFWC). The women's club district covered the same geographical area as the political Ninth District. Coya's speech impressed the women, Marge recalls, and that was not an easy task because many of them attending were "dyed-in-the-wool Republicans" who would not be impressed with anything a Democrat had to say. Young women who had recently come into GFWC work were convinced that there was a place for women in government and that through their political efforts, they could acquire the health, education, and welfare programs they sought. Until this meeting, Marge remembers, the GFWC meetings comprised discussions of art and literature.

Marge saw Coya, a legislator who spoke with such genuine enthusiasm, as a catalyst encouraging the GFWC to use their powerful force to improve government programs. The women responded to Coya's speech with a tremendous ovation.

Coya was impressed with Marge, a pert, red-haired volunteer leader who was Secretary of the Ninth District DFL and President of the district Federated Women's Clubs. She was an energetic person who smiled a lot and Coya liked her. After the program, Coya surprised Marge by asking for her advice. Coya felt that Marge could best assess her political potential in the southern part of the district. The two women arranged to meet the following month.

Coya thought that the GFWC meeting augured well for her political future. She furthered her candidacy by speaking at chapel services at Concordia College. Harding C. Noblitt, the professor of political science, had invited her to speak to his classes about her work as a state legislator. When Joseph L. Knutson, the president of Concordia, was asked by Noblitt for his permission, the president replied that he would be happy if she would also speak at chapel, "provided it is not a political speech. She has done a lot of church work so I think she could give a good devotional message in chapel".[8]

Noblitt suggested that it would be to Coya's political advantage to appear, especially since the chapel talk would be broadcast over radio. Because no funds could be provided for expenses, he hoped she might come as a favor to her alma mater.[9] Coya in turn asked Noblitt about the possibility of "making the definite announcement" of her congressional candidacy at the close of her talk.[10] Noblitt responded that they had to be very careful about the candidacy announcement because of the attitude of the radio station on political matters of that sort. It was arranged that an announcement of her candidacy would be included in the introduction to her speech. Coya capitalized on the opportunity by printing up business cards and passing them out on the day of the broadcast.

In early May, Coya and Bill Kjeldahl arrived at Marge Michels' back door in Breckenridge, a railroad town not far from Fergus Falls. Marge's husband John joined them at the kitchen table for a long talk about Coya's campaign strategy. John, who was active in trainmen's affairs, said that he knew the railroad workers would support Coya because many were of the old Farmer-Labor party, and both Michels were confident they could generate a good deal of support from other labor strongholds. Marge was angry with DFL chairman L.J. Lee for not backing Coya. He had not consulted her, the district secretary, nor Kay Peterson, the vice-chairman of the District, who were both members of the Ninth District executive committee. Marge said later, "I am sure if he had asked us, we would have said, 'Give her a chance,' but Lee ruled it out in his own quick decision."[11]

Later that spring the Ninth District DFL convention endorsed Curtiss T. Olson. Olson had also been the DFL nominee in 1950 and 1952, but he had lost both races to Harold Hagen. Olson, who had studied law through correspondence courses, was an insurance salesman. He later became the manager of the *Roseau Forum*, and farmed his 800 acres in Roseau County. Active in DFL politics, he had served ten years in the Minnesota legislature and had been the Ninth District chairman. Coya did not like him because he behaved in a condescending manner toward her throughout the campaign. Party regulars—DFL District chairman L. J. Lee and most county leaders, including Marvin Evenson, the dominant DFLer in the Clay County party—worked for Olson. Evenson was a salesman, and Coya saw him as a "man's man who let her know that he thought women should stay in their place."

Even though the DFL endorsed Olson, a number of Democrats left the mainstream of the party in order to support Coya. These were mostly the former Farmer-Laborites who had bolted the DFL because they did not believe the party served their best interests. To counter an ad that Curtiss Olson had run in 1952, a group calling itself the Independent Farmer Labor Federation accused Olson of getting himself appointed the DFL Ninth District chairman in a secret session. In a statement they charged that he called them "red-baiting peace lovers" and created his own machine that denied them the right to be seated in the 1948 DFL state convention and in the 1950 Ninth District convention. In conclusion, they "sincerely and hopefully" urged defeat of Curtiss Olson.[12]

Three more farmers—Thomas A. Letnes, Oscar A. Johnson, and T. Austin Teigen—also filed in the 1954 primary for the DFL nomination in the Ninth District. Letnes, a resident of Neilsville and Coya's seatmate in the legislature, was a business college graduate. Like

Olson, Letnes had served ten years in the Minnesota legislature. Johnson, a Crookston farmer, had been the endorsed and defeated DFL candidate in 1948. Teigen, from Georgetown, had studied political and social economics in college and had run unsuccessfully for office many times. Coya comments, "Teigen ran all the time and always lost. At a parade in Barnesville, he was hollering 'Coya, you are going to win'—he was the only one with a decent sense of humor."

This large number of hopefuls—five—was unusual in a primary and was probably due to the efforts of Byron Allen, the 1954 Democratic National Committeeman for Minnesota. Allen felt responsible for seeing that a strong candidate from his district ran against the Republican incumbent whom most people deemed unbeatable. It was getting late in the political season and Allen knew it was his duty to recruit strong candidates to fill the ticket.

Of the three men who had been approached by the party—Curtiss Olson, Thomas Letnes, and "a Mr Nelson from Breckenridge"—none had seemed eager to run. They figured they would be sacrificial lambs or in Allen's words, "moat fillers," running against well-known incumbent Harold C. Hagen. It was Allen's idea to smoke out a candidate by leaking a story to the press that focused on the candidates being considered for the Ninth District race. He called a political journalist in St. Paul and asked him to write a "from-a-reliable-source" article and, "for color," to throw in the name of state legislator Coya Knutson. Allen explained to the reporter that his name must not appear; he was "honor bound not to take sides in an open primary contest."[13]

A few days later the story about multiple candidates appeared in the *Pioneer Press* and in papers across the state. Arthur Naftalin wrote, "DFL activity aimed at capitalizing on anti-GOP sentiment is especially noticeable in the Ninth District where several candidates are being advanced as potential opponents of Harold C. Hagen." He named Coya Knutson as one of them.

Soon Allen's telephone began to ring. The three candidates, all of them flattered to be under consideration, came to him wondering how and why the story had appeared. Allen declared himself just as surprised as they were and joined them in speculating about the identity of the reliable source. In the end, five candidates filed and a strenuous primary campaign was under way.

The interest in the contest that was generated was a "shot in the arm for the DFL," according to Allen.

The four leading candidates for the DFL spot each took out newspaper advertisements emphasizing the fact that they owned farms. All said they supported 100% parity for farm products. But Coya's ad stood out: hers was a half-page, twice the size of the others, and she included her picture. [14]

Coya wrote the ads and paid for them herself—$150. She knew that while not many people fully understood parity, everyone was for it and wanted top farm prices. At the same time, debt-free farms were impossible to achieve because farm production had to be reduced to accomplish it. However, in the 1950s farmers began using chemicals to achieve high yields. Coya's father got good yields at 20-30 bushels of wheat to the acre, and by this decade 40-50 bushels were common. High production forced prices down.

A second ad for Coya was titled "The Lady Legislator from Oklee" and was a reprint of an editorial that had appeared in the *Oklee Herald.* The editor predicted that Coya Knutson would win the primary "by a comfortable margin" because her legislative record "proves a willingness and adaptability to meet sometimes confusing challenges of driving toward a goal." Given the nomination, would she win the general election? According to the editor, the incumbent "would win in normal circumstances, but these circumstances are not normal—there is Mrs Knutson to contend with." Underlined in the ad was this statement: "We are satisfied that she is incorruptible."[15]

That spring Coya enlisted a number of people to help her who also became her close friends. One of the first was Marge Michels, who promised to travel with Coya in the southern part of the district whenever her daughters, (ages 13 and 14) could baby sit with her 13-month-old "darling baby boy." Marge was to spend a good deal of time on the road with Coya as soon as school was out and the sitters available. Marge's husband John would work for Coya in the overall campaign and especially within his labor organization, the Brotherhood of Railway Workers.

Another stalwart she enlisted was Spot Reierson, whom Coya had first met in 1948 when she was the Red Lake County DFL chairwoman. Although Spot had been instrumental in bringing the Ninth District Farmer-Labor party into the new Democratic Farmer-Labor party ten years before, he had become so disillusioned with the DFL he had left that party and campaigned for Republican Congressman Hagen. Coya decided to drive to Fosston, a town twenty miles from Oklee in Polk County, to meet with Spot and decide for herself whether their political positions were compatible. After a visit with his wife Esther and a long conversation with Spot, Coya asked him if he would support her instead of Hagen. He said he would because he thought the people were disillusioned with Hagen and he wanted to see someone with "spark" run for the office.

Spot, a successful farmer in Fosston, had a talent for working quietly and without fanfare to gather political supporters together. Weatherbeaten and unassuming, he was so ordinary looking that he could enter a room almost unnoticed. He had a reputation for never dressing up even for important occasions, yet he commanded considerable respect and power.[16]

Marge Michels enlisted another key person, Kay Peterson of Karlstad, who was the vice-chairman of the district and an astute politician. Bill Kjeldahl scheduled Kay to travel with Coya and acquaint her with the county organizations in the northern part of the district. Rae Arlis, Spot Reierson's daughter, set up booths at county fairs under her father's direction during the summer months when she was home from college. Oklee friends Elvina Zimmerman and Millie Melby would also take turns traveling with Coya. Cliff Bouvette, a Hallock newspaper editor who wrote favorable articles about her, offered to exert his influence through the Kittson county DFL organization. Although Cliff Longtin did not take an active part in this campaign, Coya still looked to him for sound political advice.

Coya's cadre of dedicated workers was headed by Bill Kjeldahl who devoted full time to managing the campaign once the university spring term ended in June. She could not afford to pay him, and that was fine with Bill who valued the experience he would gain. He enlisted his father, a retired farmer, to join the team on a part-time basis. Kjeldahl's room and board were provided by the Knutsons. He moved into one of the guest rooms in Andy's Hotel and set up campaign headquarters there.

One day Coya stood in the doorway of the café kitchen and looked at Bill sitting on the couch in the hotel lobby poring over voting records, unaware that anyone was watching him. A wave of happiness and well-being washed over her and with it the revelation that somehow this bright, patient young man must have been sent to help her. He was hard-working and had all the energy and enthusiasm needed to run her campaign. More than anything, she trusted him and knew she could depend upon him. The feeling of well-being that she had not experienced before meeting Kjeldahl stayed with her.

Coya liked having Bill around and Bill, in turn, made no secret of his admiration for Coya. He enjoyed her warmth and friendly, out-going personality. Although Andy paid little attention to Coya, he was jealous of the young man's obvious devotion to his wife. He made no secret of his displeasure that Bill was now living under their roof and working to advance his wife's political career.

Bill analyzed the voting results in the district, precinct by precinct, and on myriad pieces of paper figured out how many votes they would need in each precinct in order to win, a procedure that thirty years later would take minutes on a computer.

The Ninth Congressional District was made up of fifteen counties located in the northwest corner of Minnesota, a district dominated by the Red River Valley, and one of the richest farming lands in the world. Its fertile land was virtually treeless, stoneless and flat, making it ideal for raising grain. In 1954 spring wheat, winter wheat, oats, barley, and flax were the principal crops in the western half of the Ninth District.

The Red River Valley can be viewed from one of the high eastern sand ridges of the drained lake bed of ancient Lake Agassiz. The valley extends as far as one can see, gradually sloping into a gigantic basin that stretches to the horizon. Looking northwest from the sand ridge near the town of Trail in eastern Polk County, the enormous fields stretch endlessly, divided by straight roads following section lines. Only a cluster of houses, elevators and tree-lined avenues that form the neat small town of Oklee interrupt the pattern of fields. Standing on that same ridge near Trail but facing southeast, one sees a much different terrain: rolling, wooded hills with an occasional patch of oddly shaped field or meadow. This hilly terrain outside the old bed of Lake Agassiz, in the southeastern part of the district, accommodates small farms that produce dairy products, poultry, beef and hay.[17]

The White Earth Indian Reservation occupies a portion of the southeastern section of the district, with parcels of privately owned farm and recreation land adjacent to the Native American-owned land. To the northeast, where the Red Lake Indian Reservation is located, acres of marshland and huge shallow lakes provide a contrast to the farming areas of the district. A few fishing resorts and summer homes rim the two large lakes, Lake of the Woods and Upper Red Lake. Some of the land adjacent to White Earth is state forest. The city of Bemidji, located in the southeast corner of the district, is surrounded by forests, small farms and resort areas.

Because the Ninth District traditionally supported congressmen who voted for liberal domestic welfare issues, and especially those that affected rural interests, a politician who was also a farmer would have great appeal to the voters. Since the settlement of the Valley in the late nineteenth century, low wheat prices had triggered agrarian radicalism in successive waves of reform movements through the Populist, Progressive, Nonpartisan League and Farmer-Labor parties. Voters of the Ninth District were likely to choose a person rather than a party. In fact, Congressman Hagen had switched from the Farmer-Labor to the Republican party in 1944 without diminishing his popularity at the polls. Once a representative was elected, it was not likely that the opposing party would regain the seat until the congressman had retired.

1950 census records reveal that the majority of the residents in the fifteen counties were Norwegian farmers, and that their living conditions were better in the more prosperous western section of the district. The second largest foreign-born group were Swedish, followed by German people. More than 2,000 Native Americans lived in the district. Homes in the eastern portion of the district were equipped with fewer modern conveniences than those in the western portion. In 1950 only 8% of the houses in Clearwater County and 15% in Lake of the Woods and Mahnomen counties had hot running water and private toilet and bath facilities. The most modern housing was in Wilkin and Clay counties. [18]

Andy's Hotel was centrally located within the district and became the major base of operations. Because the district was so large in area, her committee also set up additional campaign headquarters at the Comstock Hotel in Moorhead. The manager, a Democrat, was willing to give good rates on several rooms. In other communities, such as Breckenridge, volunteers distributed literature from temporary storefront locations.

After Curtiss T. Olson was endorsed by the DFL, Coya's campaign started in earnest with strategy centered on meeting personally as many voters as possible. Although Coya knew what a rural woman's role was expected to be, it did not inhibit her persistence or assertiveness. Coya reached out to people; years later her campaign style is remembered for its warmth, good humor and down-home friendliness. "She came to our Ladies Aid at Trinity Church. Everyone knew her." "Coya was simple and direct; she was friendly and nice to everyone." "She stole our hearts."[19]

Coya sang at the rallies, accompanying herself on the guitar or, when available, the piano. Her favorite campaign song was "The Happy Wanderer," and she also sang "Red River Valley." Perhaps some people found her too brassy, but Coya's ability to entertain and her rambunctious style in the hustings attracted many voters. She was smart, funny and folksy. "Yah, I voted for her," an elderly woman said. "She sure can play and sing."[20]

Bill Kjeldahl subscribed to all the local newspapers in the district and in the evenings the campaign staff perused them for notices of festivals, parades, Farmers Union picnics, county fairs, and any other local events. These gatherings were the basis for scheduling Coya's campaign trail. Priority was given to county fairs because they attracted the most people. It could be rather awkward when Curtiss Olson and other party regulars were campaigning from the DFL booth at fairs, but Coya would work the fringes showing up at the milking demonstration, the grandstand, or the 4-H Dress Revue Parade to hand out her brochures and shake hands.

The summer of 1954 was sunny and bright, with good weather for outdoor campaigning. Coya was in every parade her staff could find; sometimes walking, sometimes riding in a car, and once waving to the crowds from a fire engine. But Coya believed that she found the best rapport with the voters by walking up and down Main Street during a parade, shaking hands. The other candidates did similar things, but Coya did more of this type of campaigning and it was evident to everyone that she enjoyed it.

On Sunday afternoons, Coya's sister-in-law Orianna would sometimes pack a picnic lunch and join the campaign team on a drive to Diamond Point, a picnic spot in Bemidji, or visit the roller rink at Pine Lake in Gonvick. At Farmers Union gatherings, Coya would drive into the picnic grounds honking her horn to attract a crowd. While she was meeting people, Terry's job was to tour the parking lot, placing campaign literature under automobile windshield wipers. He enjoyed doing that, but chose not to put bumper stickers on cars, afraid that owners would not like it and Coya would lose their votes.

Coya was on the move day and night, stopping only to have an occasional midnight hamburger which would taste extra good after running all day without food. She lost thirty pounds on this regimen. Her mouth was always dry "with all that air coming in there and talking so much." Soft drinks were not generally available in those days, and the best she could manage was a swallow of coffee now and then.

When Coya and her workers could not make it back to Oklee or Moorhead at night, they would usually stay at a friend's home where they were welcomed with a cup of coffee and given breakfast in the morning. They stayed many times at the Michels' and the Reiersons'. When showing her home to visitors, Marge Michels was fond of saying, "Coya slept here." In Bemidji, the Ken Thompson family, relatives of Andy, opened their home to the campaign staff. In Lancaster they stayed with a wealthy friend of Cliff Bouvette who lived on the former James J. Hill farm which had a swimming pool and a railroad siding that had once been used for a private railroad car when Hill, the "Empire Builder," had stayed there. If there were no friends in the area, the campaigners looked for a "tourist room" sign outside a private home and usually paid about $2 for bed and breakfast.

Coya was already well-known in the northern part of the district, but she needed to work hard in the southern area. Through Kjeldahl's careful statistical study Coya knew that if she could take certain "swing" precincts in the southern portion of the district, she would have a fine chance of winning the election. "I never did crack the Fergus Falls area—that is heavy Republican territory," she said later, "but we tried."

Indeed she tried. She used a plat book of Otter Tail, the biggest county in the district, as a guide while traveling with Terry from farm to farm for nearly a month. Coya was determined to meet every farmer in the district. Because they did not know people to stay with in that area, Coya and Terry sometimes slept beside the road in their Plymouth. They used gas station rest rooms to wash up. Occasionally Coya would be awakened in the middle of the night by a truck thundering by on the road. As the very earth vibrated beneath her, she resolved to restrict truck traffic if elected.

Coya would be aroused by the sun at about five o'clock in the morning and head for the nearest barn in hopes of finding a farmer milking his cows. Often a surprised farmer would find a smiling woman waiting outside his barn to talk with him about dairy prices. During her month on the road, she concluded that farmers' lives had changed since she was a girl; they didn't get up and start work as early as they used to.

During the day, she would trudge into the fields to meet farmers. She showed an interest in their work and in the condition of their crops, and sometimes shared her own farm experiences with them. She did not often directly ask for a woman's vote, and relied on her instincts to determine how to handle each encounter with a woman voter. Coya realized that there were some women who thought she should be at home taking care of her family, or who were jealous of a woman pursuing a career outside the home. "I felt okay with women until I realized that to many of them I was a threat to their status in the home or community. Some women were polite, and did not directly confront me, but more than once I heard, 'What are you doing out when you should be at home?' I tried not to let it bother me." In fact, she spent more time with male voters who, according to the census statistics, outnumbered the women of voting age, 54% to 46%.

Coya had both the advantage and the disadvantage of being the only woman running. Even though ten women had served in the Minnesota Legislature prior to Coya's race in 1954, there were still voters who would not vote for a woman because she was a woman.

Apart from the home-town editorial and the small flurry of ads that appeared during the week of the primary election, little mention of the five-way Ninth District DFL contest was evident in area newspapers. Neither the daily papers—*The Fargo Forum*, the *Bemidji Pioneer*, and the *Crookston Times*—nor sample area weeklies—*Baudette Region*, *Thief River Falls Times*, or the *Bagley Independent*—had much campaign coverage other than brief filing notices. The exception was the *Grand Forks Herald*. It described the Ninth District DFL primary race as the "hottest contest of the election."[21]

Most of the local papers were Republican, such as the *Thief River Falls Times*, whose editor Bill Dalhquist served as a Conservative member in the legislature with Coya. Although he would "not give me the time of day," Coya says, "he was happy to get my advertising dollars." Newspaper coverage did not worry Coya. She was not counting on it, and relied instead on radio advertising and person-to-person campaigning. "We didn't care whether the newsapers gave us publicity or not because we were out meeting people directly—but then reporters started to follow us after awhile." The local newspapers began to pay attention when others outside the district started to take notice of the race.

In the primary election of September 14, 1954, Coya soundly defeated the four other DFL candidates, garnering 45% of the vote. Receiving nearly twice as many votes as the endorsed candidate, Coya polled 11,069 to Olson's 5,938. Coya's win was hard on Curtiss Olson who won only 24% of the vote. Following the election, Olson, once a major political leader in the district, faded away. Eventually he moved to the central part of the district and then left the state. Letnes received 17%, and the other two candidates each polled less than 10% of the vote. On the other side of the ballot, Harold Hagen won 18,082 of 21,557 Republican votes. The DFL total was 24,557 votes.[22]

Predictably, the press did not give special attention to Coya's victory. "Few Upsets Develop in Primary Election" announced the *Thief River Falls Times*. The *Grand Forks Herald* emphasized that the DFL vote was heavy statewide, and for the first time had out-polled the Republicans.

Coya's family had been managing on their own while she was busy with the campaign. Andy had no summer employment, but took occasional odd jobs painting or fixing a roof. Andy was out of Coya's life, except that she continued to support him financially. Coya also saw to it that there was sufficient money available for Anna to provide food and clothing for the family. She regretted that she had so little time to spend with Gunhild and Anna, and that she saw so little of her sisters or mother. Coya, who had never been fond of writing letters, realized she wrote to them even less frequently.

The one to whom she gave emotional support and from whom she received love in return was Terry. Because he preferred to be with her, Terry joined Coya on the campaign trail wherever she could take him with her. That summer's campaign cemented the relationship between mother and son by its shared work, making them closer than ever before. Fourteen-year-old Terry was taking on new responsibilities and Coya bought him a Ford, a two-door Model A. It was similar to her own first car, but modified by the installation of a utility box where the rumble seat had been. It came in handy for hauling campaign materials. In the Oklee community there was little criticism of Terry driving at this young age; farm youngsters, Coya included, generally learned to drive early. However, when an editorial appeared in the *Crookston Times* criticizing Coya's judgement in giving her young son a car, Terry thought he had done something wrong. He did not yet understand that such stories were often politically motivated.

Besides using the Model A to distribute posters for his mother's campaign, Terry needed a car to drive nine miles to work. When he was not campaigning with Coya, he earned pocket money by working on the Brievold's farm. Terry liked to work outside through the long daylight hours and, in spite of his hay fever allergies, continued to shovel grain from a threshing rig into a truck. When he was paid $20 for the summer's work, he was sure he could never spend that much money and, thinking he was overpaid, tried to return some of the money to his uncle. Like other Oklee youths, he also worked in town mowing lawns. He had fun, too, biking with the other kids to the Lost River to swim, and going to the movies. When Terry was in Oklee and Coya was on the road, Anna continued to look after him.

Terry wholeheartedly supported his mother's campaign efforts. In turn, her son became the focal point of Coya's life. Her sister Crystal and her mother showed little interest in her political aspirations, and, except for Torkel, Andy's side of the family was lukewarm. Aside from Terry, the people who had come forward to help with the campaign—especially Bill Kjeldahl and Marge Michels—were the people she felt closest to because they understood her drive and supported her efforts.

She had worked hard to win the primary and now, bursting with vitality, Coya felt ready for the fall campaign.

The Gjesdal family: (*left to right*) Crystal, Helen, Christian, Coya, Christine, Eva.

The Gjesdal sisters with their adopted brother
Richard, known as Sonny. (*clockwise from bottom
center*) Sonny, Crystal, Helen, Coya and Eva.

Aerial view of Coya's hometown Edmore, North Dakota, in 1939.

Coya (*left*) with her father Christian, standing in front of the Reo Flying Cloud and the pickup truck.

Andy Knutson (*fourth from left*) with farm hands on the Gjesdal farm in 1926.

The Gjesdal farm in Edmore, North Dakota.

Coya in the Minnesota State
Legislature.

Minnesota Legislative Manual

Loaned by Eris Super

Coya, in front of the Oklee High School in
1945, taught English and public school music.

Minnesota Historical Society

Friend and colleague Sally Luther,
the only other woman serving in the
Minnesota State Legislature at the
same time as Coya.

Coya and Andy with a campaign worker inspecting silk-screened
campaign posters.

Coya on the hustings.

Coya with Terry in his Model A Ford jalopy.

Newly-elected Congresswoman Knutson on Main Street, Oklee,
November 1954.

Coya in Andy's Hotel celebrates winning
the election.

Coya and Andy. "She won the election
by singing at every wedding and funeral
in the district."

After her 1954 victory, Coya and her
mother, Christine, brewed four or five
pounds of coffee for well-wishers.

Coya and Andy outside Andy's Hotel on Main Street in Oklee, Minnesota, 1954.

Coya gets acquainted with her two-room air-conditioned Washington, D.C., efficiency apartment. It was on the fourth floor of a new building that boasted a self-service elevator.

Senator Margaret Chase Smith's luncheon for the women in Congress.

Mrs. Alben W. Barkley and Senator Lyndon B. Johnson with Coya and former President Harry S. Truman.

Coya and Speaker of the House Sam Rayburn.

Orville L. Freeman, Coya, Al Gerner, Coya's campaign manager, and presidential candidate Adlai Stevenson.

Coya (*far right in the light jacket*), in front of the Bagley, Minnesota, *Farmers Independent* newspaper office, listens as Hubert Humphrey campaigns. Minnesota State Legislature Respresentative Ben Wichterman stands behind and to the left of Senator Humphrey.

Marty Nordstrom

Walter F. Mondale with
power-broker Spot Reierson.

Knutson Family Collection

Coya and Humphrey at the podium
campaigning.

Knutson Family Collection

During an Agricultural Committee fact-finding trip to the
Dominican Republic, Coya inspects Generalissimo
Trujillo's prize herd of bulls.

Knutson Family Collection

Coya attends a formal dinner at the Presidential Palace in the
Dominican Republic.

AP/Wide World Photo

In her Washington office, Coya entertains her
Norwegian cousin Tor Gjesdal, Director of
Public Information at the U.N., who was on his
way to Paris to become Principal Director of
Mass Communications for UNESCO.

Knutson Family Collection

Coya entertaining her Capital Hill colleagues.

Coya with Senator Estes Kefauver at a press conference in the Pick-Nicollet Hotel,
Minneapolis, in March 1956 after Kefauver won the Minnesota presidential primary. Standing
behind Coya is her controversial aide, William O. Kjeldahl. Looking over Kjeldahl's shoulder
is Kefauver-supporter and owner of the Leamington Hotel, Bob Short.

Following the release of the "Coya Come Home" letters, Andy Knutson pledges support to Coya's opponent, Ninth District DFL Chairman Marvin Evenson, in a hotly-contested primary race.

Ninth District U. S. Congressman Odin E. S. Langen, who defeated Coya in 1958.

AP/Wide World Photo

At a press conference, Coya announces that she has requested that the House Elections Committee investigate the election in which she lost her seat to Republican Odin E. S. Langen.

AP/Wide World Photo

During the Congressional Hearing, husband Andy testified that he had been "taken" and had been a "dupe" in the Coya, Come Home affair that cost his wife the election.

Coya and Andy at the Hearing in which he told the committee he wished that "it would not have taken me all these months to tell her and everybody that I am sorry."

The family—Andy, Terry and Coya—"working together" on Coya's unsuccessful campaign in September 1960 to unseat Odin Langen, who had defeated her two years earlier.

Coya revisits Oklee in 1989, and is photographed in the same place on Main Street that she was in 1954.

Coya at home.

Chapter 7

COYA FOR
CONGRESS

*But the up-to-date woman of four score and ten years
hence will think the most peculiar thing about this generation was the patience and good nature of their
grandmothers' clamoring for things they wanted and not
getting them.*

> *"Woman Suffrage"*
> *Nonpartisan Leader: October 4, 1913*

Every chair was taken and some people stood in the back, leaning
against the wall. The Legion Hall at Bagley was jammed and Coya
was at the microphone. "Everyone must be a missionary for the
liberal candidate," she declared. The crowd applauded and several
people whistled. "I was reluctant to run; I liked it in the state
legislature," Coya went on. "But I saw that a change was needed in
Washington and I am ready to make that change." The crowd
applauded wildly and stamped their feet.[1]

Coya was hardly a reluctant candidate, but she knew that was what
people expected to hear. When she finished her speech she noted
that even though it was well past eleven o'clock, the hall was still
filled. After the dinner, many prominent DFLers had taken the micro-

phone, among them the DFL candidate for Lieutenant Governor, Karl Rolvaag, and the Minnesota national committeeman for the Democratic party, Byron Allen. Rolvaag drew attention to Coya's Norwegian heritage and her family's strong ties to the Nonpartisan League.

Coya sat on a folding chair waiting for the speeches to end, thinking about how far she had come on her own. Here she was, the featured speaker at the first big DFL event of the fall campaign. DFLers had arranged a September victory dinner in Bagley, a county-seat town which she had recently represented in the legislature. It was a sell-out crowd, and so many DFLers were scheduled to speak that it looked as though the program would go on until midnight. But no one was leaving the hall; everyone was staying to hear the last of the speeches. DFL leaders had withheld their help in the primaries, but now, she noticed, they were rallying round. DFL district chairman L.J. Lee, one of those who had refused her party endorsement, was master of ceremonies for the program.

Coya wasted no time in gearing up for the November contest. In order to campaign full-time she resigned her teaching position. Andy would have to manage the hotel and Anna could take care of the housework. Campaign headquarters were already set up at both Andy's Hotel and the Comstock Hotel in Moorhead. Coya and Bill Kjeldahl figured that they could not win in the larger cities such as Fergus Falls and Moorhead, which were Republican strongholds; they had to concentrate on the small towns and farms. This campaign had to be fought not on television, but on Main Streets, on farmsteads, in Legion halls and church basements of rural Minnesota.

The idea of a woman campaigning for Congress was not new. In 1954 twelve women were serving in the U. S. Congress. But in Minnesota, a woman running for national office remained a novelty. Coya's credibility as a female candidate was aided by Eleanor Roosevelt's advocacy of women's rights. After she became the United States' delegate to the United Nations and chairwoman of its Commission on Human Rights (1949-1952), Mrs Roosevelt continued to champion causes she had espoused while in the White House. In a speech to the United Nations General Assembly she said, "Too often great decisions are originated and given form in bodies made up wholly of men, or so completely dominated by them that whatever of special value women have to offer is shunted aside without expression."[2]

Coya had enlisted many people to aid in the campaign, including all those who had worked for her in the primary. An active new recruit was Amy Janneck, Ninth District Chairwoman, who farmed with her husband near Barnesville. Bill Kjeldahl remained in charge of the campaign and drove Coya to meetings. As they had in the primary, Marge Michels, Kay Peterson, Milly Melby and Elvina Zimmerman took turns accompanying Coya on campaign trips.

The primary campaign had worn out the old Plymouth. Coya was tempted to replace it with a four-door 1950 Chrysler Imperial, but worried that a "luxury car" would give voters the wrong impression. She discussed this problem with Bill Kjeldahl and they finally decided that because her opponent drove a Cadillac, the used Chrysler would not cost her votes. Bill rigged up the Chrysler with a rooftop loud-speaker to attract crowds and Coya remembers that "we went into town blaring away." It was Bill's choice to broadcast songs such as "The Happy Wanderer" and "The Missouri Waltz." Coya reluctantly agreed with Bill that the opera music she preferred "was a sure way to lose supporters."

Bill, Coya and various campaign workers drove from town to town, making no advance announcements and working on an improvised schedule. As they drove into a town, Bill would take the microphone and call out: "Come to the corner by the restaurant and meet the woman who will be your next congresswoman."

Marge Michels, who often accompanied them, recalls that "we were a curiosity. People would gather on the street, and Coya was very friendly—she had a big smile, and people liked her."[3] In order to appear at scheduled community affairs, the campaign team scanned the local newspapers for announcements of upcoming events.

Coya spent most of the time shaking hands and chatting with people. Voters in the villages were not accustomed to having politi-cians seek them out and Coya sensed that her "personal touch" was more important than "long-winded speeches." On the road, she was talking non-stop for ten to twelve hours each day. She credited the techniques she had learned in her vocal studies for her ability to do this without getting hoarse and worn out. She recalls that she did not think about fatigue or getting tired; the campaign was like a musical performance and the show had to go on. She enjoyed the people she met. She was also grateful that she had her mother's happy temperament.

Until she listened to a taped radio speech, Coya had not realized that she had a Norwegian accent. It was often a distinct advantage in her district to be able to speak Norwegian. At a bean feed in Thief River Falls, the second row of folding chairs was filled with bachelor farmers from the old country who warmed to her immediately when she spoke to them in fluent Norwegian. However, it could also be a disadvantage with those voters who disapproved of an American politician with a foreign accent. To some she sounded uneducated.

Whenever Coya appeared at political events, attendance was high. At a DFL "Meet Your Candidate Night" in Thief River Falls, a capacity crowd of 300 filled the new Zion Lutheran Church basement. In her speech Coya challenged the incumbent, Harold Hagen, on his vote for Tidelands Oil. In 1954, at Eisenhower's insistence, Congress had transferred the title to valuable Tideland Oil reserves to the states. Coya claimed that taxes on offshore oil should go to the nation's schools; that is, oil taxes should go to the federal government rather than to the states located adjacent to the oil fields. [4]

She comments, "I was not in favor of the 25% tax write-off that Texans got. Of course the Speaker of the House [Sam Rayburn] was from Texas and was in favor of it."

Bill Kjeldahl and several women on the campaign staff searched the Congressional Record to establish Hagen's voting record. It provided Coya with the ammunition she needed to discredit her opponent. But the Tidelands Oil issue was secondary to what Coya cared about and what was closest to the lives of her constituents— prices for farm products. Parity—a balance achieved when farm commodity prices have the same purchasing power as the average in the base period from August 1909 to July 1913, when a so-called economic balance between rural and urban prices existed—was a big issue. At a speech in Moorhead Coya acknowledged that Republicans had campaigned for 100% parity for farm prices. That was not what farmers got. "We farmers got sliding-scale parity, which in a few short years will be no parity," she said. [5]

In 1954, Congress had enacted an Eisenhower-supported bill to provide flexible supports of farm prices between 82 1/2% and 90% of parity. The reasoning was that by tying crop prices to a parity index, the farmer would be fairly paid.

Campaigning against Republican farm policies, Coya often

brought up the name of Ezra Taft Benson, Secretary of Agriculture, and linked his name with sliding-scale parity. Coya effectively satirized Benson and Hagen by composing a nine-verse song, the "Saga of Silent Harold," which she sang to the tune of "Casey Jones."

Old Flexing Ezra, cut the dairyman's income by half
For he wants each dairyman to live on curd and sell his calf.
Flexing Ezra, he's not the farmer's secretary
Flexing Ezra, he's cut our income by half
Flexing Ezra, he's not the farmer's secretary
For he wants each dairyman to live on curds and sell his calf.

Gather round and let us scan
The record of old Silent Harold, our Congressman
Who gave away the Tidelands oil to those wealthy millionaires
But never said one word for our children and their heirs.
Silent Harold, gave away the Tidelands oil
Silent Harold, gave it to those millionaires
Silent Harold, gave away the Tidelands oil
But never said one word for our children and their heirs.

"That song really devastated Hagen," Coya said. "It took hold and got people talking—they have to have something to chew on. When you poke fun a little bit and you have fun doing it, people pick up on it." She told her staff, "If the candidates would laugh and enjoy themselves a little, they would be surprised at the voters' interest."

Her campaign committee had the song printed in a brochure and added the note: "Since Silent Harold got his pension bill passed, let's put him on pension and get someone who will work for us in Washington."[6] Campaign songs were common in the days before television. If the jingles were catchy, word of mouth spread the campaign message in short, succinct bursts that people remembered.

Her song referred to the flexible or sliding-scale price supports Republicans favored. The Secretary of Agriculture took the brunt of farmers' criticisms because he was the one who announced the cuts in farm subsidies that would soon take effect. The Republicans hoped a drop in price would lower the surplus. In February 1954 the support price of butter was dropped from 90% of parity to 75% of parity. By April the price of a pound of butter dropped 8 cents from its previous price of 68 cents. Eggs also dropped in price. And so Coya sang, "Silent Harold wouldn't talk for man or wife back home."

According to Harding Noblitt, Professor of Political Science at Concordia College, "one only had to mention the name of Ezra Taft Benson and a lot of people would go into orbit."[7] Republicans advocated flexible farm supports, but farmers insisted on rigid supports, and that is what they wanted to talk about. Even while angry farmers focused upon Ezra Taft Benson, President Eisenhower maintained his personal popularity. His administration contended that high farm supports added to mounting farm surplus, and therefore the government must reduce rather than increase farm income. Behind this argument was the belief that, due to the impact of technology on agriculture, there were too many farmers. The Republicans reasoned that a reduction in farm subsidy and a greater reliance on a free market would eventually reduce the number of farm units while increasing their acreage size.

On the other hand, Democrats declared there was no sure evidence that high supports were responsible for farm surplus. However, there was considerable evidence that reduction of supports meant a further reduction in farm income during that time of industrial boom. Farm incomes were already dangerously low; therefore, some—not all—Democrats favored a rigid, 100% of parity, and Coya was one of them. Democrats also asked whether economics was the only criterion, insisting that a farm subsidy could be justified on the ground that farming as a way of life needed to be retained.

Campaigning was a seven-day job. Terry remembers that one Sunday Coya and her staff drove up and down the streets of the town of Newfolden shortly after church was over. On the car's loudspeaker, Bill played records and invited people to come downtown to "meet the future Congresswoman." The people of Newfolden gathered at cafés after church, just as they did in Oklee. As people entered a café, Coya reached out to shake their hands.

A Sunday campaign task more to Terry's liking was driving around the district with his friend Wanda Melby to nail onto telephone poles the long strip posters with C-O-Y-A printed vertically in large red letters. The campaign staff put a great deal of thought and energy into making posters, and several types were produced in a shop Bill set up in an empty building south of Andy's hotel. Bill knew how to silk-screen, and he sometimes stayed behind in Oklee, assisted by Terry and his friends, working on posters while Coya was out stumping the district.

Oklee neighbors would help with the distribution of the posters. They would drop by the shop and say they were going to such-and-such place, Coya remembers, "and they would take some posters and tack them up one here, two there wherever they went." In a backwoods area north of the Rapid River where a staunch Republican lived, several of Coya's supporters went out under the cover of darkness and nailed dozens of posters to the trees around his house.[8]

Her committee also had red-white-and-blue buttons produced with Coya's photograph on them. They were effective, according to Marge Michels, because the buttons were sold, not given away, to raise money for her campaign. The committee sought to appoint a chairperson in each community and, if possible, set up store-front campaign offices. In Breckenridge the wives and children of railroad workers distributed Coya's literature. The Wilkin County organization held a dinner with Coya as the featured speaker. More than 200 people attended, and the proceeds deposited in the county political chest. Public interest generated by this event later resulted in a record county turnout at the polls.

The amount of cash donated to Coya's campaign totaled $800. "Friends handed me a few dollars as they walked by," Coya says, and various amounts were raised at rallies. The records show that funding for her campaign came in small amounts, mainly from DFL county and city organizations, such as $50 from Becker county; $150 from Kittson county; $100 from Moorhead.[9] Some county DFL groups paid local bills for the campaign: the Red Lake County DFL paid a $17 bill and Kittson County picked up the tab for radio advertisements at a station in Hallock, but many bills for printing brochures and advertising remained outstanding.[10] In-kind donations were made, such as offers to distribute literature or to open their homes and provide lodging when the candidate was in town.[11]

Coya preferred radio rather than newspaper advertising because her distinctive lilting voice caught people's attention and she could talk to them directly. Besides, many of the papers were owned by Republicans. Radio ads cost $78.25 at station KTRF in Thief River Falls, and that was a reasonable rate. But even with relatively low expenses, Coya had difficulty paying the bills. She mailed $32 as a down payment on a bill of $132 to station KGDE in Fergus Falls. In an accompanying note, Coya apologized, explaining that the Volunteer Fund was $400 short and that we are "in debt up to our necks."[12]

In the end, she had to pay her campaign debts with her own money. To settle her bills, Coya decided to sell the North Dakota farm land that she had inherited from her father. Each of the Gjesdal daughters had been given a quarter section of land, and Coya's 160 acres included the field south of the farm buildings. It was there that the horses ran away from her once when she was a young girl.

The state DFL distributed ballots on which Coya's name as the candidate for Congress appeared beside Hubert Humphrey's name for Senator and Orville Freeman's for Governor.[13] Statewide, the DFL spent $15,800 for these sample ballots. However, Coya's campaign received almost no money and little support from the state DFL. In fact, their monetary contribution was so small that Coya considered it an insult. Of $16,898 disbursed to DFL candidates that year, Coya received only $25. The other eight congressional candidates each received amounts ranging from $175 to $4,013.[14]

It seemed to Coya that sometimes state DFLers hardly noticed she was in the race. Shortly after she had soundly defeated the endorsed Democratic nominee in the ninth district primary election, DFL columnist Arthur T. Naftalin wrote in his weekly column: "Unendorsed candidates made little impression."[15]

During the campaign, Coya saw that she was attracting the support of several influential groups, especially those of her father's party, the Nonpartisan League. Many of the old Nonpartisan League followers had become part of the Farmer-Labor group but, since the DFL merger, had been sitting in the wings. At the start of her campaign, Coya would not have been able to identify these supporters individually, but they soon revealed themselves to her and to Spot Reierson, still the most influential among the former Farmer-Laborites in the district. When Spot deserted Hagen for Coya, he also brought some of Hagen's supporters to Coya's side. At the same time Coya was responsible for bringing Spot back into the party, and he was happy about it because now both factions in the DFL—former Farmer-Laborites and Democrats—began to come to him for advice.

In addition to the Farmer-Laborites, Coya had the railroad unions behind her. Aside from both of the Michels who were very influential with trainmen, she had contact with other unions through her old friend Bob Olson in the legislature. She also had some teachers behind her, although many teachers who were Democrats were careful about overtly supporting their party because so many school board members were Republican. It was Coya's experience that because of the nature of their work and their visibility within the community, teachers generally avoided political involvement altogether. However, she felt that there was an undercurrent of restlessness and hoped that it would occur to many within the profession that sending a former teacher to Congress would help them improve their pay and working conditions.

Television was just getting started when Coya made her first appearance in front of the cameras at station WDAY in Fargo, North Dakota. When she arrived at the studio, she found it was still under construction. The temporary facilities were housed in a tent and, as she stepped on boards spanning puddles to keep her feet dry, she thought to herself, "If this is not pioneering, I don't know what is."

Andy did not accompany Coya or escort her to any of the campaign events. She had "reached the last straw" one afternoon when she had arrived home to find mail addressed to her lying opened on the dining table. Several of the letters indicated that money had been enclosed by supporters for her campaign. When she confronted Andy, he pulled a few crumpled dollar bills out of his shirt pocket but did not offer to return the money. Coya angrily shouted at him that the money was intended for campaign expenses and not for their personal use. Andy handed her the money and, without a word, walked out the door to go to Fritz's tavern. Coya went immediately to the bank, deposited the money in her campaign fund and requested forms so that she and Andy would have separate checking accounts.

Terry preferred to be out on the campaign trail with his mother to remaining at home with his father. She was so different from all the other mothers he knew in Oklee and, although he didn't quite comprehend what politics was all about, he was proud of the way people responded to her. "Washington" was a remote place he often heard mentioned but gave little thought to because he could not believe his mother would win the election.

The campaign intruded into every part of Terry's life. In October he invited sophomore Barbara LaJambe to the homecoming dance and asked his mother if he could borrow her Chrysler for the evening. He didn't want to take a girl who was all dressed up in a formal to the dance in his old Model A. Unfortunately, the Chrysler came equipped with a loudspeaker system and a large campaign sign, "Coya for Congress," mounted securely on the roof. Terry certainly made an impression on his first big date as the young man drove his girl to the dance in a luxury car decked out with political slogans.

Between April and November Coya addressed more than 20,000 voters and traveled about 25,000 miles.[16] By the time the campaign was over, she had worn out all the clothes she owned and lost a considerable amount of weight. Coya paid little attention to her personal appearance, but she quickly learned that once she became a public figure everyone felt free to comment on it. "Sure, I lost a lot of weight and people were not afraid to come right up and ask me, 'What's the matter with you? Working too hard?' Or, 'What is the matter with your hair?' They'd say anything to me." The truth was that after a summer spent outdoors campaigning 10-to-12 hours a day, her hair was sun-bleached the color and texture of a pile of straw. It was taboo to wear a hat; people had to see the campaigner's face.

While her style was bold, her political opponent used passive tactics. Harold Hagen did not seek out personal meetings with his constituents. His campaign was conducted during office hours and he relied on newspaper stories and ads to convey his message to the voters.

The two candidates had backgrounds that were remarkably similar. Harold Christian Hagen was born in 1901 to the Gilbert (Gulbrand in Norwegian) T. Hagens, who had emigrated from Norway to the Red River Valley in the same decade as Coya Knutson's father—the 1880s. The Hagens settled in Crookston, a town on the eastern edge of the valley, 120 miles from the Gjesdals' farm at Edmore. It was ironic that a daughter of Norwegian immigrants was challenging a son of Norwegian immigrants.

Gilbert Hagen was the publisher of a Norwegian language newspaper, *Vesterheimen,* and wrote a humorous novel, *Per Kjalseth.* When Harold was only eighteen, his father died and his family sold the newspaper. Harold worked part time in order to further his education at St. Olaf College in Northfield, Minnesota. During summer vacations from college, he worked as a starter for auto races, where he became acquainted with J. Alex Sloane, a famous race promoter. Under Sloane's tutelage, "Chick" Hagen became nationally known as a manager of auto race circuits.

After graduating from college in 1927, at the age of twenty-six, Harold worked at a variety of jobs until he returned to Crookston in 1933 to manage a newspaper, the *Polk County Leader.* Hagen's political career began in 1934 when he moved to Washington, D.C. to work as the administrative assistant for Congressman Richard T. Buckler of Minnesota's Ninth District. Buckler, remained in office for eight years, partly because of the fine Farmer-Labor county organization built by Spot Reierson, Harold Hagen and Hagen's brother, George Hagen. When Buckler retired in 1942, Hagen won the seat. Hagen was the only Farmer-Labor congressman in the Minnesota delegation; the other eight were Republican.

When the Farmer-Laborites merged with the Democrats only two years after taking his seat in Congress, Hagen switched his allegiance to the Republican Party. Even so, Hagen was re-elected in 1944 by a larger margin of votes than he had enjoyed as a Farmer-Labor candidate. It was apparent that the party switch helped him. Hagen gave a variety of reasons for switching, but mainly he felt that because left-wingers had taken control, his party had left him.[17]

After several years as a Republican, Hagen regained support of several individuals from the old Farmer-Labor group. Spot Reierson bolted the DFL party and became the leader of Hagen's DFL Volunteer Committee. This meant that Spot, one of the 1944 architects of the DFL party in the Ninth District, was actively campaigning for a Republican. In 1950 Spot sent out letters under the letterhead, "Hagen for Congress DFL Volunteer Committee," that asked for votes for Hagen.

The Reiersons and Hagens were good friends and socialized together. In 1953, Hagen wrote thanking Reierson for the "wonderful gifts you gave Audrey yesterday."[18] Remarkably, the two men maintained their friendship after Reierson told Hagen that he had decided to support Coya. Reierson claimed that his switch in allegiance was political and not personal. He told Hagen that he felt the GOP no longer met the needs of the district, but the fledgling DFL could.

After enjoying support from both the Republicans and the Farmer-Labor side of the Democratic party, Hagen, a maverick, was now being challenged by another maverick—and a woman, at that.

Hagen, like Coya, campaigned for better prices for milk, eggs and poultry. But early in his career Hagen had made the mistake of saying favorable things about Secretary of Agriculture Ezra Taft Benson. He tried to backtrack, but his earlier statements always cropped up. Besides, he could not run counter to Republican policy and promise the high, rigid supports that Coya favored. Democrats in Congress reported that Hagen was under pressure to abandon his call for more liberal farm programs. Hagen knew farmers were sore about the farm program and concluded, "They've a right to be. So am I."[19]

The race looked like a longshot for Coya. The schoolteacher from Oklee faced a contest with a six term congressman whose record for vote-getting was sensational. He had won the election of 1952 by the largest margin ever recorded in the Ninth District, getting 25,000 votes more than Curtiss Olson.

Hagen's office arranged for public gatherings in the larger towns "for the purpose of meeting constituents and giving them an opportunity to discuss problems personally."[20] Hagen's campaign focused on Republican rallies and events rather than on informal encounters with the general public. His staff was complacent because Hagen had won by such a large margin two years earlier.

Hagen made the normal pitches that a Republican in his district would make, but he also targeted three other groups: labor, veterans, and women. To woo the first two groups, he wrote an open letter: "Harold Hagen Publicly Thanks for their Support the Organization of Railroad Conductors, American Legion, Veterans of Foreign Wars and others." This ad, he wrote in a memo, was to be inserted in newspapers in "Labor areas like Thief River Falls, Bemidji, East Grand Forks and Moorhead"[21] But this strategy backfired.

The Thief River Falls Railroad Workers ran a newspaper ad, too: "In order to clear up the confusion of conflicting statements as to the endorsement by the Brotherhood of congressional candidates, we wish to inform you that Coya Knutson has been endorsed by the Order of RR Conductors, Brotherhood of RR Trainmen."[22] Hagen received angry letters from Legion Commanders that demanded retraction of the implied Legion endorsement of his candidacy, but Hagen replied that he would not comply with their request.[23]

Hagen also sent letters to friends in various towns of the Ninth District to submit as "letters to the editor" in local newspapers. One such letter read: "When I think of the faithful service that Representative Harold C. Hagen has rendered to all of us in this part of the Ninth District generally, the idea of substituting a reputable lady schoolteacher for solid worth seems very out of place. To be inserted in the Crookston paper."

A recipient of that letter responded to Hagen in pencil on lined paper, informing him that he had added a sentence in his letter to the editor: "She can't do what Harold Hagen has done for the farmer in water wet lands and if she is a smart woman she should be able to work in some bank that is intended for a woman and not stick herself in a man's place."[24]

Hagen went after women's votes by designing a newspaper advertisement headlined "Women for Hagen," to be signed by local Republican women: "We, the undersigned, are among the thousands of women of city, town and country in the Ninth District supporting U. S. Representative Harold C. Hagen for re-election. All women can conscientiously back him on November 2nd because Representative Harold C. Hagen is a Christian, a family man, devoted to his family, his country and his God. He serves every citizen regardless of politics, race or creed, and is a credit to state and nation. We urge other women to call their neighbors and friends in his behalf."[25]

These ads appeared in many small city newspapers, with the women's signatures appended: 27 in Baudette; 24 in Thief River Falls. Hagen spoke of women as "upholders of the family and of the nation," an echo of the anti-League campaign rhetoric of 1920.

His wife, Audrey, campaigned for him, attending women's coffee parties and making radio and television appeals. In an appearance on WDAY-TV on October 26, she told viewers, "Don't let a little singing, loud talking and false charges influence or capture your vote when seriously you know that Harold C. Hagen has done a good job..."[26] Andy made no public appearances on behalf of his wife and Coya seldom made reference to her family in the campaign. This was not unusual; female candidates seldom portrayed themselves in a family setting, while male candidates did.

Editors of area papers did not often endorse candidates, but their editorials favored Hagen. The *Fergus Falls Journal* noted that Coya "fairly shrieked" when she made charges against Hagen. The *Journal* also reported that "no congressman has ever kept in closer touch with people of his district than Harold Hagen."[27] But editorials, news coverage, and paid advertisements would not win this election.

The week before the election, Hubert H. Humphrey made a swing through the district with Coya. He was running for a second term in the Senate against Republican Val G. Bjornson. Before she left Oklee on the morning of the tour, Coya fried up two chickens and brought them along for lunch. The fried chicken was a big hit with Humphrey and his staff. Parked beside the road with the roaster full of chicken on the hood of the car, the campaign party had a feast.

Their DFL caravan drove from Warroad to Detroit Lakes, stopping in small towns along the way. In each town the caravan would cruise the length of the main street and then park so the two politicians could walk around and meet people. Coya was amazed by Humphrey's energy and by his ability to talk nonstop on any subject.

Walter F. Mondale, an eager young law school student who had recently returned from military service in Korea, worked as a volunteer on Humphrey's staff. He recalls Coya as a "sparkling, exuberant, bubbling, happy Scandinavian—heading for the moon. She was full of life. She was electric and people liked her. She was kind of like Humphrey. She could go into a room and get the dead to wake up."

Coya looked forward to Humphrey's visit to Oklee. She awoke that morning to a bright, warm autumn day and was pleased to discover that her family from North Dakota had arrived in town on a surprise visit. In anticipation of a large crowd, a public address system with microphones was set up in front of the school. Classes were dismissed in the early afternoon so that children and faculty could attend the rally and enjoy their popular teacher's big day.

Shortly before Coya and Humphrey were scheduled to speak, Andy told his wife that her recently widowed brother-in-law had committed suicide. Despondent over Eva's death, Milford Morford had lain down on his bed and aimed a small caliber gun at his head. His body had not been found for several days.

When Coya heard the news so suddenly and unexpectedly from Andy, she says, "I think all my life drained out of me. It was a real blow, coming as it did: it was horrible. My family knew it would be hard on me and they were waiting to tell me after Humphrey's speech was over—but Andy could not wait to tell me the bad news. The election was only a week away and by then I knew I would win it. I had already planned ahead and thought I would help out my brother-in-law by bringing him to Washington to work in my office. He was a good person. I knew he was very depressed after my sister's death, and I had wanted my mother to go to him, but she was not able. At that moment I did not know if I could keep going to the end of the campaign—I felt this was something that should not have happened."

Coya introduced Humphrey that day and let him do the speaking. Coya could not talk: she was in anguish. "I had time by myself for a little while, and then I had to move ahead." During the final week of campaigning, she was so grief stricken that she barely managed to fulfill her obligations.

Coya won—48,999 to 46,664—carrying all but four counties: Otter Tail, Wilkin and Clay, the Republican counties in the prosperous southern section of the district, and Beltrami county in the resort area on the far eastern side.[27] Hagen even failed to carry Polk, his home county, that he had won easily in the previous six elections. Coya carried her home county of Red Lake, two to one.[28]

Coya was front page news. The telephone rang around the clock and reporters appeared on her doorstep at all hours. The *Grand Forks Herald*, under the headline, "New Minnesota Congressman Widely Hailed," declared, "Minnesota political history was made this week by a housewife in the little town of Oklee, Minnesota, where she won election as the first woman congressman from the Gopher state. Political wiseacres said it couldn't be done—that Mrs Coya Knutson of Oklee 'didn't have a chance.'"[29]

The Fargo Forum related on page one that "peppery Mrs Coya Knutson rode to victory as a self-described 'down to earth public servant' and a lusty campaigner. 'I guess it takes a woman to beat you fellows,' she quipped at her home Wednesday after she served sandwiches to well-wishers."[30]

National media gave her coverage also: *The New York Times* reported, "Republicans surrendered the Ninth District to the first woman elected to Congress in Minnesota. Coya Knutson, 42, former schoolteacher, whose energetic campaign included song fests and piano-playing, upset Harold Hagen, veteran of six terms."[31]

Coya reflects, "I could not figure out why *Time, Life,* and newspapers far away mentioned me—other women did not have that happen. Some of my female friends did not like it, and I tried to tone it down, but there was no holding it back. I heard of feature stories in far away North Carolina and Florida—there was no let up."

Columnists praised her. In fact, Democratic columnist Arthur Naftalin adopted quite a different tone from the one he'd used after the primary. He called the Coya Knutson victory "a highlight of the election," and attributed statewide DFL victory to GOP dairy policies and the leadership of Hubert Humphrey.[32]

A newspaper reporter who covered women's activities wrote that Coya's warmth and friendliness "leaves you basking in its comfort. We didn't talk politics with her. We were interested in this woman who may be a paragon, but is a comfortable one to sit with at coffee. She is not above 'woman talk' but was sharp enough at politics to win places for herself on university, welfare, health and education committees in the Minnesota legislature."[33]

Republican editors mourned defeat of their candidate. The *Bemidji Pioneer* tersely captioned its front page article, "Hagen Loses," and reported that Hagen had been defeated by "a hotel operator at Oklee."[34]

The *Fergus Falls Journal* declared, "Everything considered, it is surprising the Republicans did not lose more than they did. Minnesota has joined Georgia and the solid South." The *Baudette Region* lamented, "Over the years he [Harold Hagen] has done dozens of nice things for folks here, and yet he lost the county. It isn't fair." [35]

But no one was more surprised than the defeated Republican. At an interview in Crookston, Harold Hagen said he did not know what he would do in January when the time came to give up the House seat that he had held since 1942. "I had never anticipated I'd lose, and as a result, I wasn't thinking about any job except the one I had."

Coya had depleted her reserves of physical and emotional strength. She was exhausted from the campaign and was suffering chest pains from stress and fatigue. She badly needed rest. The campaign and its merry aftermath had exhausted her and she could not recover because she found home was no longer a restful place. It was hectic. The telephone rang incessantly, and people continued coming to the hotel to see her. After a week of sleepless nights and days with constant interruptions, Coya drove to Detroit Lakes to stay with Elsa and Barney Allen at their lakeside home. She slept through two nights and a day and awoke refreshed. She returned to Oklee after several more days of rest, her elation subdued but her head full of ideas and plans.

Chapter 8

FROM OKLEE
TO WASHINGTON

The farmer's wife is just waking up to the fact that she
has any interests which need looking after. For a long
time she had been as disdainful as the men have been to-
wards the type of woman who frequents our legislative
halls. "Oh they are fashionable women with nothing bet-
ter to do. They had better be at home darning their
husband's socks," is the general comment.

"Now that the Farmer 'Has Arrived' Must his
Wife Always Stay in the Kitchen?"

Nonpartisan Leader: October 11, 1917

The café area of the hotel had changed little since the time of Andy's
Café when Anna had baked a coconut cake fresh each day for the
customers. Now the big kitchen appliances were used to prepare
family meals, and two of the restaurant tables had been pushed
together and covered with a flower-sprigged oil cloth.

Coya had many visitors in the days immediately following her
election and they were often invited to join the family for a meal. So
many well-wishers had stopped by to congratulate her during elec-

tion week that her mother had brewed four or five pounds of coffee, the *Grand Forks Herald* reported. With the new frozen foods available across the street at Melby's Store, Anna was able to cook for four or twenty people on short notice.

Coya had appropriated two of the booths on the back wall for her own use as office space. Stacks of envelopes, telegrams and papers left a permanent clutter in the booths where Coya spent long hours writing letters, outlines, and notes to herself. Now that she had had a chance to rest, to think, and to talk over her prospects with Bill Kjeldahl, she had a good idea of what she needed to do to prepare herself for Washington.

Improving the farm economy would continue to be her top priority. She wanted price supports returned to 90%, a relaxation of controls on corn production, increased acreage allotments for sugar beet growers, and hikes in support for feed grains as well as for durum wheat.[1] When she considered the needs of the district and her own promises to the voters, Coya knew it was imperative that she be assigned to the Agricultural Committee in order to work on these farm issues. However, a woman had never served on this committee; in fact, the requests of three congresswomen—Virginia E. Jenckes, (D. Ind., 1932); Kathryn O. McCarthy (D. Kan., 1936); Katharine St. George (R. N. Y., 1950)—had been dismissed. Coya's Republican predecessor had also failed in a bid for the Agriculture Committee. No Minnesota congressman was serving on the committee that had a great effect on Minnesota's biggest industry.

Coya rolled a fresh sheet of paper into the typewriter and wrote a letter to Congressman John Blatnik of the neighboring Eighth District, asking him how she could be appointed to the House Agriculture Committee. She composed her letter carefully; his support and counsel were essential. Blatnik replied by return mail advising her to write immediately to Speaker of the House Sam Rayburn and Majority Floor Leader John McCormack.[2]

Her letters to Rayburn and McCormack were soon rewarded with the coveted appointment. Many years later, Coya learned that Agriculture Committee chairman Harold Cooley, a Democrat from North Carolina, protested to Speaker Rayburn that he did not want a woman on his committee. Rayburn told him that "Coya Knutson did the impossible by getting elected, and she's going to get her pick of committees." Coya and Cooley, who had served on the Agriculture

Committee for 22 years, eventually became the best of friends.[3]

Coya's next item of business was to appoint Bill Kjeldahl as her administrative assistant. Bill would be responsible for management of her Washington office and would also be in charge of her schedule. She felt that Bill had done an exceptionally fine job of managing her campaign; in fact, without his help she would not have been elected.

Surprisingly, considering the opportunity the young man was being offered, Bill was not anxious to go to Washington. His service in the Korean War had already delayed his plans to attend law school and now, at the age of 25, he felt he should not postpone his education any longer. However, he decided that working as a congresswoman's administrative assistant in Washington would be excellent experience for his own future political career.

Coya had been taking notes on the specific needs of her constituents: increased electric power for Moorhead; more frequent air service for Bemidji; a new port of entry on the Canadian border; flood control for the Red River Valley; and funds to aid the Red Lake band of Ojibwes. But however serious she was about serving their needs, the public appeared to be obsessively interested in her home life. Newspapers were more concerned with her method of combining homemaking and a career in Washington than with her political agenda. Katie Louchheim, the Director of Women's Activities for the Democratic National Committee, said her office was besieged with reporters who wanted human interest stories about the congresswoman. They particularly wanted to know what her husband did and whether or not he would move to Washington.[4]

Coya, in an edited version of the truth, told reporters that her husband, a member of their township board, went along with the idea of her being involved in public service from the very beginning. "He talked politics and egged me on. When we first began to talk about this campaign last Christmas vacation, and as it took more definite shape at Easter time, he was backing me," she said.

The truth was that Andy's passive temperament had undergone a swift change once Bill Kjeldahl had joined Coya's staff in April. Andy had taken an immediate dislike to the college kid his wife doted on and had deemed indispensable. Bill, in turn, had little time for Andy. The young man's diffidence irked Andy, who felt even less significant in the Knutson household. Bill, who had moved into one of the hotel's guest rooms, preferred working through the night on his voting statistics and often slept late in the morning. Coya would not permit her husband to sleep late, but indulged her young assistant's irregular hours. One morning, when Bill slept until nearly noon after an all-night working session, Andy became enraged. He stormed through the hotel shouting, "that good-looking lout has no business laying around in bed all day." Bill tried to keep his distance, but Andy's resentment grew as the campaign wore on.

In answer to the question of how the family would "manage with Mother away in Washington," one women's-page reporter wrote: "The new congresswoman makes her plans after careful consideration and no one knows better than she does that you can't just walk out and leave your husband and teen-age son to shift for themselves. She [Coya] was the first to see the funny side of that, for she said laughingly, 'After all, they have had to learn to look after themselves and do it pretty well. I am serving my second term in Minnesota's legislature and this past year I haven't spent much time around here.'"[5]

For Coya, victory was sweet, and any problems of being a wife and mother while living a thousand miles away from home were subordinate to the happiness of her hard-won victory. Dozens of congratulatory letters and telegrams arrived in Oklee. One friend wrote, "It took a woman to beat friend Harold. That's what really tickles me. In spite of all the dire predictions of defeat, you did what we have failed to do."[6]

She heard from her lobbyist friend, Bob Olson, who told her he was "still picking crow's feathers out of his teeth." Her cousin, Tor Gjesdal telegraphed from Norway, "Heartiest personal congratulations. Family in old country proudly rejoices."[7] His telegram meant much to Coya. Tor had been a great source of inspiration for her, and she believed that his campaign appearances on her behalf had contributed to her victory.

Terry finally realized something really important had happened to his mother when the *Minneapolis Tribune* chartered a plane to bring in newsmen to interview Coya in Oklee. When Coya and Terry drove to the nearby Thief River Falls airport to meet the reporter and photographer and drive them to Oklee, Terry asked lots of questions and began to think about what "going to Washington" might mean. He was even more impressed when the mayor of Oklee designated the town the "Capitol of the Ninth District."

Tom Melby, known as "Mr Republican," cut across party lines to join with others in sponsoring a community celebration in Coya's honor. On the day of the party, which included a bean feed, Oklee's high school gym was packed to overflowing. More than a thousand people—twice the town's population of 497—came to pay tribute to the new congresswoman. Many well known politicians—including Congressman John Blatnik and DFL Executive Secretary Ray Hemenway—were among the speakers and guests. Coya's former pupils presented her with a desk set, and local businessmen gave her luggage and a brief case.

Townspeople were exuberant, telling each other that "Coya put us on the map." Andy was conspicuous by his absence. According to Terry, everyone in town attended the gala except his father, who elected to stay at home.

Coya enjoyed the party, and was overwhelmed by the outpouring of pride and affection from her neighbors. Throughout the day Coya felt little pushes of happiness swell inside and suffuse her with a warm glow. She had no time to get anything special to wear, but she figured she was among old friends and it wouldn't matter. Besides, she did not have the money to buy a new dress.

After the initial distraction of victory celebrations, the women and Terry became increasingly apprehensive, aware of the tremendous change about to take place when Coya left for Washington, D.C. In addition, the approaching holiday season offered Andy an excuse to drink. For several years Coya had not dared invite friends or family to the house for holiday festivities because she was afraid Andy would be drunk.

Coya felt responsible for leaving things in good order at home. She wondered if she had done as much as she could to help Andy. There was little she herself could do for him any more, but she thought that perhaps she could find someone else to help him. She talked to Andy's brother Torkel about her husband's deteriorating condition. They agreed that she should consult the mental hospital in Fergus Falls, the nearest alcohol abuse center.

When Coya called the center, the doctors advised her that they could help him only if he would agree to six weeks of in-patient treatment. She made the arrangements, but Andy ridiculed the idea. He was so infuriated by Coya's intervention that she dropped the plans. But she knew that he could not keep on drinking without destroying himself. She asked the manager of the local liquor store to stop selling alcohol to Andy. When Andy found out about the action she'd taken, he was so angry that he shouted and threatened Coya and Terry.

For Coya, Christmas preparations went by in a blur, mostly because Andy was predictably drunk. Coya thought again about divorce, but she found too many reasons to avoid facing it: moral reservations; concern about the adverse effect it would have on her political career; and the lack of time and money for the legal preparations. She decided to provide for Andy as best she could; she paid the taxes and utilities on the hotel and gave him sufficient money for other expenses. His mother, Gunhild, had a small, private income. Coya felt that Anna was closer than anyone to Andy, and was the best care-giver he could possibly have. Anna, who had no income of her own, would continue as before, keeping house for the family and looking out for Terry.

Coya planned to take Terry with her to see the nation's Capitol; they would leave shortly after Christmas to allow plenty of time to drive to Washington for the January 5th swearing-in ceremonies. She hoped that in the meantime she could make the holidays as pleasant as possible for the family.

Andy watched these preparations and knew that he was being "provided for." He would have a roof over his head and hot meals prepared by his sister. Perhaps his mother would give him some pocket money to buy cigars, but none of it compensated him for the loss of his wife. The last shreds of his self-esteem would go out the door with her. She was his wife and belonged at home, but she couldn't see that. The house would be very quiet without her—and she was taking Terry with her, too. For all her faults, Coya was a bright, lively whirlwind and he would be lonesome without her. He did not know how to tell her that. Instead, he left the house after supper to drink some Christmas cheer in a bar where it was lively and friendly.

The house looked bright and cheerful for the Knutsons' traditional celebration of Christmas Eve the following night. A small spruce tree decorated with tinsel, blue lights, and blue and silver balls sparkled in the entryway of the hotel. There were several gift-wrapped packages underneath the tree. As she did every year, Coya had bought Andy a new shaving kit. She had not had time to bake her Norwegian specialties, but friends had given her boxes of homemade cookies carefully layered in wax paper. Everything was ready for Christmas. By nine o'clock Anna and Gunhild had gone to bed, but Coya and Terry were sitting in the living room, talking and listening to the radio.

They were startled by the clattering back door and knew at once that Andy had arrived home drunk. He entered the kitchen cursing loudly and yelling "Where is that wife of mine, that woman that thinks she can leave me?"

Coya tried to steady Andy, but he broke away from her and stumbled down the hallway. She followed him to the side door where he tripped over the threshold and went outside. She heard the trunk of the car slammed shut.

Minutes later, Andy returned, a little steadier on his feet and brandishing a shotgun. "Stand here, you two," he growled, motioning to them to move against the laundry room wall. "You think you're leaving, huh? Now what do you say?" Terrified, Coya and Terry did exactly as he asked. Then Andy's expression changed, and just as suddenly as he had erupted in anger, he dropped the gun on the counter, shaking his head. "I did not mean it; I did not mean it," he whispered. He hung his head.

Terry hid the gun while Coya ran to the telephone. "I knew it was time to get out," Coya says. She called her friend Bernadette Stromme, who arrived within minutes to drive them to meet the midnight train for Minneapolis. Anna had been awakened by the noise. She came into the kitchen and helped Andy to bed. Meanwhile, Coya and Terry tossed clothes into suitcases. One valise and a shopping bag held everything that Coya would take to begin her new career in Washington, D.C.

Coya and Terry sneaked out of the hotel into the frigid night air, jumped into the waiting car and raced to catch the 11:59 train out of Brooks. As the car pulled away from the curb, Terry rubbed a little hole in the frosted window and looked up at the hotel. A light was on in Andy's room and through the drawn shade Terry could see figures moving. Just before the car reached the corner, Terry looked through the cloud of exhaust and saw his father framed in an upstairs window watching their departure. Terry felt dread as he thought ahead to his return to Oklee in a couple of weeks. Coya did not look back.

As they boarded the train, a young porter recognized Coya and reached out to shake her hand, saying, "Coya, get us a student loan bill, will ya?" Coya answered, "I will."

In Minneapolis they stayed with her sister, Crystal, and went through the motions of celebrating Christmas Eve and Christmas Day. Coya telephoned Bill Kjeldahl at his father's house and asked him to meet them with her old Chrysler and drive them on to Washington, D.C. He would bring Alice Lindquist, a single woman from Oklee who had secretarial skills, whom Coya had asked to be her secretary and roommate.

While waiting for her traveling companions, Coya had time to think about and evaluate the parting scene with Andy. It had been a frightening experience and she was still angry with him. But she realized that he had acted out his own anger and frustration at her leaving. She decided to continue being supportive of him—but from a distance. Coya did not call home before leaving Minneapolis.

On the two-day trip to Washington, D.C. Bill and Coya took turns driving. Terry remembers that "even though we had packed bare essentials, the car's tailpipe was almost hanging on the ground. The car fishtailed on curves when they forgot to slow down."[8] The skies were gray and they drove through rain and snow. But Coya did not mind the weather, nor the long, tedious drive. She was relieved to be away from Andy at last and was looking forward to her new work.

Even though it was late at night on December 27th when they arrived in Washington, Coya took them on a tour of the town so they could enjoy the beauty of the Capital city all lit up for the festive season. The four Minnesotans were impressed. Coya especially enjoyed showing Terry the beautiful Capitol building where she would be working. She was thrilled to see it herself—she had forgotten how enormous it was compared with its smaller Minnesota version. She was weary, but eager to begin her new life in this exciting place.

Chapter 9

A Woman
in Congress

The women will be running things and getting what they want. They will have no more need for patience then than men do now. They can just be natural.

"Knitting or Women's Rights?"
Nonpartisan Leader: October 4, 1917

It did not take Coya long to unpack. When she hung up the three new dresses and her good three-quarter length coat trimmed with mouton lamb in the small closet she would share with Alice, there was still plenty of space left. Coya folded her new green knit suit, carefully protecting its angora collar, and thought of the old worn out things she had left at the hotel in Oklee. The only remnants of her former wardrobe were a few items of lingerie and her pajamas. It seemed a good omen for beginning a new life.

She and Alice had taken a two-room apartment on the fourth floor of the Coronet, a well-kept residence only a block from her office. The apartment was air conditioned and the building had a self-service elevator—luxurious and very modern features to Coya—but the rooms were small. Two single beds and a dresser barely fit into the bedroom. In the living room there was a small table with drop leaves, a chair, lamps, and a sofa where Terry would sleep. The Pullman kitchen, concealed by a venetian blind, contained a small stove, sink and refrigerator, and minimum cupboard space.

For a moment, Coya was overcome by all the old apprehensions of high school days. But she calmed herself by repeating softly, "Coya, you are going to be okay." She felt better and went out to buy a coffeepot.

Office space remained a problem. There were no interim quarters for incoming congressmen and Hagen did not offer the use of his office nor cooperate with Coya in achieving a smooth transition. He seemed, in fact, to view Coya's two-year term as an unwelcome but unavoidable hiatus in his political career, after which he would be re-elected.

Congressman Blatnik provided Coya with a desk and a telephone in his own offices. There she set to work on Volume I, Number 1 of "Coya's Capital Chat." Its format included a photograph of the Capitol and a candid shot of Coya with the caption "Minnesota's First Congresswoman." The column reported that her first official visitor had been Ben O. Little Creek of Red Lake, who had brought Native American handicrafts that she would subsequently display in her permanent office.

After more than a week of makeshift, Coya was assigned to Room 324 in the Old Senate Office Building. When she proudly used her key for the first time to inspect her office, she found the former tenants (a defeated California congressman and his staff) still moving out. A handsome leather sofa caught her eye. Then, during the change-over, it was replaced by a shabby substitute. Coya registered a complaint but did not follow up on it. She realized that she "wouldn't have time to relax on any sofa, old or new."

Bill Kjeldahl was responsible for setting up the office and hiring the staff. In addition to Alice Lindquist, Coya's secretary, there were two other women. One was bright-eyed and enthusiastic Marge Sieber, who handled correspondence and became Coya's confidant. Another was Nicki Wilson, a dedicated and efficient legislative assistant.

Coya was still settling into her new office when she discovered that an announcement of her appointment to the Agriculture Committee had made her front-page news, with her picture appearing in nationwide publications, including *The New York Times*.[1] She found the unexpected burst of publicity unsettling. While the press focused their attention on the first woman member of the Agriculture Committee, she was singled out for brief meetings with House Speaker Sam Rayburn and Majority Leader John McCormack. She worried that encounters with these illustrious public figures would make her tongue-tied, but both men put her at ease. Her voice shook slightly when she was introduced to Rayburn, but Coya didn't think he sensed her fright. "Everyone's wrapped up in their own worries, so just get on with your own business," she told herself.

In the rare intervals between professional and social commitments—which were, and still are, often indistinguishable in the U. S. capital—Coya evaluated the 1954 political climate. The Korean War was over. There was less tension in the Middle East. On the other hand, the Cold War was clearly escalating. Dwight D. Eisenhower was still a favorite of the American public. His 1952 campaign had emphasized a popular "peace and prosperity" theme, while Vice-President Richard M. Nixon had denounced the Democratic Party as "selfless servants of Communist propaganda." Republicans had hoped that the candidates' combined messages would retain House and Senate majorities.

GOP tactics were successful on the Executive level, but the Democrats took control of Congress by a majority of 19. That was an advantage Coya had not enjoyed in the Minnesota House. Women in the national legislature were not the rarity they had been in 1950 among Minnesota lawmakers. In 1954 the four new U.S. congresswomen joined thirteen already in office.

Coya was fascinated with House Doorkeeper, William "Fishbait" Miller's tales about women in previous Congresses. He observed that the gentlemen of Congress were not at all pleased that the House was invaded by more and more female members. He cited Clare Boothe Luce as a prime example of a woman who was especially resented because she acted "uppity, and walked around with her nose in the air" as if she had just as much right to be there as the men.[2]

Clare Boothe Luce, a Republican from Connecticut, swept into their midst in 1942 when Coya was still a farmwife and AAA field worker in Minnesota. Coya had read about the dynamic congresswoman, who also had careers as playwright, editor, author and war correspondent. She seemed to have everything: looks, charm, wit, intelligence, and an indulgent husband with considerable wealth and power. Miller described her as "beautiful and elegant, but with a tongue like a dragon's. She could cut down anybody she did not like or who crossed her."

In 1946, after serving two terms, she decided not to run again. But she would remain the definitive Congresswoman. Eight years later, when Coya came to the Hill and Luce was serving as Ambassador to the Vatican, "Congresswoman" and "Mrs Luce" were still synonymous. Luce had proved once and for all that a woman in politics could be as successful as a man. She had also broken new ground: of the seven congresswomen in 1942, Luce was the only one who was married.

Three of those seven were still in office when Coya began her term: Edith Nourse Rogers, Margaret Chase Smith and Frances Payne Bolton. All three had succeeded their husbands in office, and all three had long and distinguished careers as legislators. Coya came to know and admire each of them.

In 1925, at age 44, Edith Nourse Rogers, a Republican from Massachusetts, joined the House of Representatives, and eventually became a more prominent politician than her husband who had served seven terms. Having cared for the wounded in Europe as a Red Cross volunteer during World War I, she staked out veterans' affairs as her turf, later becoming chairman of the Veterans Affairs Committee. To thousands in her Massachusetts 5th District, Rogers was a combination business advisor, mother confessor and friend-in-need. In 1952 the Democrats nominated a woman to run against her, but Rogers was re-elected. When Coya entered Congress, Rogers was seventy-four-years old and still going strong.

Republican Margaret Chase Smith of Maine described herself as a "product of nepotism" because she had served on her husband's staff as his secretary (at $15 a week). A congressional freshman in 1940, she hoped to carry on his work in the Labor Committee, but was not given the assignment. A growing interest in military preparedness led her to her next request, a seat on the Naval Affairs Committee, which was granted in 1943. There she could watch over ship building and other interests vital to her state. With Rogers, Smith also worked to give women regular (not just reserve) status in the armed services. She overruled a colleague's opposition to her proposal to send WAVES overseas with the rejoinder: "Then we'd better bring all the nurses home."[3]

In 1948 she became the first woman to win a first-term election to the Senate rather than to be appointed to office, defeating three opponents, including the state Governor. Like Coya, Smith had an able, young, male campaign manager who later became her administrative aide. Bill Lewis, son of an Air Force General from an oil-rich Oklahoma Indian family, was a promoter for the Air Reserve Association when he helped Smith win the Senate election.

Smith is remembered for her early condemnation of McCarthyism at a time when few others dared speak out. She startled her colleagues by saying, "I do not like the way the Senate has been made a rendezvous for vilification, for selfish political gain at the sacrifice of individual reputations and national unity." Retribution came swiftly when Senator Joseph McCarthy instigated her expulsion from a key subcommittee. Her replacement was Senator Richard Nixon.

Francis Bolton of Ohio entered Congress with Smith in 1940. Good-natured, matronly, and the richest woman on Capitol Hill, Bolton was lonely. Her chauffeur remembers that "we killed time by riding around town and talking because she did not want to go home to an empty apartment."

Bolton was in favor of drafting women for military service. "In the war, women will be out with guns defending their homes. They ought to be drafted so they'll know how to defend their men and their children." She did not want to be called "Congresswoman." "I'm a congressman," she said. "A poet is not a poetess and an author is not an authoress. It's degrading."[4]

Although World War II had given women more political scope, many were working only in local and state capacities. Of the fifteen who had run for Congress in 1946 only seven had been elected. But in 1948 three women who had become influential in their respective parties were elected to Congress: Indiana Republican Cecil Murray Harden, New York Republican Katharine St. George, and New York Democrat Edna Kelly.

When these three women were added to the six incumbents, the Halls of Congress included only nine women—the same number who had served 20 years earlier. Four more congresswomen were added in 1950 and 1951, and then throughout his 1952 presidential campaign, Eisenhower actively courted women voters: "I know what can be done with a good broom in the hands of a morally indignant woman." Women, reacting against the Korean deadlock, swarmed to the GOP candidate. An increase of women elected to Congress that year meant that in 1953 there were 12 women in the House. Two of these women were to work closely with Coya: Gracie B. Pfost, an Idaho Democrat, and Leonor K. Sullivan, a Democrat from Missouri.

The 1954 roster listed a record total of 17 women with congressional seats; all 12 women incumbents had been re-elected. One new female member, Iris F. Blitch, had been elected from the one-party state of Georgia, and three female Democrats had ousted male Republican incumbents: Edith Green of Oregon, Martha W. Griffiths of Michigan, and Coya Knutson of Minnesota. Elizabeth P. Farrington of Hawaii had been elected as a delegate to Congress in August, 1954. The International News Service reported that, "If the gentlemen of the 84th Congress appear a little better behaved and a little better mannered than usual, there'll be a reason: women."[5]

Yes, it was a good year to be joining her fellow congresswomen, Coya decided. For the first time ever, all entering congresswomen were married, which broke the "widows succession" tradition. These female freshmen were younger than in previous years: Knutson, 42; Griffith and Blitch, 43; and Green, 45. Before 1954 the age group rearing children were not very well represented in Congress; entering congresswomen were more likely to be in their fifties.

The attitude of a Congresswoman's spouse was to be a crucial factor in her campaign as well as a major determinant to her success in office. Could a satisfactory family-life be maintained while the wife and mother was in Washington or out campaigning? Would the husband be able to accept having a well-known, influential wife? Much would depend on the relationships of the individual couples and the willingness of the partners to adapt.

Coya prized her copy of the Congressional Directory, a small book that contained the names, photographs, home states and party affiliations of House and Senate members. She studied the booklet at home, learning to match faces with names. If she could not "hook a name up with a face," she referred back to the directory and refreshed her memory. In her column she pleaded, "Congressmen, please take some new pictures; I cannot tell who you are."

Popular with the press because of her appointment to the Agricultural Committee, Coya also became a personal favorite among reporters. The concept of a small-town farmwife at work on Capitol Hill was good copy. Especially in the Midwest.

Coya's portrait appeared in color on the cover of the *Minneapolis Tribune's* "Picture Magazine." The story listed the farm problems and district needs she had on her agenda, and she was described as an "energetic figure up on the edge of the big, high-backed swivel chair at her desk, handling a steady stream of early business."

The writer compared her old life with her new life, as though trying to bring them together for her. Scenes from her daily life in Oklee and Washington D.C. illustrated the story: a photograph of Andy and Coya strolling in front of their white-frame hotel in Oklee contrasted with a picture of Hubert H. Humphrey showing Coya around Washington. A photograph of Coya standing on Main Street appeared in the layout next to a picture of Coya standing on the Capitol steps. Terry and Coya were pictured in his jalopy and also in front of the high school where she had taught. She was portrayed frying eggs at the kitchen range in Oklee and examining the oven in her tiny kitchen in Washington. She was seen singing at the piano in Andy's Hotel and seated at the big desk in her Washington office, some thousand miles east. A caption read: "She spent the first couple of days mentally rearranging the furniture, so that when she actually moved in she was ready to push it around into a new pattern—like any woman."[6] In another article, the *Grand Forks Herald* noted that she had taken county fair prizes for her apple pie and doughnuts.

Coya enjoyed the press attention and she recognized that the slant of these feature stories was accurate. Her life had changed, and her new life bore little resemblance to the former one. She had left her marital unhappiness behind and embarked on a life that promised new challenges and the hope of achievement in public service.

Terry stood beside her for the swearing-in ceremony on the floor of the House. The boy was awed not only by the ceremony, but by the grandeur of the building itself. He was not prepared for the breath-taking expanse of sculpted marble and magnificent murals nor for the highly-charged atmosphere of immense power and authority. He was also not prepared for a glimpse of the dark side of the building's history. After the ceremony someone showed him bullet holes in the back of a chair which made him realize how vulnerable people in office are. For the first time the 15-year-old felt a chill of fear for his mother's safety.

Coya was pleased that Terry hit it off with the son of Congresswoman Edith Green, with whom Coya felt an affinity. Democrat

Green, from Oregon, had also been a schoolteacher and had brought one of her sons with her to Washington, D.C. Terry admired James' polish and manners, and confided to his mother that he felt awkward in the company of other Congressmen's children; he envied their facility in handling social situations.

The day after the swearing-in ceremony, the President delivered his State of the Union address. Members of the Cabinet, the Supreme Court, the Diplomatic Corps and the Senate joined House members in their chambers for President Eisenhower's 56-minute speech. The House Chambers, illuminated by bright television lights, resembled a huge Hollywood movie set. Television cameras mounted on dollies, microphones, radio equipment, and electrical cords snaking through the aisles added to the excitement and glamor of the scene. Coya was glad to have Terry in the gallery to watch the spectacle.

On this occasion she had time to look around, and she was unhappy to see brass spittoons placed here and there throughout the chamber. She could hardly believe that some men in Congress shared her father's filthy habit of chewing tobacco.

That evening a dinner for the women of Congress was sponsored by the Women's Press Club at the Hotel Statler. This was Coya's first big Washington social event, and she enjoyed visiting with other congresswomen. The four new women members of the House were honored guests, along with Vice-President Richard M. Nixon and his wife Patricia. Betty Farrington had orchid corsages flown from her home in Hawaii as gifts for her women colleagues in the House and Senate.

The ornate room and beautiful table settings, with white cloths and fresh flowers, reminded Coya of the much simpler appointments of her first formal dinner in the gymnasium of Edmore High School, which to a graduating senior had seemed the height of sophistication in 1930. Table conversation—mostly shop talk—was so engrossing that Coya forgot to eat. These dinners, she realized, were the equivalent of work sessions.

However, she noticed that her own three-quarter-length dress did not compare well to some of the other congresswomen's long formal gowns. She did not really mind. She was who she was and she would never be comfortable trying to look elegant or glamorous. No one asked her about Andy. In fact, she had noticed that few of the married women's husbands had escorted their wives. The husbands were back home working or had other obligations of their own.

Coya also attended the Red Mass, a prayer for guidance in the year to come, given at St. Matthew's Cathedral for all the diplomatic dignitaries and members of the judiciary, legislative and executive branches of the government. The annual Mass was by invitation only and seating arrangements followed strict protocol. Congressmen were seated alphabetically according to seniority. Coya sat among the other freshman legislators with her new friend, Betty Farrington. On the way to the service, the two women talked about Hawaii, a place Coya thought of as a tropical paradise at the far end of the earth. She recalled that the President in his State of the Union message had talked about Hawaii becoming a state, but had not mentioned the territory of Alaska, another far-off place that captured her interest. She made a mental note to find out whether statehood would be offered to Alaska.

Another highlight of Coya's first days in Washington was the reception for members of Congress hosted by President and Mrs Eisenhower at the White House. Edith Green and Coya happened to arrive together and Congressman James Roosevelt strode by them cheerfully calling out, "I see you girls made it here by yourselves." In her column Coya criticized the manners of the 200 people who did not bother to send their regrets that they could not attend. She noted that an invitation to the White House was, in fact, a command performance, and told her readers, "Pardon me, our manners are showing." [7]

One weekend Coya, Terry and Bill Kjeldahl were invited by Tor Gjesdal to attend a gala United Nations party in New York City. The three took the train to New York and hurriedly changed clothes before the party. Terry was very proud of his mother's ensemble, a jacket and dress of soft silver faille with black fur cuffs that she had bought in Bemidji. When they arrived, Tor immediately took them to meet the Secretary-General of the United Nations, Dag Hammerskjold. "No one keeps the Secretary waiting," Tor explained.

Hammerskjold, a quiet, formal gentleman, bowed deeply when they were introduced. After a brief visit, the two U.N. officials and Coya walked together to the front of the room where the group was photographed. Coya was deeply impressed.

The remainder of that evening was spent as other social evenings were to be spent in Washington, with Coya buzzing around the ballroom talking to people, eager to find out what everyone was thinking about the issues of the day. While quantities of food and drink were available, Coya ate little at parties and drank no alcohol.

Elmer and Elsie Thompson, the cousins Coya had visited on Long Island during her Juilliard days, had also been invited to the U.N. gala. It was the beginning of their renewed friendship. While Coya was in Washington, the Thompsons stopped in to see her whenever they traveled back and forth to Florida.

Terry liked being in Washington. Coya and Bill gave him odd jobs to do to occupy his time, but more than anything Terry liked to talk with James Roosevelt, the congressman who had offices across the hall from Coya. Everyone called the congressman Jimmy, and Terry could not believe that the son of President Franklin D. Roosevelt would take time to talk and joke with "just anybody" like himself.

Coya would have liked to have Terry stay on with her in Washington, but she had so many new things to adjust to herself that she felt a lively teenage boy was more than she could manage. Moreover, it was too expensive to have a family in Washington. She could get by on very little by herself, but to provide food, clothing and schooling for Terry in Washington was beyond her means.

Coya counted on Terry being self-sufficient. When the time came for him to return to Oklee, Terry took the train home alone to finish his freshman year of high school. Terry would be "keeping his father company while Mother is in Washington," a reporter explained.[8]

Coya was exceptionally busy the rest of the winter, "learning the ropes" of Congressional work—its committees, floor action and debate— and attending the many ceremonies and events that marked the beginning of a Congressional session. Coya was learning fast and working at a fierce pace.

Soon after she arrived, Coya had the briefcase that the Oklee townspeople had given her altered to accommodate her massive load of paper work. Because she could barely hold the bulging briefcase in her arms, she took it to a shoemaker to have sturdy handles attached.

Chapter 10

THE FRESHMAN

*When Woman consigns her crochet hook and embroi-
dery hoops to a museum and begins studying the economic conditions that make child labor possible, then
can we hope to feel her power in the councils of the nation.*

*"Progressive and Practical Ideas for
Women"*

Nonpartisan Leader: December 9, 1915

The minute Coya was ushered into the State Dining Room, she was
swept up in its picture-perfect splendor. With the other twenty-five
freshman members of Congress, Coya had been invited to lunch at
the White house. The Eisenhowers and their guests sat in high-
backed gold chairs around an oblong mahogany table that was
decorated with three huge bouquets of salmon-colored tearoses. The
silver was very simply engraved, "President's House."

Coya was delighted to find that she was seated near the President.
She had expected a terse and formal military man and she was
surprised to discover that Ike was friendly and good at keeping a
conversation going.

While they dined on pheasant and wild rice, the President talked
about his farm and mentioned that he had five head of Aberdeen

Angus cattle. Coya replied, "How about a few Holstein as well; they look more picturesque against the green grass." Ike, familiar with Coya's interest in price supports for milk products, had the final word: "That's a dairy strain, and we have enough of that already."[1]

Coya was awed that she, a farmer's daughter, was a guest at the White House having lunch with the President of the United States. She also found it amusing that, given this precious time with the President, the subject of their light-hearted conversation was frivolous uses for paper money. "Let's settle our national debt by using one side of our paper money for commercial advertising," someone suggested. "Should we have "in God We Trust" on paper money as well as on the silver pieces?" someone else wondered. Another guest thought that "we could wipe out our national debt in a matter of a few years by canceling the transaction value of outdated paper money and making it a 'collectors' item' only." Coya had a very good time, and she knew it would be one of the highlights of her life.

In her "Capitol Chat" column in March 1955, Coya told her constituents about the good time she'd had talking with the President at the White House luncheon and mentioned that "the President's spectacles needed cleaning." She slyly commented that she could not imagine how he could see anything clearly through his glasses. Her wry observation about Ike's smudged spectacles was reprinted in newspapers throughout the country.

On a typical workday, Coya was on the Hill for an early breakfast meeting and, after a full morning of committee meetings and conferences, she would have a quick lunch at her desk before 11 a.m. when Congress convened. From her office Coya would run across the street and sprint a block to the side door of the Capitol, in that way getting her daily exercise. If there was a roll-call vote while she was in her office working, she had to run—legislators were not given much warning. When she arrived at the Chambers, it was customary to linger and chat at the entrance with other Representatives until the buzzer sounded. Then, at the last moment, everyone would flock in at once.

The Agriculture Committee usually met at 10 a.m. and stayed in session until noon, well after Congress had convened. The majority of Coya's work during those early months in Washington had to do with farming bills, and the Committee meetings afforded her the opportunity to "learn the ropes" of getting legislation to the floor.

Chairman Cooley, a tall, forceful man with a square jaw, headed the 34-member Committee. At the first session Cooley told them that he considered agriculture paramount to all other problems facing the government because ample food production and distribution was essential to the welfare of the nation and closely linked to world peace. Coya knew she was in the right place. She had found her niche.

She was particularly interested in the hearings, in which people from all over the country testified about their specific needs and problems. She empathized with farmers from seven counties in the dust bowls of Colorado and New Mexico who were in Washington to protest the withdrawal of their crop insurance. Their slogan was "The land is grey, the clouds are spent, I wonder where my farm went?" Coya saw the elimination of crop insurance as another move to uproot and drive out family farmers.

These hearings reminded Coya of the debate forums and discussion panels she had attended during college, and she enjoyed the down-to-earth give and take between the people and their government representatives. Her participation in the Agriculture Committee made Coya feel that she was an important member of Congress. Because she was the only woman member, the men on the Committee politely deferred to her and teased her, but she felt they also listened to her and respected the expertise she contributed. A favorite among the Committee members was Democrat Pat Jennings who sat next to her at meetings. Jennings, whom Coya called "The Mountaineer," entertained her with stories about the moonshine stills in the hills of his native Virginia.

During the 1955 session she worked through the Committee on a bill to be presented to Congress calling for an explicit statement of national policy to preserve and strengthen the family-farm tradition and on an amendment to the Agricultural Act of 1937 to provide additional credit facilities for farm enlargement and development. Her name was attached to a request for an extension and amendment of the Sugar Act of 1948—sugar-beet growers in the Red River Valley and elsewhere in the U.S. would have their crop subsidized at $40 a ton. She also worked for an improved soil-conservation program.

Coya emphasized that agricultural problems lay not so much in production as in distribution. She pointed out that higher prices, although not popular with labor, would help not only the farmers in this country, but those in developing nations who could not compete with the low prices of U.S. products.

She joined Congresswoman Leonor Sullivan in seeking to enlarge the school-lunch program by using dairy products and basic foods—including free milk to school children—as a solution to farm surpluses. Like Sullivan, Coya wanted a food stamp plan for distribution of surpluses. Overly abundant foodstuffs should not be stored, she maintained, but should be used to feed the less fortunate. The bill was passed.

Coya's fight for recognition of problems facing small farmers led to the establishment of the first congressional subcommittee to study the family-sized farm. Grass-roots opinions were heard in congressional hearings held throughout the nation, including one in her own district. That hearing in Fergus Falls, combined with her syndicated column, helped to convince her constituents that she was working hard on their behalf.[2]

Coya had a lifelong knowledge of farming issues and understood that farmers are proud people who do not expect handouts, only a fair price for their produce. She worked hard for the price supports that she believed were essential. Invited to speak on farm problems at the 1955 vocational seminar of the National Council of Churches in America, Coya stated that "rising costs and falling prices had brought the farmer at the end of 1953 to the smallest share of national income on record."[3]

The first testimony to the Agriculture Committee on the 90% parity bill was given by Secretary Ezra Taft Benson. Coya called his testimony "disappointingly evasive." She stated again and again that until farm products earned higher prices, she would continue to demand 90% parity.

Throughout her first months in Congress, Coya had listened, observed, asked questions and worked until, in May 1955, she felt ready to give her maiden speech on the floor of the House. The lawmakers were considering a repeal of flexible price-support systems. Coya made an impassioned plea for restoration of rigid, high farm-price supports declaring that "adequate farm income is a task we must achieve for the economic health and welfare of the country."

Coya's first trip abroad was to the Dominican Republic where cane growers wanted U. S. representatives to see what they had accomplished for themselves, and to view first hand the ways the island was trying to diversify its agricultural business. The growers were especially interested in influencing sugar prices, which at that time were set by Hawaiian cane growers. The Agriculture Committee took off in a chartered plane and Coya, who was fascinated by airplanes, was delighted when the pilot invited them to visit the cockpit and explained how the various dials and instruments worked.

They were warmly received at the airport, and the wife of the ranking Committee member, Mrs Poage, received a bouquet of yellow roses. After dedicating a new sugar-cane plant, the committee inspected several farms on the island. On the tour people turned out everywhere, and because a female member of Congress was a novelty, many women and children wanted especially to see Coya and present her with home-grown bouquets of flowers.

The roads were bad, and each time they hit a deep rut, Coya thought "our car was done for." The chauffeurs drove recklessly, and as they speeded through village streets, chickens and debris in the road went flying. Even at that pace, the committee somehow ran behind schedule. When the members decided to skip a planned stop, Coya volunteered to go on her own to represent the delegation, with the Dominican Consul accompanying her as an interpreter. When Coya saw the large group of people who had gathered in the village to greet them, she was very happy she had decided to go.

A highlight of the trip was an evening at the palace where they were entertained by Generalissimo Rafael Trujillo. When Coya was introduced to him, the Generalissimo said through his interpreter, "You are a lady with a heart," referring to her solo visit to the village. After a sumptuous dinner, Coya was thrilled when he gave her his arm and together they led the entourage to the hall where a symphony orchestra played for them.

In contrast to the elegant evening, the following day the Committee went to see the Generalissimo's purebred cattle, a herd of 700 animals that supplied stock for the whole country. To the amusement of all Coya sat down on the milking stool and proved that she could milk a cow.

By the end of the trip, Coya found herself popular with the male Committee members for a reason that she didn't like. "Because I was the only woman, I was the center of attention. The men vied to sit by me and talk to me. If you've got any looks whatsoever—and I wasn't too bad looking—you're going to attract the wrong kind of attention no matter what you do." She sensed that she was looked upon as fair game, and felt that "traveling as an unattached woman with a group of men" could jeopardize her career. "It didn't look good." She resolved to take along a female traveling companion in the future.

Back in the Capitol, Coya realized that her lack of social know-how would be a continuing problem. It was in her nature to be boisterous and out-going and she knew that her good-humored antics could be misinterpreted. The casual hugs and kisses of Washington, D.C. were a far cry from a handshake, the acceptable greeting back home. She did not want to appear priggish, but it was sometimes hard to distinguish between the compulsory pats on the back—and else-where—that were "just friendly" and the overtures that had sexual innuendos. She was not sophisticated enough to handle unwanted attention and deflect amorous advances. She would try to pass it off and not pay attention to the fondling, but it made her feel self-conscious. It also angered her because being made to feel awkward and insecure put her at a disadvantage in her dealings with fellow legislators.

Nevertheless, she enjoyed a busy social life during her first session. Senator Hubert Humphrey and his wife Muriel entertained the DFL Minnesota congressional delegation and members of the Minnesota press at a buffet supper of pheasant sent to the Humphrey family from South Dakota, and wild rice, a product harvested by Native Americans in Minnesota.

She also attended dinners and parties hosted by special-interest lobby groups. It was a good way to meet people and find out what they were thinking, but she soon found that staying out late made her less productive the following day. By the end of the session she had become selective, attending only those parties where a lobbyist might be of help with specific legislation. There were those who denigrated lobbyists, but through her association with Bob Olson, her lobbyist friend in Minnesota, she saw that they had a productive role in the legislative process. They presented research and laid the ground work for legislation that would benefit their special-interest groups in a concise form that she could pass along to her staff for investigation. She did not, however, want to "be beholden to anyone," and there-fore, she did not accept favors. She would not solicit campaign funds from lobbyists as some of her colleagues did, and she was careful to decline help or gifts that might be construed as payment for her support or assistance.

Another social highlight for Coya was the formal luncheon for all congresswomen that Margaret Chase Smith arranged for her colleagues. It was Smith's custom to wear a fresh rose in her lapel each day, and the first thing that Coya noticed was the rose. Smith impressed Coya as a calm, matter-of-fact person who was competent and hard working.

Coya looked around at the other women: there were nine Democrats and eight Republicans, the largest number of women at any one time in Congress. A third of these women had worked in education; a tenth in farming; and the others had backgrounds in law, communications and applied social sciences. The majority had been homemakers and community volunteers, and almost half had not been born in the state from which they were elected.

Coya thought about these colleagues, whom she was beginning to know individually. Elderly Edith Nourse Rogers, beginning her 30th year in Congress, was becoming a bit forgetful, but she was still a warm, bright woman who always found the right words for the right occasion. Coya talked often with friendly, energetic Elizabeth P. Farrington. Before succeeding her husband as a nonvoting delegate from Hawaii, she had worked with him toward acquiring Hawaiian statehood. Three years before she went to Congress, *McCalls* had named her "one of Washington's ten most powerful women." Katharine St. George was a gracious gray-haired woman, sophisticated in appearance, and hard to get to know, Coya thought.

She felt she had the most in common with Gracie Pfost, the Populist from Idaho, an early conservationist who had built her reputation by "battling private interests for the public good." Coya considered her a "real trouper," always out meeting people and working hard. But Coya did not see her socially because Pfost's husband accompanied her day and night. Pfost acknowledged that her work in Congress was a joint venture with her husband, and that he spent as many hours on the Hill as most administrative aides—but without pay.

The other three newcomers, Coya found, were putting in as many hours on the job as she was. The more experienced members had learned to delegate a good deal of work to their staffs. Coya enjoyed being among other women, and because she enjoyed Smith's luncheon so much, she looked forward to similar noon hours. However, a social life with other congresswomen was not to be. In the four years she was in Washington, the women seldom met because everyone was simply too busy. They did not get together at their homes, either. Except for Missouri's Leonor (Lee) Sullivan, who had a big apartment in Arlington Tower, the single women seemed to live in cubby holes like Coya's. When Sullivan talked about exercising on the floor of her living room, Coya was amazed; her own place was far too small to allow any such activity.

To keep in touch with voters, Coya continued writing her "Capital Chat" column. Throughout the Ninth District, farmers and townspeople read her column in their weekly newspapers. Writing mostly about pending bills and her work in Congress, she kept a conversational, chatty style. Especially popular with her constituents were the columns she wrote about newsy tidbits of local interest, reports about the folks from home who visited her and anecdotes about her life in the capital city. Sometimes she waxed poetic, as in a story she wrote about band concerts on the mall: "When it is just beginning to get dark with different colored lights playing on the fountains, one gets a feeling of peacefulness."

She described the cherry blossoms blooming in the Tidal Basin and all over Washington, and told about the preparations for crowning the Cherry Blossom Princess. She related the story of the "real, live horse in Washington" to the delight of farming families back home. Around 6 a.m. six days a week, Coya would hear the "clack, clack, clack" of a horse's hooves on the pavement under her apartment window. It seemed she was not so far from farm life, after all; in cosmopolitan Washington, D.C., a horse was used to pull the garbage wagon.

Coya had considered passing the task of writing the column off to staff people, but they convinced her that she could write it better than anyone else. Distributing it was easier than it had been when she was a legislator in Minnesota; she not only had franking privileges in Washington but also a staff to mimeograph and mail the column out to the sixty rural weekly newspapers. Copies were also mailed to radio stations in her district, and to key DFLers in Minnesota. Moreover, a copy was sent to the Capitol newsroom where daily newspapers could pick it up.

She did not have to drum up press interest for herself; the press was following her. A February wire service article called Coya the country girl who was on her way to becoming "Miss Congress of

1955."[4] It went on to explain that this was not an official title because Washington did not run contests for brains, beauty or popularity, but that there was no doubt Coya had "made a hit." The feature reported that although she had arrived as an unknown quantity in national politics, most people in Washington became aware of her overnight; photographers snapped her picture, cooking editors requested recipes and political pundits quoted her. And then, the article added, she "bowled everyone over" by becoming the first woman named to the House Agriculture Committee.

Feature editors liked to get an angle about her country background. The same article asked, "How did she make such a dent? There is only one answer. Eggs. Simply eggs—and the price thereof. Soon she became not the Democrat's egghead, but its egg woman." When she is not being serious about egg pricing intricacies, the article continued, she will tell you how she likes her eggs: "not too nervous, but well done."

After all this publicity, an egg lobbyist asked Coya to present a double case of eggs to the White House. She agreed, but she had a hard time persuading other Minnesota members of Congress to accompany her. When Coya and her secretary Marge Sieber drove to the airport to pick up the eggs, they happened to meet Hubert Humphrey stepping off a plane. When Humphrey heard what her mission was, he enthusiastically joined her. The drive was thrilling for Coya because they had a police escort, with sirens to announce their arrival. The press had gathered at the White House to take photographs of the group with Mamie Eisenhower.

Coya did not set out to make publicity for herself, yet she did nothing to discourage it. Because the press flocked to her, Coya wondered if some congresswomen were miffed by all the attention she got. "Pretty soon," Coya says, "reporters were following me around; they would come even when there was nothing in particular happening and I did not have anything to say. Sometimes the publicity was a whole lot more than I wanted."

When the Fergus Falls Chamber of Commerce shipped *lefse* (Norwegian potato pancakes) by air express to Washington, Coya wrote that she served the delicacy with Minnesota butter to the full Committee. Washington reporters called her for a *lefse* recipe and she, in turn, got in touch with the Norwegian embassy to ask for theirs. Because the two recipes were very different, a good-natured dispute about a definitive *lefse* recipe made news for several days. As a result of the publicity, Coya received *lefse*-making tools such as special rolling pins, spatulas and irons. "I really enjoyed it—I played it for all it was worth and had fun," she commented, "because it was a good way to promote farm products." She knew it was corny, but it seemed to be what people enjoyed, and she was comfortable being "a country girl with a down-home sense of humor."

There was no doubt about it. Coya was having the time of her life, enjoying every work-packed weekday minute. In her March 31, 1955, column she wrote "This is another week that I feel like an Egyptian mummy— 'pressed for time.'" Congress was working as if it were the closing days of the session. She was frustrated by the laborious, time-consuming roll calls for quorums and votes that interrupted her day from 11 a.m. until early evening. Recalling how efficiently the votes were registered in the Minnesota Capitol, she suggested streamlining the roll call system by installing a board with electric lights to register votes.

She relayed to her readers the rules of the House: the maxim "Order is heaven's first law" summed them up. She took to heart the instruction that "each member is clothed with tremendous power over the lives and destiny of a mighty people and that with that power goes a corresponding responsibility to discharge the trust given by the people."

She reported that she was disturbed by the private conversations constantly going on among congressmen on the Floor. "Those guys always sat under the nose of the Speaker, talking a mile a minute." It seemed to her the only time the House was quiet was during the opening prayer.

In her "Capital Chats" column she wrote about House Majority Leader McCormack taking the press and a Senator to task because reference had been made to the Senate as the Upper House. McCormack pointed out that the Constitution states that the two branches of Congress are equal. But Sam Rayburn said "Tut, tut, Mr McCormack, no aspersions, please. Rule of comity."

Coya, who was quickly learning the rules of the House—courtesy, always—gleefully reported the exchange and repeated the rules of conduct and good taste for her readers: Address the presiding officer as "Mr Speaker" or, in a committee, as "Mr Chairman." No person shall be allowed to smoke on the Floor of the House at any time. No feet on seats. Reading newspapers during session is in bad taste. The proper way to address a colleague is "the gentlewoman or gentleman from_____." She explained that however vitriolic the conflict was among members on the Floor, the language was couched in respect-ful terms. Every day she saw examples of "congressional courtesy," when a member referred to another member as "my distinguished colleague from _____" and then proceeded to deliver a blistering tongue-lashing.

One day when Coya walked across the Floor of the House during a session, she tripped over one of the brass spittoons, making a terrible clattering noise. Everyone looked up and stared at her, and some of the members seated nearby laughed. Her embarrassment turned to anger the more she thought about the filthy cuspidors; those using them did not always hit their mark. Coya rejoiced when the unsightly and unsanitary objects were permanently removed from the Floor a few months later. She was relieved that the hateful habit she and her sisters had so despised had at last gone out of style. She triumphantly presented a nice, clean spittoon the doorkeeper had reserved for her to a constituent who wanted one for a souvenir.

It was fully three months into her first Session before Coya had a free Sunday. She set out to tour the places of historical interest in the capital but soon tired of sightseeing. Before long she found herself across the Potomac from the Capitol walking alone through National Airport watching people and airplanes come and go. Coya spent the rest of the long afternoon watching the huge airplanes gracefully touch down to unload passengers and then, in what seemed a matter of minutes, take off into the sky again with a new load of passengers on their way to some other destination.

By now Coya was a celebrity in her home town, and her friends and neighbors admired the way she was adjusting to the demands of her new life. Her friend Helen Chervestad remembers that the changes in Coya's appearance were subtle; she dressed well in practical but stylish clothes, her hair was styled simply, and she wore only a bit of make-up. Washington had not gone to her head; there was nothing overdone or self-conscious about her. Coya had grace-fully entered middle age; she was comfortable with herself and that was reflected in her easy-going, down-to-earth manner.

Young people, too, looked up to Coya. She was articulate and persuasive in her public speeches, with a direct, conversational style that people found appealing. Coya was certainly not altering her speaking style to emulate the great silver-tongued orators she listened to in Washington; she spoke simply and clearly so that everyone could understand her and comprehend what she was saying. In person, she continued to be accessible and easy to talk with, a common, ordinary person who was comfortable to be around.[5] A reporter wrote that Coya was "as easy to talk to as your neighbor on the next farm." Other reporters commented on her appearance: "Five-foot five, 140 pounds, and blonde and blue-eyed".[6] A Washington wire service story described her as a 42-year-old "blue- eyed brown-haired size 16."[7]

With so little time to take care of personal matters, Coya was learning to keep things simple. She kept her wardrobe down to the bare necessities. If she could travel on short jaunts carrying only a brief case and a change of underclothing, she would. She chose dresses with jackets, skirts with interchangeable jackets and blouses, and comfortable shoes with low heels. Her favorite costume was a tan suit with a black blouse; it was practical and did not show soil. She usually did her shopping at the Hecht store near the Capitol. Once in a while she shopped at Peck and Peck, but never at Garfinkels because she could not afford their prices. Her one extravagance was a weekly hair-styling appointment at one of the two convenient beauty salons in the Capitol building. She appreciated getting her hair done every week, especially because the "set" lasted longer than if she did it herself. It was the first time in her life that she had allowed herself such a luxury; even so, during her first six months she was so busy that it took great effort to keep the regular appointments.

She called Oklee frequently and was relieved to find that Terry was getting along all right with Anna and Andy while finishing his freshman year in high school. He told her that the latest craze in Oklee was to sit in front of Seeger's store with his buddies, watching programs on TVs displayed in the store window. He joked that the tube had so much snow that the kids wore sunglasses so they wouldn't go snow-blind. When they got tired of that, they would go to Joe Dufault's Oak Theatre to see a movie.

Coya missed Terry and decided that her son should spend the summer with her. When she returned to Minnesota during the summer of 1955 to give several speeches, she stopped in Oklee only long enough to help Terry pack for a move to Washington. They drove together to North Dakota, and after she spoke at a meeting in Fargo, they went to Hector Airport to catch a flight to Washington. However, when it came time to board, Terry became so frightened of flying that he could not get on the plane. Coya was surprised by his sudden, unaccountable reaction and tried to allay his fears. Not knowing quite how to handle the situation, Coya chose tough tactics. She boarded the flight alone and left Terry behind in the terminal. She hoped the thought of being left alone was worse than his fear of flying, and that proved to be the case. Soon Terry followed her on board and, once airborne, he decided flying was not so bad after all.

When they changed planes in Chicago, they saw Senator Bill Langer's wife in the terminal. Coya had never met either of the Langers, but she had heard about "Wild Bill" from her father. Mrs Langer looked very stylish and was carrying a hatbox, but she also appeared to be in distress and in need of assistance. Langer's wife was not accustomed to being on her own and she did not know how to place a collect call to her husband in Washington. The Knutsons helped her, but Coya was amazed that an otherwise sophisticated woman could not cope for herself. In Washington Bill Langer met his wife at the airport and offered to drive Coya and Terry to their apartment. Coya was delighted to meet him and enjoyed reminiscing about her father and the Nonpartisan League as well as discussing pending legislation concerning the sugar bill.

Back at work, Coya introduced several bills to aid Native Americans in her district. She asked for an authorization of $100 per capita payment to members of the Red Lake band of Chippewa, based on the proceeds from the sale of timber and lumber on the Red Lake Reservation. She also introduced legislation to promote the welfare of Native Americans and to facilitate orderly termination of Federal supervision and control over Native Americans and their property in Minnesota.

That summer Terry and Coya found a close rapport. Coya took her son to her office every day, and he was kept busy cranking the handle of the addressograph, stuffing envelopes, and taking charge of distributing "Coya's Capital Chats" to her mailing list recipients each week. He was also on call to run messages back and forth between her office and the chambers; at about 2 p.m. he would run over to the House with letters that needed to be signed. He fit into the routine of the office and learned quickly. He did not get paid because Coya was concerned that there would be cries of nepotism if she put him on the payroll.

Coya and Terry would have a carryout lunch together at her desk because she did not want to spend the money or time to go out to lunch. If she had a luncheon meeting or if there were visitors from home, she would go to the House Dining Room.

When Coya had to make weekend trips to Minnesota that summer, Alice would look after Terry. Flying became routine for Coya. She would work in Washington Monday to Thursday and then fly to Minnesota on weekends to attend county fairs, Farmers Union picnics, and other meetings that Bill had scheduled for her. She would catch the midnight Capital Airlines flight, change planes in Detroit, and arrive at sunrise in Minneapolis to pick up her car and drive north. On Sunday she would leave Minneapolis at midnight and arrive exhausted in Washington the following morning. Traveling back and forth and losing two nights of sleep on each weekend trip began to take its toll on her health.

Whenever she could, Coya would try to be with Terry. For the Fourth of July holiday Coya, Terry and Bill went to Atlantic City, grateful to get out of hot, muggy, Washington, D.C. Terry was entranced by the vast expanse of ocean, the first time he had ever seen it. Coya did not like the beach, and the ocean made her restless.

In general, Coya was happy. Whether teaching school in Penn, farming at Edmore or representing her constituents at the Capital, work was her life and she thrived on it. Besides working on Saturday, Coya would also go to the office on Sunday mornings after she and Terry had attended early services at Luther Place Church. The phones seldom rang and she could take her time skimming through the fifty or sixty hometown newspapers from her district. Since there was a Sunday postal delivery, Coya would leisurely attend to her mail and read while Terry worked with the office machines. The office building was quiet because few Capital Hill old-timers came around—only freshman representatives seemed to work on weekends.

For entertainment, mother and son would visit the National Zoo where they would walk about all afternoon and look at the animals. Most often they would drive to the National Airport, have dinner and people-watch. The dining room was one flight up from the passenger terminal and diners could gaze out the plate glass windows at the Capitol, the Washington Monument, and the Potomac River. Airplanes taking off and landing taxied so close to the building that Coya and Terry could watch people getting on and off. If it rained, they would watch airline personnel hurrying back and forth, holding large umbrellas over deplaning passengers. Terry imagined traveling to far-away places; Coya did not. She found her pleasure in seeing how people dressed and watching them behave. Coya enjoyed visiting the airport with Terry much more than visiting it alone.

Once in a while they would go to a drive-in movie in Alexandria, an outing they liked because they did not have to dress up. One of their favorite restaurants was a neighborhood café called "The Dirty Spoon." Sundays were long days, and both preferred the weekdays working.

Coya decided that it would be best for Terry not to go back to Oklee. She wanted to have him closer to her, and Andy did not seem to care whether the boy lived with him or not. She also wanted a good education for Terry, who wanted to attend school—preferably a military academy—near Washington. Terry and Coya set out to evaluate various private schools. When they stopped at Randolph-Macon in Front Royal, Virginia, the first military academy on their list and only 60 miles from Washington, he liked it so much that they settled on the school without investigating the others. After securing recommendations from colleagues in Congress, Coya enrolled Terry in the school of his choice.

The end of the summer meant a halt to Terry's life in Washington. Coya gave up the lease on her apartment, planning to lease another when she returned to the Capital City in January. When Coya and Terry arrived in Oklee that August, Coya was appalled at Andy's deterioration. It seemed that he no longer cared about anything. Coya's success and public visibility seemed to sap Andy of his own self-esteem; he felt diminished in the eyes of the community. He worked less, drank more, and spent most of his time with drinking buddies. He made no new friends, and communicated less and less with people outside his tight circle. His cousin, Raymond Strande, told Coya that Andy "was in with a bad bunch in Oklee" and would disappear for days at a time.[8]

Yet to Oklee townspeople, Andy was still seen not as a staggering drunk, but rather as "one of the boys" who "celebrated too much once in a while." A tall, handsome man, he often strolled about town, dressed casually but neatly, and smoking a big cigar—an expensive brand called "Y-Bs." He continued to work at the hotel, did odd jobs around town, such as helping to build a garage or shingle a roof, and found intermittent work at a farm-implement store. Coya regularly deposited an allowance in his checking account, but it grated on her when Andy accompanied her to the bank and giggled nervously as she deposited the money.

In his spare time Andy read crime magazines—his favorite was *True Detective*. Coya speculated that his preference for reading crime stories was Andy's way of working out his frustrations through fantasy. He wanted to be a big shot, but he was a shy man who couldn't communicate easily and always felt more comfortable hanging out on the fringes.

Coya spent only as much time at home as was necessary. She tried to share her success with Andy by buying him a new car, a 1955 Nash two-door for which she paid $1800. He did not drive it much because he had few places to go that he couldn't reach on foot. He liked to stay in Oklee and rarely ventured out of town.

It was not necessary for Coya to return to Washington, D.C. until January when the session began. When it was time for Terry to start school, Coya remained in Minnesota while her son, accompanied by Alice, flew to Virginia. From Washington Terry took the bus to Front Royal alone to begin his sophomore year at Randolph-Macon. At first, Terry did not let his mother know that he was lonely and felt like an outsider. The other students called him a "Yankee," and he did not think of himself as a Yankee, but few boys from the North attended Randolph-Macon. Also, Terry missed the easy way of congregating with other kids that he had associated with back in Oklee. It was not long before Coya knew how lonesome her son was. Terry ran up huge telephone bills calling his friends in Oklee.

His daily routine was completely different from life in Oklee. At Randolph-Macon he had to march to breakfast, clean his room, polish his shoes, brush his uniform, and attend daily Chapel services. Everything was new to him. Nevertheless, Terry enjoyed military school because he learned to be a gentleman and felt more comfortable socially. Coya's friends were impressed with Terry's manners and self-confidence, but they also teased her about choosing a southern school for her son.

Once Terry was in a boarding school, Coya regarded their home in Oklee as no more than a stopping place when she was in the area.

Andy begged her to stay around more, and she found his change of heart puzzling. She wondered if he was beginning to regret his abusive behavior and hard drinking. Perhaps he was beginning to see what he had missed out on and that accounted for his attempts at conciliation. However, Coya was no longer interested in salvaging her marriage with Andy. They had gone their separate ways and the gulf between them was too great. He had not wanted to share her dreams or support her in her ambitions; Coya perceived him now as one more obstacle she had had to overcome. She had achieved success on her own and in spite of him.

Again she considered the idea of divorce and again she put it off. She would wait until she had more time and money. She knew he never would divorce her because he was dependent upon her for support. Because she had given up her Washington apartment and did not want to live in Oklee with Andy, Coya chose to stay with friends around the district that fall. While she waited for the session to begin in January, she fulfilled speaking engagements and took the opportunity to visit with her constituents.

Terry joined Coya for Christmas and they spent the holidays in Devils Lake with Helen and her family. They made only a brief stop in Oklee. Coya had a business meeting and Terry wanted to visit friends. Coya learned that Andy had colitis and that he was nervous about running the hotel entirely on his own. When they tried to discuss a course of action, Coya found Andy to be contrary and "anti-everything." In the end, Coya and Andy decided to close the hotel, but maintain it as a residence for Andy and Anna.

It was a sad and difficult time for everyone. Terry was not interested in seeing his father or Anna, but was eager to be with his friends. However, as the visit ended, he confided to his mother that he felt like an outsider with his old buddies; they treated him differently, he thought. Coya and Terry were both looking forward to resuming their lives on the East Coast. Coya took delivery of a new four-door Oldsmobile from Malkerson Motors in Minneapolis, and she was glad to have Terry along for company on the drive back. The new "Olds" was luxurious, but otherwise they traveled economically. When they got hungry, they would pull to the side of the road for a sandwich. The trip was fun, now that they both knew what was ahead for them.

Back in Washington Coya lived alone. After a year in the Capital, Alice Lindquist, Coya's secretary and housemate, returned to live in

Oklee. Coya did not look for another roommate. She moved to the south of town into an apartment so small there was room for little more than a bed. She did her own cleaning but cooked very little; it was so much easier and faster to eat in restaurants.

The problem with living alone, Coya learned, was that Sunday was the longest day of the week. Even without Terry, Coya resumed her pattern of attending church, working in the office, and driving to National Airport where she would dine and watch people coming and going. She did not like to spend time in her apartment; on her own, she felt restless. Occasionally she went to the movies, particularly if there was a Jeanette McDonald film playing; she loved the romance and the beautiful songs.

She was not unhappy that her life was often solitary outside of office hours. She considered her real life the work on Capitol Hill and wished there were no weekends to interrupt it. In the halls of Congress she had many friends: everyone called her "Coya." But she did not spend time with any of them outside of working hours. If she saw anyone socially, it was the occasional visitors from home.

Coya relied on Bill Kjeldahl to manage her office, taking care of details and scheduling and helping to implement her ideas for legislative proposals. Although she thought of him as a "kid," the 27-year-old had become indispensable to her work. He was also the first male she had known who was reliable. Kjeldahl, in turn, idolized Coya. He thought her personality "was the most dynamic he had ever met." He loved to watch Coya at work, buzzing from one congressman to another, chatting, laughing and talking to everyone. In his eyes, she radiated good will and showed such genuine interest in people that smiles and warm feelings surrounded her. Kjeldahl saw her as "resourceful and dependable... a bundle of life and full of enthusiasm."[9]

Coya was happy in Washington, happier than she had ever been in her life. She loved her work. She had kept her down-to-earth quality, her boisterous laugh and her sense of fun while she was also developing a wonderful new sense of herself.

During her second year in Washington, Coya knew that she had found her natural home.

Chapter 11

BARNSTORMING
WITH KEFAUVER

*Let's work against woman suffrage—if women get the
vote they might try to elect a woman president. This
could take away from the manhood and womanhood of
America.*

Mrs P. M. Freer, Stroud, South Dakota
Nonpartisan Leader: April 15, 1918

It was late January, 1956 and Coya came into the office as usual on
Sunday. She leaned back in her big leather chair and reread the *New
York Times* front page article, wondering how the DFLers back home
were taking the news. The story reported that Coya Knutson and
Hjalmer Petersen, the Minnesota Railroad and Warehouse Commissioner, were to be chairwoman and chairman of the Minnesota
presidential primary campaign of Senator Estes Kefauver of Tennessee. [1]

The story had also made the front pages of the Minneapolis papers,
and the news did indeed take the DFLers in Minnesota by surprise.
They thought Coya was a loyal DFL supporter championing the
candidacy of Illinois Governor Adlai E. Stevenson for the Democratic
nomination for President of the United States. Instead, Coya had

withdrawn as a delegate for Stevenson and her decision to do so was
in direct opposition to the DFL party leaders' goals. Stevenson had
been the Democratic nominee in the 1952 presidential election but
had lost to General Dwight D. Eisenhower. He was reluctant to run
against Eisenhower again in 1956, but the Minnesota DFL was one of
the powerful groups within the party urging him to head their ticket.
Stevenson, who felt that the requisite campaigning in presidential
primaries was demeaning to the candidates, took great pains to
ensure that he was the dominant choice of his party before he
committed himself to another try for the presidency.[2]

It was Stevenson's contention that without uniform laws among
the states regarding primaries, delegates arrived at the conventions
without adequate guidelines to reach a concensus. However,
Minnesota's presidential primary, regarded nationally by some as a
reliable barometer of political trends, was to be in March before the
primaries in the more populous states. Stevenson's advisors assured
him that Kefauver would not seriously challenge his candidacy and
he decided to run in the 1956 Minnesota primary. It turned out to be
a great embarrassment not only to Adlai Stevenson, but also to Hubert
Humphrey and the DFL stalwarts, who strongly supported the
governor's candidacy. Coya figured prominently in the election
upset.

More than a year before the election, Hubert Humphrey and
Orville Freeman had invited Stevenson to attend a special meeting of
DFL leaders in Duluth on October 29, 1955. Earlier Coya had run into
Humphrey at another meeting and told him that she felt Stevenson
would be a liability in Minnesota because he did not have a farm
program. Humphrey disagreed with her, and he was so firm in his
conviction that the DFL should endorse Stevenson that, in Coya's
opinion, he left no room for discussion. Coya felt that Humphrey was
unwilling to hear the objections she thought should be raised on
behalf of the farmers she represented, and that he had highhandedly
dismissed her viewpoint. She walked away from that encounter
thinking, "Shucks, I'm only a woman, and he figures women are not
to be taken seriously."

Coya was up for re-election in 1956 and she did not want to be on
a ticket headed by a Democrat who did not have a farm program.
When she had arrived at the meeting in Duluth, Coya buttonholed
other DFL leaders and told them, "You know, Stevenson does not

have a farm program." But she got no response. With considerable fanfare, the Minnesota DFL Central Committee endorsed Adlai Stevenson for President. During the evening program, one DFL official after another offered tributes to their distinguished guest, and Senator Humphrey announced that the entire state DFL leadership was committed to Stevenson's candidacy. Great favor was shown to Ninth District DFL Chairman L.J. Lee of Bagley; he was chosen to give the nominating speech for Stevenson.

Immediately after Stevenson's visit to that meeting, the DFL state central committee gathered for an extraordinary session to vote for an unprecedented early endorsement of Stevenson for President in 1956. Two weeks later Stevenson announced his candidacy and added that he proposed to enter the Minnesota primary.

Humphrey continued to give Stevenson strong support. He wrote, "Adlai Stevenson is a great American. He is a constitutional liberal. He refuses to permit emotion, prejudice, and rabid partisanship to control his actions and thoughts. His sense of moral and intellectual integrity are the source of his strength. It was on the basis of these known virtues and qualities of character that the responsible leadership of our party asked him to file in the Minnesota primary."[3] Humphrey had a personal reason to enlist Stevenson's favor. Humphrey and Freeman had offered the early Minnesota DFL endorsement in exchange for Stevenson's support of Humphrey as his running mate.[4]

Following the Duluth meeting, district conventions met in early December at the request of the DFL Central Committee to select Stevenson-instructed delegates. Senator Humphrey and Governor Orville Freeman headed the 57-member delegation and delegates-at-large were selected by the executive committee. Never before had the DFL party endorsed a candidate without a state party convention.

While the Minnesotans were lining up the Stevenson endorsement, Senator Kefauver was deciding whether or not to run for President. Four years earlier Kefauver and Stevenson had battled for the Democratic nomination; Minnesota, Nebraska, and Iowa had voted for Kefauver at the convention. In order to have a chance at the 1956 nomination, Kefauver needed early victories in several presidential primaries. If he could prove his strength in Minnesota, in the heartland of America, Democratic bosses would have to pay attention. He was already a proven vote-getter in his own state of Tennessee where he had first been elected to the House in 1939.

When Kefauver visited Humphrey to discuss a bid for the Minnesota primary, Humphrey tried in vain to persuade him to opt for Wisconsin's primary where he would be unopposed. In late December, Kefauver visited Governor Freeman to suggest that district DFL meetings be held to name Kefauver delegates. When Freeman hedged, by replying that there was no time for that, Kefauver decided to plan a Minnesota campaign on his own.[5] Kefauver had been urged to campaign in Minnesota by former Governor Hjalmer Petersen and two state legislators from St. Paul, Peter S. Popovich and D. D. Wazniak.

Kefauver turned to Hjalmer Petersen and Coya Knutson to head his Minnesota campaign, and they both accepted his offer without consulting their party's leaders. On a late January morning Ninth District chairman L. J. Lee read in the *Minneapolis Tribune* that Coya Knutson was to be Minnesota chairwoman of the Kefauver for President committee. Lee was furious, but there was not much he could do. As a result of Coya's action Lee felt he had to resign from his post as chairman of the district, a position he had held since the formation of the party in 1944. "I could no longer serve both my congresswoman and my party," he sadly explained.[6] Marvin Evenson became 9th district chairman.

The unexpected news of Kefauver's supporters was met with dismay in DFL circles. National Democratic Committeeman Gerald Heaney, Central Committee Chairman Ray Hemenway and others tried to dissuade Petersen from chairing Kefauver's campaign, but he held firm. When Coya withdrew her name from Stevenson's slate of delegates, party leaders told her that she must remain neutral on the Stevenson-Kefauver fight. They also insisted that she dismiss Bill Kjeldahl because the party leaders believed that it was her assistant who had persuaded her to back Kefauver. Coya publicly accused DFLers of threatening to drop the party's endorsement of her and run another candidate against her in the election.[7]

Humphrey discussed the presidential primary and Coya's defection in a five-page letter to L.J. Lee, to be read at the Ninth District DFL committee meeting on February 12, 1956. He outlined reasons for supporting Stevenson, and then explained that he had talked with Mrs Knutson, "a lady for whom I have the greatest respect and whose record in Congress is a distinguished one...As you all know, I vigorously supported her, and I am happy I did so. We needed her in Congress, and she has vindicated the good judgment of the voters in her district. I explained to Congresswoman Knutson that she was at liberty to make any choice she desired and that I would respect her judgment. I had hoped that we could work together on the same team with the same slate—just as we did in 1954. I deeply regret that her choice makes this impossible in this particular situation.[8] Twenty-six years later, L. J. Lee referred to that letter to point out that Humphrey stated, "We needed her in Congress," not "we need her in Congress."[9]

Soon after the announcement that Coya was Kefauver's Minnesota chairwoman, rumors began to circulate about Coya and her secretary, Bill Kjeldahl. The editor of the *Willmar Daily Tribune* wrote to Hjalmer Petersen about a rumor he had heard from Ray Hemenway, Executive Secretary of the DFL Central Committee. In his letter O. B. Augustin wrote that he had "attended a regular DFL county meeting the other evening. Hemenway was there and talked about Coya. Said something about the row over her secretary. Have you got the dope on that—anything wrong there?"[10]

In reply Petersen wrote that he didn't know anything more than what he read in the daily press "and what I have heard—a little here and there. I believe the short of the thing is that the Central Committee wanted her to be a Stevenson delegate and when she refused to do that, some of the leaders became antagonistic...She, as well as any other citizen in the state, has the right to want a presidential prefer- ence primary contest and certainly, she has the right to be for either Stevenson or Kefauver."[11]

Bits of gossip and innuendoes floated about the Ninth District, but the source of these rumors was impossible to pin down. In the meantime, Kefauver's Minnesota committee ignored the rumors and waged an aggressive statewide campaign on his behalf. Co-chairmen Petersen and Knutson signed letters sent to thousands of voters urging them to vote for Kefauver, and stating that as their elected state officials, "We have a grave obligation to ensure the workings of democracy by providing the people of Minnesota with a choice."[12]

Petersen and Kjeldahl did much of the scheduling, arranging many stops in rural areas, particularly in northwestern Minnesota. Kjeldahl was the advance man, traveling around the state ahead of Kefauver to meet with sponsors and make arrangements. He typed voting statistics on bits of paper and then glued them on a road map as a guide for Kefauver and his staff.

Stung by the gossip about her and Kjeldahl and wary of any further criticism of her propriety, Coya arranged to have Elvina Zimmerman accompany her on the campaign trail throughout Minnesota. Coya had learned that on any political tour, she was invariably the only woman present. With her personal life now the subject of common gossip, it was prudent and more pleasant for her to have a woman companion along.

When Kefauver came into Minnesota, Hjalmer Petersen, Coya Knutson, businessman Robert E. Short and others stumped the state with him. They took turns warming up the audience and introducing Kefauver. Again and again they referred to the issues of "bossism" and "dictatorship," asking whether the state DFL should dictate to the voters by imposing its endorsement of Stevenson rather than permitting voters to choose the Democratic candidate in the primary. The committee used extraordinary means to bring Kefauver to the people, employing the barnstorming tactics that had worked so well for Coya in her earlier congressional campaign. At rallies Coya sang a campaign song about Kefauver to the tune of "Davy Crockett."[13]

In the week prior to the primary, Kefauver campaigned in 54 Minnesota communities. It was astonishing that Kefauver and his entourage arrived at their various stops on time. They were tightly scheduled and they traveled in winter weather that included sleet, ice and snow. Wherever it could be landed, a twelve-passenger Beechcraft Super 18 was used to fly Kefauver throughout the state while his entourage followed in automobiles. Terry joined the Kefauver caravan for a few days during the final week of the campaign while the Randolph-Macon Academy was on spring break. For the youngster who had come to love airplanes so much, the most glamorous event of the campaign was riding along in the Beechcraft to pick up Hjalmer Petersen and bring him to a meeting in Hibbing.

To show his kinship with frontier values, Kefauver wore a coonskin cap in the style of Davy Crockett. It became his trademark, and he often wore the cap as he traveled around Minnesota—shaking hands with voters in the high school auditorium in Willmar, at a street meeting in Paynesville, at a rally at Sacred Heart High School in East Grand Forks, at a gathering of people at the Slovenian Home in Chisholm and at a dinner at St. John's University in Collegeville.[14] He liked to shake as many hands as possible, emulating Coya's style.

While watching Coya move through a crowd at one stop, Kefauver shook his head in amazement and exclaimed to Kjeldahl, "When has there been a personal campaigner like her?"[15]

The Kefauver committee in Oklee knew how to draw a crowd; they solicited food supplies and donations from local companies and organized volunteers to prepare a free noon meal of cheese sandwiches, baked beans, cookies and milk. More than two thousand people were attracted to the March 17 event and were waiting to greet Kefauver in the high school gymnasium when he arrived wearing his famous coonskin cap. The sheriff of Red Lake County, Carl Kankel, who ushered Kefauver into the gym, wore full frontiersman regalia— a buckskin suit and the ubiquitous coonskin cap—prompting one observer to comment that Kankel looked more like Crockett than Crockett himself. Kankel led a procession of young boys in similar garb; however, the students had been taught to remove their hats when they entered a building, so the news photographers lost their opportunity to photograph Kefauver leading a pack of junior frontiersmen. Carrying the theme further, Kankel sang "Davy Crockett," the popular ballad about the legendary hero from Tennessee, substituting "Estes Kefauver" for Crockett's name. Kankel and Coya then sang a duet.

Introduced by Coya, Kefauver began his speech by saying, "My people are farmers." The crowd was with him from that moment on. He explained his graduated farm-price support system in which small farmers with less than $7,000 annual income would receive 100% of parity, while medium-income farmers with up to $20,000 income would receive 90% and farmers with larger annual gross would receive decreasing percentages of parity. At the closing, Coya sang "God Bless America." After the program Kefauver missed the baked-beans dinner; he was too busy shaking hands.

Kefauver made a good impression in Oklee and Coya was praised for her efforts in organizing the event. Arthur Talle, writing in the *Crookston Times*, complimented the committee because in the Kefauver program the "give 'em hell" technique was conspicuous by its absence. He noted the moderation and courtesy shown by every speaker. Omer Sundrud, editor of the *Oklee Herald,* said Kefauver's supporters saw in him the popular appeal of Lincoln and Roosevelt, and a quietness that was in contrast to Harry Truman's boisterous style. Sundrud also saw the contest as a test not only of the virtue of the presidential primary laws but also of the political strength of Coya Knutson. He expected that the election would prove that voters wanted to express their choice in a contest among the candidates. Sundrud admitted to an admiration for the "courage required by Mrs Knutson in helping to provide Minnesota with a contest."[16]

Wherever he went, Kefauver drew crowds and touched the concerns of rural Minnesotans. He flattered them by saying, "One thing I've noticed about Minnesota is the large number of fine looking boys and girls," and he also told them what they wanted to hear by stating that "Federal officials should be interested in the farmer, not people like Ezra Taft Benson who is serving Wall Street bankers."[17]

At the conclusion of each of the rallies, a few of the local girls passed shiny tin milk pails through the audience to collect money that was used to buy gasoline. Someone would holler, "You'll want to put the light stuff in because the pails jingle real loud;" thus most of the donations were paper money rather than coins. Coya got caught up in the spirit of the campaign and pitched in to pass the silver pails among the crowd. Although some critics said it wasn't respectable for a congresswoman to help collect money at a rally, a Kefauver aide recalled that Coya got away with it because everyone loved her personality.[18]

The wind driving across the prairie was keen, Coya recalls, but that campaign moved even faster than a prairie wind. In order to keep to the schedule the campaign staff often had to leave a rally abruptly, and one time they had traveled several miles down the road before they realized that Elvina Zimmerman had been left behind. When they made a hasty return trip, they found a forlorn Elvina standing in front of the auditorium with a money bucket in her arms.

Stevenson made no serious effort to match Kefauver's expenditure of time and energy in Minnesota. Adlai had a personal distaste for the folksy, handshaking, coonskin-cap style of campaigning favored by Estes. In contrast to Kefauver's energetic showmanship, Stevenson delivered issue-oriented, carefully prepared speeches. Occasionally the Kefauver people would run into the main-line DFLers who supported Stevenson.

On one occasion, Kefauver and Stevenson were scheduled to be in Moorhead at the same time. The Stevenson committee had already rented the Concordia College fieldhouse for a rally. Kefauver supporters requested that Kefauver appear on the same platform with

Stevenson, but the college honored the original contract because the DFL refused to have Kefauver appear at their rally. But that did not stop Coya and the other Kefauver stalwarts. They parked the Kefauver sound truck near the fieldhouse entrance and loudly invited people going into the Stevenson rally to come to a bean feed for Kefauver.[19]

The confrontation proved to be embarrassing to administrators at her alma mater as well as to DFL party regulars, but Coya interpreted her action in a different light. "What we were doing was hard for them to swallow, but we were having fun while at the same time showing them that you do not have to let people walk all over you. I knew the party was working against me, and I fought them with Kefauver. I proved that I was on the right track with the people."

Minnesota voters had not seen anything like the Kefauver storm since the Nonpartisan League political prairie fire of forty years past. In the final days of the campaign, Humphrey, who was the glue that held the party together, was a thousand miles away in Washington waging a futile fight for a bill backed by the Farmers Union.

The efforts of Kefauver and his supporters paid off. When the vote was in, Kefauver did not just win the Minnesota primary: he captured the state in an overwhelming victory with 65.6% of the popular vote. Kefauver secured twenty-six of the thirty convention delegates, or seven of the nine congressional districts. Stevenson won only the Iron Range and Minneapolis (the 8th and 5th districts.) Observers were surprised that Kefauver triumphed in St. Paul; like the Iron Range, it was a DFL stronghold. Kefauver won virtually all of the farming districts (the 1st, 2nd, 6th, 7th and 9th districts). In Coya's district he garnered a resounding 70%, representing a genuine farm protest.

Some of the Kefauver tally was also due to crossover votes. In Republican Otter Tail County, the *Fergus Falls Journal* reported that "many voters were puzzled and some were even irate over having to indicate whether they wanted a Republican or Democratic ballot."[20] Metropolitan suburbs went for Kefauver too, an example of crossover voting by Republicans. Members of one party were free to vote for either party, and word had gone out to Republicans to vote for Kefauver. Yet this was a solid Kefauver victory; the strongest vote came from rural Minnesota where farmers offered a protest against the urban, intellectual candidate that the state DFL had offered them.

Coya had accurately sensed the strong objections her constituents held against a candidate without a farm policy and she had ensured that their protest would be heard.

Stevenson's defeat was of crushing, humiliating proportions. Kefauver's slate of unknowns piled up a lead of some sixty thousand votes over Stevenson's—245,845 to 186,763. The DFL higher echelon smarted under the double slap from the traditionally independent electorate and from the rebellious group in its own ranks. Humphrey's ambition to advance nationally had been thwarted, and Democrats could not ignore who was responsible. Humphrey's highly disciplined, tough-minded Minnesota party of the 1950s had been defeated, and Minnesota Democratic leaders were more than embarrassed; they were devastated. L.J. Lee, the Ninth District chairman, lamented twenty-six years later that, "None of us could be delegates for the national convention."[21]

For Coya, it was a coup. Newspaper headlines throughout the country called attention to the Minnesota debacle: "Staggering Setback for Stevenson," the *Philadelphia Enquirer* proclaimed. "Stunning Defeat," a Detroit banner headline read. "Adlai Did Badly," the *Milwaukee Sentinel* heralded. The cover of *Life* magazine showed Kefauver with a bandaged hand and was captioned, "Shake the hand of the man who shook the Democrats." So many people commented about that cover to Coya that she began to greet people by saying, "Shake the hand of the woman who shook the Democrats."

When Coya and Terry returned to Washington after the election, she was greeted at the airport by photographers and reporters. Terry describes this interlude as "heady wine" for his mother. He wondered if perhaps the limelight blinded her from the reality that she had now totally cut herself off from her party. For her part, Coya saw her stance as a bold defiance of people within her party who had tried to tell her what to do. Coya resented DFL leaders like L. J. Lee who had not helped her get elected, yet tried to dominate her once she was in office. "I had had people like that around me all my life; now I felt I had earned the right to decide things for myself," she says. "Voters trusted me and I wanted to work for the people."

However, she did not like to hear colleagues on Capitol Hill tell her, "Well, it looks like Minnesota's got a new political boss." Coya, who liked Humphrey and respected him, did not want to be known as the "lady who had defeated Hubert." "Oh," she would say, "I don't want any talk like that."

In the spring of 1956, Coya became the most talked about Congresswoman on Capitol Hill. And she paid a high price. To sixteen-year-old Terry, the estrangement between his mother and Humphrey was evident. "After the primary, the Humphreys had us out to their house in Chevy Chase, but it just was not the same; the warmth was not there, and the relationship was strained." Coya was aware that her defiance had hurt Humphrey both personally and politically, but she also knew that, to his credit, Humphrey was not the sort to retaliate. Humphrey and Coya continued to work together.

Minnesota's primary had abruptly removed Stevenson from his front-running position, and his defeat there had far-reaching consequences. Fifteen of the seventeen presidential primaries were yet to be held. After Kefauver upset him in Minnesota, where he had been heavily favored to win because of support by the state organization, it was clear that Adlai would have to change his tactics and drastically revise his campaign strategy.[22] At a large press conference the day after the Minnesota election, Stevenson said he felt he had failed to communicate. Thereafter, Stevenson ran, as he said, "like a singed cat." Minnesotans had made Kefauver a viable candidate and, indirectly, had turned Stevenson into an active, hand-shaking politician. The new Stevenson donned cowboy boots in Arizona, carried a stuffed alligator in Florida, and everywhere shook hands by the hundreds. His tactics paid off. To the astonishment of his own staff, he scored a series of minor but significant victories and, in the crucial California primary in June, he scored an overwhelming victory that assured him of the Democratic nomination.

Humphrey had not given up his goal of being a vice-presidential candidate. His hopes were revived after a pre-convention "unity feast" when Stevenson had told him that he was his choice for Vice-President. Humphrey had stars in his eyes and seemed to have forgotten about the state of his fractured party. Kefauver's supporters wanted their man on the November ticket with Stevenson.

Prior to the national Democratic convention in August, the *New York Times* reported that a chief source of pressure for Senator Kefauver's nomination for Vice-President on a ticket headed by Stevenson came from Minnesota and Wisconsin. This was another embarrassing development for Humphrey. Kefauver had again turned up in Humphrey's own backyard.

A *New York Times* pre-convention report preserved in the Humphrey papers had the following sentences underlined: "Robert Short, chairman of the Minnesota delegation, predicted it would be difficult to get delegates to switch to Mr Stevenson without assurances of second place for Mr Kefauver. He said there would be no difficulty in switching from Senator Kefauver to Governor W. Averill Harriman, if the Senator had suggested it." Senator Humphrey flew to Minneapolis from Washington to try to stem the tide.[23] These were hard words for Humphrey to swallow. The chairman of his own state's delegation had implied that Minnesota would not support Humphrey for Vice-President.

Coya arrived in Chicago several days before the convention was to begin in order to work on the Democratic platform, and was upset to discover that there was a problem with her credentials. She viewed it as a tactic to harass her. The problem was soon smoothed over by Sam Rayburn, and Coya went on with her work. Then, after several days of intense labor, Coya was bitterly disappointed to find that a strong farm program would not be on the platform. "If they had let Kefauver's ideas have more influence," she says, "some of the conflict could have been avoided later." When the convention began, Coya was exhausted and frustrated by the pre-convention work.

As an elected Kefauver delegate from Minnesota, Coya was a particularly visible and vulnerable politician. A bodyguard, John Baker, was assigned to her during the convention. At night he stayed outside the door of her hotel room where she was staying with Terry and Bill Kjeldahl's sister Doris. Emotions were running high and when the Minnesota delegation went out to eat, Baker "stuck to me like glue because sometimes things can get real hot when people don't like the way things are going." The convention was confined to two hotels across the street from each other, so she did not have far to go to any event. She ventured beyond the confines of the hotels only once and that was to join other conventioneers on a Lake Michigan boat ride. She remembers that the climate was so damp and windy that her hair "looked like it had been starched."

Convention interest focused on the selection for Vice-President, since Adlai Stevenson indeed was the convention's choice for President. His nomination was speedily confirmed. Hubert Humphrey did what nobody had done before: he declared publicly that he was a candidate for the vice-presidency. The *Minneapolis Tribune* of

August 15th reported that the Minnesota delegation took a secret ballot on their choice for Vice-President and then, after weighing the consequences, ordered the ballots burned. Minnesota delegates had a tough choice. They could vote for the Tennesseean they were pledged to support, or they could vote for Minnesota's favorite son. Delegate Coya Knutson side-stepped backing either Kefauver or Humphrey publicly. "I'm just backing the Democratic Party," she said.[24]

Then Stevenson dropped a bombshell. He unexpectedly announced that contrary to tradition, he was not going to name his Vice-Presidential choice. Instead, he would permit the Democratic nominee to be chosen by the convention in a wide-open contest. Coya thought that Stevenson was crazy to throw the nomination open just because he did not want to have to face conflict and choose among his friends. Because he was letting things happen and not asserting himself, Coya saw Stevenson as weak.

Stevenson's announcement was a major setback for Humphrey. His carefully built plan had gone awry. Even worse was the fact that his idol had passed him by. Humphrey's friend, newsman Eric Sevareid, found him weeping just after Stevenson's announcement.[25] To add insult to injury, Stevenson asked Senator John F. Kennedy of Massachusetts to give his nomination speech. Humphrey had hoped to have that honor.

The convention's stunned surprise had not passed before Senators Humphrey, Kennedy and Kefauver had become active Vice-Presidential candidates. "Adlai's statement sets up a terrific battle for the number two spot," the *Minneapolis Tribune* reported on August 17. Following Stevenson's announcement, scores of Humphrey's dedicated volunteers rushed to his hospitality headquarters at the Hilton, where literature was quickly mimeographed for distribution to the 1,372 delegates. They went home at 4:40 a.m. only because Humphrey himself dismissed them by saying that "nobody will be worth anything if they don't get sleep."[26]

All that night the Loop hotels were scenes of frenzied activity as intense campaigns for delegates went on. "There was so much discussion, and so many power plays going on," Coya recalls, that she, like many others, stayed up all night. "There were so many rumors flying, it drove us buggy." Coya, like most of the delegates, was so tired that she could not function well. "Everything was swimming in front of my eyes and I could hardly stand on my feet."

Before the first ballot was well underway, it was apparent the race was between Kefauver and Kennedy. Humphrey was running a poor fifth and his own delegation passed. The first ballot for Vice-President showed Kefauver 483 1/2, Kennedy 304, Gore 178, Wagner 162 1/2, and Humphrey 134 1/2. Humphrey's chances for the candidacy, damaged by the Minnesota primary results, had swiftly waned.

As switching began after the first ballot, the Minnesota delegation caucused to see where its sympathies lay. Minnesota was not yet willing to desert its favorite son, but sentiment for Kefauver was obviously strong and rising; after all, delegates were committed to him. Moreover, by deserting Humphrey and jumping on Kefauver's bandwagon, Minnesota could help stop Kennedy, whose votes for a flexible price-support system made him a liability to farm voters.

A fatigued and almost beaten Humphrey sat with close friends in Sam Rayburn's private room behind the convention platform. Michigan Governor G. Mennen Williams pleaded with Humphrey to throw his backing to a stop-Kennedy move. Williams' argument was that Humphrey's friend Orville Freeman would almost certainly fail in his re-election bid as Minnesota's governor if the Massachusetts Senator became Stevenson's running mate. Kennedy's farm and labor record were not in tune with the radical Democratic-Farmer-Labor goals.[27]

There were others who begged Humphrey to stick it out. Eugenie Anderson shouted, "Leave Humphrey alone." Everyone was crying. About the only thing TV commentator Martin Agronsky can still recall of the 1956 convention is that lachrymose scene. "Hubert was crying, really sobbing, and so were some of his friends." When Kefauver entered the tear-sogged room, Agronsky quickly informed the public that Minnesota would throw its support to Kefauver and that would probably tip the balance.

The report was premature. Kefauver had to do considerable pleading before it happened. He began by saying, "Hubert, you've got to help me. You've just got to help me...Please." Kefauver, too, had begun to cry. "In fact," said a witness, "everyone was crying...I'll never forget the water gushing in that room."[28]

When the caucus began, delegates were in a quandary about whether to stay with Humphrey or go with Kefauver. To dump their favorite son, the man who had founded the DFL, seemed callous. Yet realities suggested it would be politically wise to vote for the Tennessee senator. Reflecting on the emotional tug on the delegation, chairman Robert E. Short announced, "We are about to cross the bridge I thought we'd never have to cross."[29] He cast his vote for Kefauver. The vice-chairman voted for Humphrey. Representative Coya Knutson also broke down in tears as she cast her vote for the Minnesota senator "in one of the most difficult decisions I've had to make in my life." Other delegates were near the breaking point, and chairman Short recalled that "everybody in the room was crying."

Still more tears were to come. The Minnesota caucus tabulation showed 20 1/2 votes for Humphrey, 8 for Kefauver. The three remaining delegates, with 1 1/2 votes, were absent; later they aligned themselves with Humphrey. Coya recalls that this moment was the only time in her career that she ever cried in public. Everyone, she remembers, was emotional from the excitement combined with the lack of sleep.

When Minnesota was called on again, Short grabbed the microphone, shouting "Senator Kefauver, in the interest of party unity, asks me to cast Minnesota's full thirty votes for Senator Humphrey."

Humphrey's supporters gasped. Short, they felt, had conveyed the impression to other delegates who watched Humphrey's home state that Kefauver was in actual control of most of the Minnesota votes rather than a minority of them. A Minneapolis delegate remonstrated with Short, telling him "that may have a bad effect on Humphrey's chances because it sounded as if Kefauver handed us most of the thirty votes!" Yet it was apparent that while the Tennessean did not have the majority of Minnesota votes, sentiment for him pervaded the delegation; the majority of votes for Humphrey were cast with reluctance.

Coya has since admitted that she and Kjeldahl had been behind this strategy. They had decided that if, at the right time, Kefauver threw his votes to Humphrey, later Humphrey would have to throw his votes to someone else—and that someone would be Kefauver.

As switching began at the end of the second ballot, the race was between Kennedy and Kefauver: Kennedy 559 1/2; Kefauver 478 1/2; Gore 96 and Humphrey 67. Robert Short announced Minnesota's 16 1/2 votes for Humphrey, 13 1/2 for Kefauver. Kennedy's total mounted to 618, only 68 1/2 fewer than he needed to win. While some Minnesotans wanted to switch to Kefauver, "Leave it to Humphrey," was the sentiment that prevailed. Up and up climbed the

Kennedy totals until they reached 648, just 20 short of nomination. Then Kefauver received the break. Senator Albert Gore threw his delegates to fellow Senator and Tennessean Estes Kefauver.

Humphrey, seeing that he had no chance, went up to the platform. "All right, Estes," said Humphrey, "I said I would get out if I didn't make a good showing. And we've got to save the farm vote." The Minnesota delegation then threw its entire 30 votes to Kefauver.

Minnesota's vote broke the dam. Kefauver got the majority he needed. The final totals were Kefauver 755 1/2, Kennedy 589, Gore 13 and 1/2, Wagner 6 and Humphrey 3 1/2.

With the announcement that Kefauver was the winner, pandemonium reigned in the Minnesota section. Coya threw her arms around an alternate delegate, crying, "We saved the farm vote, thanks to Hubert's switching."[30]

Minnesota voting had been embarrassing to Humphrey, but more humiliation was to come from his state's newspapers. "State Nominated Veep—but not Favorite Son," the front page of the *Minneapolis Tribune* announced on August 18. "Humphrey just didn't have what it takes in 1956: The Vice-Presidential drive of Minnesota's favorite son Hubert Humphrey faltered and died Friday—but there was little sorrow in his delegation. There was a tear here and there, but noting the eyes of the pro-Kefauver majority which—although its loyalties were severely tested by the Humphrey candidacy—whooped and shouted and pounded one another on the back as the phlegmatic Tennessee Senator, Estes Kefauver, inched his way to victory over Humphrey, far in the rear, and Senator John F. Kennedy. Humphrey just didn't have what it takes in 1956. True, he was the favorite of many farm, labor and congressional leaders, but it quickly became apparent that he hadn't gotten across to the delegates themselves."

Humphrey had not correctly assessed his power with Minnesotans. Theodore White thought that both Freeman and Humphrey had an almost romantic faith in "The People." But, White explains, "colder men noted that this party seemed held together more by spirit and emotion than by hard organized machinery, that it rested on volunteer enthusiasm for an individual and beloved leader, plus the support of other organized groups the party could not control." [31]

The Stevenson-Kefauver ticket was swamped by Eisenhower-Nixon in November. Eisenhower was re-elected by the largest margin of any Republican president up to that time. Humphrey's wife Muriel claimed that the 1956 convention was the worst, the bitterest defeat of Humphrey's career, and that he would not talk about it. However, it was in Humphrey's nature to bounce back. He was not a man who held grudges.

Immediately after the convention, Coya returned to what she hoped would be her normal routine in Washington, D.C. But she continued to be a controversial figure. Politics indeed makes strange bedfellows. L. J. Lee and Byron G. Allen, DFL opponents within the party, could finally agree. They both thought that Coya had reached high—too high—and interpreted her support of Kefauver as a bid for an important appointment in his administration.

Their assessment was wrong, says Coya. She knew that Eisenhower would win against any Democrat. Therefore, her goal was to build up support for her re-election, and backing Kefauver's farm program would help her get the necessary votes. But she also truly believed in her candidate and his platform and refused to let DFL leaders dictate to her: "Putting distance between me and the know-it-all's did my heart good." She also admits that "I love to beat the odds."

The irony was that Coya had not backed the wrong horse; her horse had won by a great margin. But while gaining support among Ninth District voters, Coya had made enemies in her own party. DFL leaders were so embarrassed by the Kefauver win that before the next presidential election, the Minnesota legislature eliminated the presidential primary.

Vice-President Walter F. Mondale, then a young law student and Humphrey aide, sums up the DFL sentiment at the time. "The DFL was a new political party—brand new—and had set for itself the goal of nominating Adlai Stevenson because they did not think Kefauver could be elected. But Adlai was not a natural politician for a rural state. He spoke in a kind of Eastern style, an academic language. Old Estes just pattered around like an old hound dog and people liked it. Coya joined up with him and, as always happens in those things, people got angry. People shouldn't have gotten angry—people have the right to support whoever they wish. Besides, the party was hot—on its way to remaking Minnesota, the nation, the world—and we were not very good at accepting dissent."[32]

The DFL did not re-unite. After the national convention the Kefauver delegation continued to meet separately. Both Hjalmer

Petersen and Robert Short were trying to build up a power base to run for the U. S. Senate. In the Ninth District, Republicans were ready to take advantage of division in the Democratic party. An editorial that appeared in the *Crookston Times* shortly after Stevenson's win in the California primary stated: "Right here in the Ninth District, Rep. Coya Knutson gained a good deal of prestige among Democrats for her espousal of the Kefauver cause and her denunciation of boss rule. Her favorite candidate's apparent elimination has probably hurt her own chances for re-election to Congress. It's not politically sound to back the wrong horse—and it's just about a lead pipe cinch that Mrs Knutson will get precious little support in the campaign ahead from those who control the DFL Party. Chances of returning the Ninth District seat to the Republican fold are looking up—way up."[33]

The new district DFL chairman, Marvin Evenson, believed that by supporting Kefauver, Coya had improved her chances of winning the coming congressional election. It wasn't only that many Kefauver campaign stops had been in her own district, but that she had also allied herself with the presidential candidate that her constituents trusted and liked. As her first term in the U. S. Congress ended, one thing was certain. Coya no longer thought that her image as a DFL member was important. She had let people know that she was on her own.

No one knew that better than Coya herself. She was alone in more ways than one. At an August DFL meeting, she met Muriel Humphrey in the hotel lobby, carrying a little ironing board under her arm. Coya envied Hubert—she wished that she too had someone to help her be at her best at all times and see her through the rough patches.

Chapter 12

COYA COME HOME

There is a woman in Congress and she is becoming a new kind of power.

"A Woman's Influence in the Schools"
Nonpartisan Leader: September 20, 1917

Coya was glad she had come in to work on Sunday and was alone in the office when she opened the letter from Jim Turgeon. Perhaps it would have been easier to take from a stranger, but this letter was from one of her high school students in Oklee who was now secretary of the Red Lake County DFL. The letter was curt and hostile. She read it through again:

"I am much more worried and concerned about disunity and poor working relationships when someone high in the party, like you for instance, lets yourself get involved in a political fracas like the Minnesota primary turned out to be. I hope and pray it will not be disastrous to any of our candidates."[1]

In preparation for her campaign in the fall her office had requested that the Red Lake DFL send caucus material to precinct captains, a standard procedure. In return, James Turgeon, now a high school science teacher at Oklee, made clear in this letter what the politicians at home thought about her.

Coya had already been warned that her backing of Kefauver had alienated DFLers from her own county. She had become more and more uneasy. After the Kefauver win in Minnesota she had had more attention than was good for her. There were far more requests for speaking engagements than she could possibly fulfill. However, even though no one said much, she could feel that attitudes toward her had changed in Washington. There was an undeniable coolness in many Democrats who had once been friendly.

Congresswoman Gracie Pfost told Coya that she'd had a similar reaction from colleagues when she was pushing for preservation of wilderness lands. Pfost gave her a poem entitled "The Congressman's Lament" that Coya liked so much that she included it in the "Coya's Capitol Chat" column:

Among life's dying embers
These are my regrets:
When I'm right, no one remembers,
When I'm wrong, no one forgets.[2]

More repercussions from the Kefauver campaign were to come at the Ninth District DFL convention and again at the Minnesota convention. At the district convention, L.J. Lee withdrew from nomination for district chairman and Marvin Evenson of Moorhead was unanimously elected to that post. At the district meeting in May, Resolution Seventeen proposed that delegates be selected by convention method, not by the results of the recent presidential primary. The reason given was that the 1956 presidential primary had "created confusion in the minds of voters," according to James Turgeon, chairman of the resolutions committee.[3] It was also resolved, in an unprecedented move, that the convention would no longer endorse incumbent congressional representatives; they were "urged to file for re-election."

Prior to the June state convention this resolution was presented to the state endorsements committee. Members Margaret Michels and Spot Reierson argued that if all other districts supported their incumbents—with only the Ninth District holding out—the "Kefauver-Stevenson wound would be reopened to counteract the efforts for harmony."[4] After lengthy discussion the endorsement committee agreed to endorse incumbents upon request of their respective districts. Following a succession of meetings on the last day of the state convention, Coya was finally endorsed by the state convention along with other DFL congressional incumbents.

Coya especially appreciated Spot Reierson's assistance in getting the endorsement. She wrote him a letter of thanks for the "wonderful help" that he had given her at the state convention. Coya complained to Spot about the DFL: "It was awfully hard to keep still hearing that Curtiss Olson had worked so closely to the party. I should have answered, 'Yes, but he tried three times and lost.' I feel under the circumstances they will never see my side of it, but I think you realize that I had to do what I did."[5]

Spot, who had succeeded Barney Allen as National Committeeman from the district, continued to stay in the good graces of the Democratic leaders: he had actively worked for Adlai Stevenson in the recent Presidential Primary by organizing a large rally for Stevenson in Fosston, and now he was working for Coya. As a mediator between factions in the DFL, Reierson was able to please both sides. Walter F. Mondale, then a speech writer for Hubert Humphrey, wrote Spot, "Thanks again for the way you compromised with the Oklee group the other day. You certainly got me off a hot spot."[6]

Mondale comments that Reierson "could have been Secretary-General of the United Nations. He was a clever, full-time politician who could hold that crazy community up there together—and did for the better part of 20 years—in spite of all this bitterness." However, Reierson would betray his dislike of someone by invariably mispronouncing their name, as in the case of State Representative Ben Wichterman of Plummer. Mondale recalls that "I would tell him, 'Spot, that guy's name is Wik-ter-man, not witch-ter-man.' 'I know that,' Spot would say. He would drive them crazy."

Because Coya was unopposed in the Minnesota primary election, she did not need to make frequent appearances in the state. She was able to remain in Washington on some weekends that summer, and she enjoyed her time off with Terry. During summer vacation from his military academy, Terry moved to Washington and found work as a reservation clerk for Capital Airlines. In September he returned to Randolph-Macon for his junior year.

When the 1956 general election rolled around that fall, Republican Harold C. Hagen was again Coya's opponent. Even her DFL detractors thought she would win. She was still popular with the press.

Better Farming, one of the popular farm journals, had run an article, "Meet the Farm Woman's Congresswoman," that presented Coya as a Democrat from a Republican district who had fought her way into Congress and on to the Agricultural Committee with 'butter and egg' electioneering." Coya's request for women's comments was quoted: "I would like to meet and talk with every farm wife in America, but since I can't, I hope they will at least write me about their problems."

They did. Thousands of letters from forty-five states flooded into Coya's office.[7] She had touched a responsive chord. Because of the readers' responses, the magazine published two articles written by Coya: "Protect the Family Farm Now" and "Farm Women Tell How to Fight the Surplus Threat to Family Farms."

The press in the Ninth District, however, was negative toward her. An editorial that appeared in a Crookston newspaper complained that "her base appeal must be some other reason than her qualities as a congresswoman or her value to her constituents. She has claimed to be a friend of farmers, but no one single act of hers has benefited any farmer in our area."[8]

Late that summer Coya addressed the Democratic Women's Seven States Conference in Kansas City. She interrupted her speech to wait for latecomers Harry, Bess and Margaret Truman to be seated. Continuing her speech with off-the-cuff remarks, Coya recalls that "I made some good points and got some good laughs." Secretary Benson was the butt of many of her jokes.

She also told a story about the night of Truman's election victory in 1948 when she had been county chairman. She had driven home late that night and noticed that the lights of all the Republican households were out because they thought they had won with Dewey, while the homes of Democrats were brightly lighted because they hoped Truman still had a chance. The story brought down the house. Above the sound of laughter and applause, Coya heard Truman say, "I've got to have a copy of that speech." Although she had spoken extemporaneously, Coya did her best to reproduce that speech for the President. Her self-confidence was bolstered by the kudos from Harry S. Truman.

That fall, when she returned to Minnesota to campaign, she drew large audiences. Agnes Israelson, a former mayor of Thief River Falls, recalls that "a street was blocked off for a rally when Coya came to campaign because there was such a big crowd. Outdoor meetings where she could mingle freely with people and say hello were her forté. Her vitality drew people to her."[9]

Coya visited with White Cloud, the Ojibwe's leader on the White

Earth Reservation and promised him that "anything I can do for you, I will." At a powwow near Mahnomen, she was invited to join the tribal dancing and spent the evening at their campfire gathering.

In Red Lake she had a long conference with Peter Graves, the leader of the Red Lake band of Ojibwes. For more than half a century, Graves had ruled firmly, sometimes with an iron hand, and had come to be popularly known as "The Chief." As an accomplished statesman and the secretary-treasurer of the band, he had helped preserve the reservation solely for the Red Lake Ojibwes by not permitting land allotments to be taken by individuals, stating that "we want this reservation protected for our children and grandchildren." He was skeptical of the materialistic white man's world and told Coya "the dogs are burying too many bones."

Coya soon discovered that her person-to-person campaign style would have to be augmented with television advertising. In the two years since her 1954 campaign, many area homes had sprouted television antennas. Even though reception was poor throughout much of the area, Coya spent $3,129, nearly half of her 1956 campaign money, at the Ninth District's only television station, WDAY at Fargo, North Dakota. Radio announcements accounted for $1,679 of the budget, while newspaper advertisements and flyers cost $1,614. Her re-election campaign was shorter and more intense than her first campaign. She made a whistle-stop tour of 86 locations in 14 days.[10]

Coya beat Republican Harold Hagen in the general election by a margin of 5,979 votes, garnering 53% of the vote. Shortly before the election Harold Hagen was involved in an automobile accident. His young chauffeur was driving him to a political meeting in Detroit Lakes when an on-coming car crossed the median, forcing Hagen's car into a ditch. Hagen, who sustained internal injuries, was hospitalized for a week. He did not want to let his party down and persuaded his doctors to allow him to resume campaigning. Five months later, Hagen's injuries contributed to his death of heart failure at age 56.[11]

In January 1957 Coya returned to Washington and brought her mother along to live with her. Coya liked having someone to come home to and appreciated her mother's home-cooked meals, a treat she had not enjoyed for a long time. Coya was very happy to be back in the capital and relished the legislative work ahead. But she could no longer ignore her problems in Oklee.

Coya's heart sank when she received the letter from Andy written in pencil on blue-lined paper:

My dear wife,

Some of the party had a meeting they called me over and asked me lots of things. Well, I didn't say much because I want to see first how you turn out. They want another meeting now about February 1 and they let me know.

Well, Coya, if I don't hear from you by that time I am going to tell them the whole works. I don't get any money from you, so I'll have to get it some other place. I'm broke and need money. The cafe's got about $50-$75 coming from me. I really can make money out of this deal.

The rest is up to you, Coya, which side of the fence you want me on.

I love you, honey.[12]

The disgruntled husband and the desperate DFL party leaders in her district had found each other. The letter was not entirely unexpected because Andy had made various demands for money, but his implied threat was a concern. Coya had decided to stop sending money to Andy and, in spite of the ultimatum expressed in his letter, she resolved not to give in to his demands.

The Knutsons' banker had warned Coya that Andy was not working and could not pay his bills.[13] However, travel expenses between Washington and Minnesota, the cost of running two households and Terry's school fees had depleted Coya's savings and she was finding it difficult to continue sending money to Andy. Furthermore, although a congressional campaign could be run for little money in 1956—only $7,515 was the total recorded for Coya's entire campaign—a loan was necessary to cover $3,359 in unpaid campaign bills. She would have to pay off the loan from her salary—which meant she would pay 40% of the campaign expenses out of her own pocket. Andy would have to find a way to provide for himself and his sister in Oklee.

Although she was well aware of the possible consequences of Andy's alliance with disgruntled Ninth District DFL party leaders, Coya deliberately turned her attention to special events in Washington surrounding the Presidential Inaugural and the opening of the 85th Congress. A snowstorm prevented Coya and Terry from attending many of the parties, but they did go to the gala Inaugural Ball.

Rather than buy a lavish evening gown, Coya wore her white dress and coat with fur-trimmed cuffs. She had never learned how to dance, but she enjoyed mingling with the throngs of party-goers and seeing such celebrities as Gregory Peck and Jeanette MacDonald.

At the swearing-in ceremony for members of Congress, the House Chambers were brightly lit for the television cameras. Sam Rayburn was beginning an unprecedented eighth term as Speaker of the House. Fourteen congresswomen had been re-elected in 1956—only Republican Ruth Thompson of Indiana had lost her seat. Elizabeth Farrington of Hawaii had also retired. At the annual Women's Press Club Dinner at the Statler Hotel honoring women members of Congress, Coya met newly-elected Democrat Katherine Granahan of Pennsylvania and Republican Florence Dwyer of New Jersey. Granahan, a former ward leader who had been elected to fill her husband's office after his death, had earned a reputation for serving tea and cookies at ward meetings instead of the traditional barrel of beer. Dwyer, a former lobbyist, had entered elective politics by beating 19 Republicans for the primary nomination before winning a seat in the New Jersey State Assembly.

In her "Capital Chats" column, Coya wrote about a variety of legislative matters, including the passage of a disaster-loan bill that would benefit drought-stricken areas where "two cows were waiting for every blade of grass that came up." She reported that President Eisenhower had received a telegram from a Minnesota farmer who complained that "if you don't get some hay to us right away, there won't be a cow or a Republican left in the district."

She wrote that a farmer from Kensington had visited her office and told her that when he learned that eggs cost ten cents apiece in the Capital, he realized that he would have to sell a dozen eggs back in Minnesota to buy two eggs in Washington.

When legislation concerning feed grains came up in Committee, Coya told a story in her column about two hog farmers. One farmer said to the other, "I hear you sold your pig." "Yep, sold it this morning," was the reply. "What did you get for it?" asked the first farmer. "Eight dollars." "That does not sound like much. What did it cost you to raise it?" "Paid three dollars for it and five dollars for its feed," the second farmer replied. "Didn't make much, did you?" "Nope," was the cheerful answer. "But I had its company all summer."

Coya introduced a proposal to restore rigid farm-price supports.

She sought aid for Ojibwe Native Americans and worked to ratify and confirm conveyances of allotted land on the White Earth Reservation. Coya worked for a new deferred grazing program that provided payment to drought-stricken farmers

In a speech on the floor of the House, Coya was quick to defend the American housewife in a lively debate on trading stamps. Another lawmaker had charged that housewives shopped erratically "with no more purpose than a bumblebee, attracted by brightly colored stamps." Coya countered sharply that she, like other housewives, were most concerned with nutrition, grade, variety and cost, and maintained that "the American housewife is a shrewd and prudent shopper."[14]

That year Coya and Terry made the most of their holidays together whenever Terry came to Washington. They went by train to New York to celebrate New Year's Eve in Times Square. That spring they took in the Easter Parade on New York's Fifth Avenue.

Coya had little social life in Washington. Most of her time was spent working on the Hill, but occasionally she would attend a dinner party. It was a chance to meet people and find out what might be in the offing for Capitol Hill legislators, but "there was just too much lobbying and too much of everything you did not need, like food and alcohol," to appeal to Coya. Sometimes she would attend special events such as the embassy party for Queen Elizabeth and Prince Philip of Great Britain where she shook hands with the royal couple. Coya was amused to overhear Prince Phillip tell his wife, "Buck up, old girl, you're drooping."

With few friends in Washington, Coya especially enjoyed seeing visitors from her district. In 1957 she escorted 55 members of the Concordia College Concert Choir on a tour of the Capital that included a foray into Vice-President Richard Nixon's empty office where she invited several students to take turns sitting in his chair. Later, when the choir stood singing on the steps of the Lincoln Memorial, Coya took the baton from Director Paul J. Christianson and led them in singing "God Bless America." One of the youthful choir members, Mary Jackson, recalls that Coya looked unsophisticated, even "slightly dumpy," and did not quite blend into the cosmopolitan scene about her. However, Coya's obvious enthusiasm delighted the young people, each of whom received a letter from the congresswoman: "The Concordia College Choir did such a wonderful job here at Constitution Hall that many people still talk about it. It really does bring back memories of the days I traveled with the Choir."[15]

On June 2nd, 1957, Coya was one of the proud parents at Randolph-Macon Academy watching her uniformed son march in as one of the graduates. She was elated that her son had adapted to this military school life, and felt that everything was turning out for the best after all. She was honored to be invited to give a greeting at the ceremony. In a news article, Terry was described as being a handsome boy having "the direct look of his mother."

After much study and discussion, it was decided that Terry should enroll at Luther College in Decorah, Iowa for the coming fall semester. In the meantime, Terry returned to his summer job at Capital Airlines.

Coya had not forgotten about the successful student-loan fund in Norway that Tor Gjesdal had told her about. She was experiencing the difficulty many parents have in finding enough money to send a child to college. The latent idea of establishing a student-loan fund grew into a firm resolution to initiate such legislation through Congress. After contacting her cousin Tor several times to learn more about Norway's plan, which had been operating for ten years, Coya became convinced that a similar program would be a tremendous help in encouraging America's youth to go on to further education. She sent Bill Kjeldahl to Norway on a fact-finding mission to learn all he could about the program.

When the 1957 session ended in August, Coya gave up her apartment in Washington and moved back to Minnesota where she stayed in the homes of friends. When she had to go to Oklee, she would not stay overnight. That fall, she helped her mother move to a retirement home at Devils Lake, North Dakota, where her daughter Helen lived. Coya also saw Terry off for his freshman year at Luther College.

Coya was happy to get back to Washington. She found an apartment on E Street, west of the White House, and each day she enjoyed driving past the home of the President. Immersing herself in work on Capitol Hill gave her the sense of accomplishment she had been seeking all her life. There were so many things she wanted to do and Washington was a place where one could get things done. She did not think of herself in terms of gender or party affiliation, but rather as the person the voters in her district had entrusted to represent them. She felt no obligation to the DFL district leaders; they had not helped her get elected. She hired her aides and office staff on the basis of their qualifications and not to satisfy political favors. She had become very much her own person in Washington, and she was aware that there were party leaders back home who took a dim view of her feisty independence.

That fall she was not surprised to see a *Minneapolis Star* newspaper headline ask: "Is Coya the target of both the GOP and DFL?" The November 18, 1957 news story reported that a number of prominent DFL leaders had been urged to challenge Coya Knutson in the primary, but that even her severest critics in the party had declared that she had done a good job. Several Ninth District politicians, including Rep. Ben Wichterman of Plummer and State Securities Commissioner Arthur Hansen of Ulen, admitted that they had been asked to challenge Mrs Knutson in the next primary election, but they would say no more for publication.[16]

The *Minneapolis Star* was on to some big news. A fight was underway that would capture headlines across the country during the coming election year, and Coya Knutson, 45, stood at the center of the controversy. The principal target of DFL criticism, the *Star* reported, was William O. Kjeldahl, 29, Knutson's administrative assistant. "The youthful Kjeldahl continues to get blistered for what many party hands charge is his deliberate effort to make her inaccessible to them for conferences and other district chores. "Coya's critics admitted that it would be hard to campaign against her in a primary election simply on the issue of whether her administrative assistant has or has not made for poor relations between the party and the congresswoman's office. Whether she had done her job well was not the issue. In fact, the *Star* called her feat in getting a House subcommittee hearing on family farms in Fergus Falls brilliant.

Coya's supporters in the Ninth District bristled at this hint of DFL opposition to their congresswoman. The DFL Ninth District secretary-treasurer, Marge Michels, wrote in a letter to the editor of the *Minneapolis Star*:

"Don't ever believe that there are very many Ninth District politicians who are generally opposing Coya's re-election. Of 15 District counties, only two have officers who would like to see her discredited. Why? For petty, personal reasons. A few individuals thought that when a woman was elected to Congress, she would be their tool, answer to them and in fact, be dictated to by them. The job of being her administrative assistant looked like an enviable plum and at least one of this handful of disloyal individuals aspired to get to Washington on her payroll. Her critics admitted that poor party relations between the party and her administrative assistant would be no campaign issue, and she has given them no other issue. Coya is stronger than ever in the Ninth District."[17]

Three other Coya supporters wrote to the *Star*:

"There is absolutely no organized opposition to Mrs Knutson."[18]

"We note that party workers are rallying to her support and that her voting record is considered with high favor in the inner circles of the party as well as with the rank and file in this county and adjoining counties."[19]

"I attended the Ninth district DFL meeting at Roseau on November 17 and found unanimous acceptance of the congresswoman by a good group made up of representatives from 11 counties of the district. If there is any opposition, it must be coming from the Republicans."[20]

But these northwestern Minnesota DFL leaders were wrong. There was a great deal of anti-Coya sentiment at work behind the scenes. Harvey Wilder, a state legislator from Marshall county, wrote directly to Coya. "You were once the sweetheart of the state legislature, and then you were elected to Washington. But in the past two years something has changed you. You are not the humble woman they once knew. Your continuous business contacts have made you a little too tough on your constituencies [sic]."[21]

Coya knew that there was strife in her district DFL party and that much of the antipathy was directed at her, but rather than worry about how her actions were perceived back home, she chose to ignore it. She had sought the nomination over her party's protestations and won the election. It rankled that certain party leaders now thought they could tell her how to do her job. Coya felt that her only obligation was to the people who had elected her to Congress and they seemed to think she was doing just fine. There was work to do in Washington and it was time to get on with it.

In January, as her fourth congressional session began, Coya was ready to initiate work on the celebration of Minnesota's centennial and to write the student-loan bill. To memorialize Minnesota's centennial anniversary of statehood, Coya saw to it that Congress authorized a seven-foot bronze statue of Maria Sanford to be placed in Statuary Hall in the Capitol rotunda. (Con. Res. 284, 4 March 1958).

Only two other American women had previously been honored in the hall. Maria Sanford, a remarkably gifted professor at the University of Minnesota at the turn of the century, had been a tireless worker for civic causes. Her faculty colleagues had often criticized Sanford because, like Coya, she was strong-willed and her energies took her beyond the bounds of usual pursuits for women.[22]

When Bill Kjeldahl returned from Norway with his research completed, Coya and her staff began writing a college student-loan bill to bring to committee. To gather support for the legislation, her office sent a memo to 1,500 college presidents describing loan possibilities and asking for their opinions. Most responded with great enthusiasm and only one wrote back saying it would not work.

One day Coya received a letter from Marge Michels telling her about a five-year-old boy she knew with cystic fibrosis. Because of the disease, the child had to sleep in a kind of oxygen tent at night and at certain times during the day. The boy's father, Ed Anderson, who was the band director in Breckenridge, had exhausted the family's funds and resources in taking care of the child. Doctors had given his parents, who had lost two other children to the disease, hope that the boy might live to be fifteen. To learn more about the disease, Coya called on the Legislative Reference Service of the Library of Congress and discovered that cystic fibrosis was ranked third among child-killers. The lungs and stomachs of babies born with cystic fibrosis fill up with a terrible mucus that has to be removed or it turns into a rubberlike substance that swells up the stomach until nothing nourishes the body.

Coya set out immediately to secure federal money for research. On March 20, 1958, Coya addressed her colleagues on the floor of the House, announcing, "We must declare war on cystic fibrosis." As people became aware of Coya's interest in the disease, letters began to pour into her office. She asked for and got volunteer help from CF parents to help answer the more than 3,000 letters that arrived from every state in the Union.

She was not the only one to get mail. Coya received a call from the chairman of the Health Committee in the Senate, asking "What have you done? My office is flooded with mail on cystic fibrosis." With the help of CF parents, she and her staff began work on a bill to attack the problem at its base by providing the means for research into the nature and causes of this disease, as well as research into the methods of controlling the lung infections and other complications.

Work on the CF bill was well underway when she left Washington to travel to Crookston, Minnesota for the Ninth District DFL convention. For Coya, attending the convention added more to her already full schedule of work; however, she looked forward to the change of pace and the chance to see old friends.

Coya was not aware that in her absence her opponents within the DFL had begun to engineer takeovers of some county organizations that spring. A Coya supporter complained to Spot Reierson that Chairman Marvin Evenson and his predecessor, L. J. Lee, had "voiced about the district that those who supported Mrs Knutson must be purged."[23] Shortly afterward, at the Norman County convention of April 19, 1958, a successful effort was made to ensure that county convention chairman C. J. Hastad, an ardent supporter of Congresswoman Knutson and vice-chairman of the Norman county DFL, would not be attending the May district convention as a delegate. The fight between district leaders and supporters of Congresswoman Knutson was in the open.

When the Ninth District DFL convention in Crookston convened early in May, the fight for control of the district was bitter and hard-fought by both sides. Spearheaded by former district chairman L. J. Lee, party leaders actively sought an opponent for Coya, the *Fargo Forum* reported.

District chairman Marvin Evenson chastised Coya for breaking with party leaders. But John Michels of Breckenridge, leader of the pro-Coya faction, criticized Evenson and opposed his re-election as chairman, saying "I feel that the only reason for the existence of this organization is to wholeheartedly support our congresswoman."

Evenson countered, "This organization exists not to build one man or one person or one leader; we need to build at the precinct grass roots if we're to get more Freemans and Humphreys for our party."[24]

Convention delegates split into two factions who differed over who should be district chairman. Delegates had to choose between incumbent chairman Evenson, who was actively working against Coya, and Coya-supporter John Michels. Balloting for district chairman went on for an unprecedented six hours.

Opposition was strongest where early support for the congresswoman had been greatest; in fact, party leaders of counties that once comprised her state legislative district—Clearwater, Red Lake, and

Pennington—all voted against her. Norman County, where the intra-party fight had ousted county convention chairman Hastad, also voted against her and cast all three votes for Evenson. Otter Tail County, which had William Kjeldahl as an alternate delegate, split its votes 2-2. The northern counties continued to be loyal to Coya—they voted for Michels.

In the end, after the hectic six hours of balloting, exhausted delegates elected John Michels as the new DFL district chairman by only two votes. The congresswoman's supporters had won. Kay Peterson of Karlstad was re-elected district chairwoman. The vice-chairman, secretary and treasurer were also women. Once her people were in control, Coya was speedily nominated as District Nine candidate for Congress. She spoke to the convention, giving her thanks for the "expression of confidence from the grass roots today."

She told the delegates that the previous evening she had driven to the Municipal Hospital in Fosston, 50 miles east of Crookston, to visit Spot Reierson, who was being treated for bleeding ulcers. He had not been allowed visitors, but Coya had "snuck in anyway for a minute because Spot wouldn't rest easy not knowing what was going on." He had told her that he wished for two peace pipes: one for the past chairman, one for the present chairman and maybe even a third for himself. She said that she, too, hoped for a spirit of good will for the future.[25] After her speech, Coya returned to Fosston Municipal Hospital to donate blood for Spot Reierson.

The DFL had challenged her, but she had beaten them. Evenson, like Lee before him, had been forced out of the district chairmanship. The DFL had openly declared war on Coya and she had beaten them one more time.

But this bitter convention fight was ignored by the press because a more sensational news story broke that Sunday as the convention concluded. Coya's husband Andy had been an alternate delegate from Red Lake County. During the convention fight he had requested that a statement he carried in his pocket be read to the delegates. Convention chairman Harvey Wilder had refused him permission.

Then, after the DFL announced its endorsement of Coya for Congress and the convention was adjourned, Andy released this startling statement to the press:

"I have as of this date, May 4, informed my wife, Coya Knutson, a Ninth District Representative in Congress, I do not want her to file for

re-election to Congress. I expect her to comply with this request. Therefore, because of my interest in the DFL Party, and as a party member, I believe it should be the business of this convention to discuss a candidate, or candidates to file at the primary so my wife's position will be filled again by a DFL member.[26]

The delicate balance Coya had maintained in public between her domestic and political lives had been shattered. An eager press seized upon the message and the letter was immediately reprinted in newspapers and repeated on radio and television newscasts across the nation.

Coya was in transit—heading for Fosston and then to the Twin Cities—when Andy's statement was released to the press and she was therefore unavailable for immediate comment. With no public statement issued by her office and no direct response from Coya herself, speculation and innuendo ran rampant in the wake of Andy's astonishing press release. *Fargo Forum* editor Lloyd Sveen used the phrase "Coya, Come Home" in an article about Andy's open letter to Coya. The Associated Press picked it up. The catch phrase, "Coya, Come Home," was born.

Chapter 13

AFTERMATH

*Don't you think it's time we farm women wake up...
Read instead of ironing sheets, pillowcases. Go over the
history of the U. S. It says "of the People," not "of the
men-folks."*

*Mrs. Sam Dean, Hurdsfield, North Dakota
Nonpartisan Leader: November 18, 1918*

Coya and Bill Kjeldahl were driving to Minneapolis to catch the "red-eye" flight to Washington. The two had talked themselves out during the grueling sessions at the convention in Crookston and had rehashed the troublesome events of the past several days. Now it was early evening and, as the miles rolled by, they had both fallen silent. Bill yawned and turned on the car radio.

Coya was driving. She loved to drive through the vast open fields on the country roads of northern Minnesota. It was May, one of her favorite months on the farm, when the newly cultivated fields had been seeded and the faintest haze of green shimmering on the dark earth showed signs of the emerging crop. As the long twilight deepened, Coya breathed in the fresh spring air and recalled her girlhood days on the farm. The musky scent of damp earth prompted a memory of herself as a child kneeling in an open field and staring at the feathery seedlings poking through the rough earth. How in the world, she had wondered, could tiny brown seeds sprout into plants that would someday turn into golden wheat stalks?

Coya's attention was caught by a news bulletin on the radio. She heard her name mentioned. Bill, who had been dozing for several minutes, also became alert. He turned up the volume and both listened intently to the report. Andy Knutson had released a statement to the press announcing that he did not want Coya to file for re-election. He expected his wife to comply with this request.

Coya and Bill were incredulous and they both laughed at Andy's absurd action. Bill asked "What has gotten into Andy?"

"It looks like he wants the spotlight," Coya answered.

They tried to make light of it, but, as Bill spun the dial, they heard the bulletin on one station after another. As they continued driving toward the Twin Cities, it became apparent that the hot news item of the evening was the marital strife between Congresswoman Coya Knutson and her husband Andy. It was no longer a laughing matter.

When they reached Lake Park, Minnesota Coya pulled into a gas station and telephoned former Democratic National Committeeman Barney Allen in Detroit Lakes. Barney had heard the news report, too, and asked them to stop by to discuss the matter.

When they arrived at his house half an hour later, Allen had sought advice from a number of people, among them Probate Judge Gus Landrum. Coya, Kjeldahl and Allen made a midnight visit to Judge Landrum. After considerable discussion, the four composed a brief press statement: "Family problems are a personal matter. I will not discuss it in the press."

Their decision was to avoid—at least for the present—any explanations or counteraccusations from Coya. "How do you deal with a thing like this?" Kjeldahl asked. "There are two sides to every story, but Coya can't tell her side without appearing to criticize Andy in public. That wouldn't be good policy."

After the statement was drafted, Coya and Kjeldahl continued their drive. Allen released the statement to the press, and then telephoned Hubert Humphrey's office in Washington D.C. Humphrey was not in. Allen left a message that Coya had agreed "to stick to this [the official] statement," and that he had consulted both Harvey Wilder and John Michels who hoped Humphrey would get in touch with her and urge her to hold fast to her statement. Allen added that "perhaps some Republican money has been smuggled to the 'old goat.'"[1]

Humphrey followed up the phone call with a letter to Allen: "I think your advice was sound and she has handled it well. The way it looks from here she came out way ahead."[2]

Coya, however, felt as though she had been kicked in the stomach. She did not think she had come out ahead with that brief press statement, but she did not know what else she could have said under the circumstances. It would have been worse to make hasty statements she would regret later, and she was glad she did not have to face reporters immediately. She needed time to think—to sort out her personal feelings as well as her political priorities.

She wanted to write a persuasive speech for the pending legislation on college loans. The bill to fund cystic fibrosis research would be coming up soon. She had planned to be back in Washington to handle legislative work for five days, then return to Minnesota to celebrate centennial ceremonies in St. Paul. And now—the letter. Everything had changed.

It was very late by the time Bill and Coya reached Minneapolis, where Coya would remain—avoiding reporters, according to their plan— while Bill returned to the office in Washington. She canceled her flight reservations and went to her sister's home. She would stay with Crystal while she sorted things out and assessed the damage Andy's press statement had caused. She tried to call Terry at college, unaware that he, too, was in Minneapolis. He was with the Luther College drama department rehearsing his role in Henrik Ibsen's *Brand* to be presented at the Lutheran Brotherhood Building theatre.

The furor created by Andy's initial announcement was magnified by a second press release that was also datelined Crookston, Minnesota, May 4, 1958. Andy complained that *"our homelife has deteriorated to the extent that it is practically nonexistent. I want to have the happy home that we enjoyed for many years prior to her election. Coya hasn't been home for Christmas for two years and for Easter the past three. I have seen our son but a few times and for only brief visits... Another reason for my request is her executive secretary, Bill Cheldahl [sic], who by his actions and dictatorial influence on my wife has taken the close relationship and affection we enjoyed before... Finally, I believe that it is useless for her to be elected as the decisions that are made are not hers but Cheldahl [sic], an individual who assumes no responsibility yet dictates the policy of her office."[3]

Andy's second statement provided a heyday for the press. Allega-

Andy's second statement provided a heyday for the press. Allegations of a romance with William O. (Bill) Kjeldahl and charges that the Congresswoman neglected her family would be the most effective in destroying Coya's personal and political image.

Terry heard about his father's statements to the press on Monday morning when a classmate showed him a copy of the *Minneapolis Morning Tribune*. He was shocked and angry and immediately telephoned Coya to ask how he could help. He tried to reach his mother at her Washington office, but it was not until later that day that her staff knew where she was. When Coya and Terry were eventually put in touch with each other, they agreed that Terry should talk with Charles Bailey of the *Tribune* in order to take some pressure off his mother. In his interview with Bailey, Terry said he felt his mother should run for re-election "on the basis of her achievements and her record in Washington. In politics, every family must be prepared to make sacrifices."[4] When Terry visited Coya he saw that "she was crushed, really crushed. I had never before seen her lose heart."

By midweek Coya had recovered her equanimity and called a news conference. She told the press flatly that she would run for office. "This is my job and I love it," she said. On the subject of whether William O. (Bill) Kjeldahl would continue as her administrative assistant, she answered "Absolutely. He is a very intelligent fellow and has tremendous ability. He will stay on."[5] She said that she considered her family life normal for two people whose interests had developed differently—her husband favored small town life and she preferred public life.

Her husband's demand that she withdraw from the race for re-election was strictly motivated by politics, and the current tempest had "background," she stated. Questioned as to whether the Come Home, Coya letter had killed her chances of re-election, she answered that she thought that "terribly wrong" because reports from newspapers all over the country had been favorable. Coya said she had a better chance than ever to be re-elected. "This has stirred up interest, and it has stirred up women."[6]

Meanwhile, Andy had made yet another announcement—a surprising reversal of his earlier statements—saying that he would, after all, wholeheartedly support his wife in her campaign if she would do two things: "fire William William O. (Bill) Kjeldahl and pay more attention to her home life. I didn't want her to quit Congress," Andy told the *Minneapolis Star*. "I just wanted her to come home more often." He had also wanted her to send her congressional paychecks to the bank in Oklee for deposit to their joint account. He claimed he did not want to hurt her politically and knew that she was busy so that she could not come home all the time. But he did want her home more often—he had not seen her in almost three years. He said that the last time he had heard from her was in a three-line note telling him how to handle the income tax return.

Andy claimed that when Coya first went to Washington, she had asked him to move there with her, but he had told her he didn't want to go because he had stomach trouble. He had told her he would stay home with their son, but after the first year, "she changed her tune and didn't say anything about me coming to Washington." He said he had asked Coya to fire William O. (Bill) Kjeldahl the previous fall, but she had told him, "I can't dump him. He is one of the ablest administrators on the Hill."[7]

This surprising about-face appeared in the newspapers only days after Andy's initial statement. From this point on, Andy backed down more and more; but it was too late. Earlier in their marriage Andy had not spoken up to his high-spirited wife, but he surely seemed to have found his tongue when it came to talking to reporters. Coya figured that "he loved the attention and that he could talk all he wanted to about wanting me to be elected again, but that he had said otherwise and the damage was done." To her his words were now a "lot of baloney" that only a few people believed. About moving to Washington, Coya thought that Andy was "singing in the breeze and that he never could or would leave Oklee."

Slowly the week passed. On the weekend, Coya rode in the Grand Parade in St. Paul to celebrate the Minnesota centennial. Coya felt she was the center of attention as she rode in an open convertible with Republican Congressman Walter H. Judd and Democratic Congressman John Blatnik. The *Minneapolis Tribune* reported: "Minnesotans along the parade route were for Coya all the way."

But Coya's spirits remained at low ebb despite this show of support. She felt humiliated by the public exposure of her marital problems. "I could have lain down and died in shame—and people calling my name and waving at me along the parade route hardly made me feel better—but somehow I had to go on. By the time that parade was over, I felt dead inside." Terry says that Coya looked stunning as she smiled and waved at the crowd.

Coya reflected bitterly that Andy's statements to the press belittled all that she had worked so hard for in Congress. She had tried to hide the strife in her marriage so that it would not interfere with her public life. Now, because of her husband's revelations, the unfolding drama of her unhappy personal life made front page news. While she was dealing with Andy's allegations and reporters who were hungry for more juicy news about the Knutson marital problems, legislation that she had painstakingly worked on for four years was coming up for floor debate in Congress. Her personal and political life were in disarray and she did not know which way to turn. It seemed that her own party had reason to ensure that public attention remained focused on the shambles of her family life.

DFLers did not tell reporters about the intraparty battle at the recent district convention. The former DFL leaders of the Ninth District did not want to release the news because they were embarrassed about the outcome of the convention election—they had again lost to Coya. In their Monday morning edition, The *Crookston Times*, which had not sent a reporter to cover the convention that was held in its city, claimed that "the Sunday Convention made no endorsements, and even Mrs Coya Knutson was not given endorsement backing."[8] The newspaper did not report the drawn-out battle for control of the district nor that the battle had been won by Coya's supporters. On Sunday, convention chairman Harvey Wilder had informed Myrtle McKenzie, the editor of the *Crookston Times*, that "there had been no discussion of support for Mrs Knutson to succeed herself," and added that no endorsements were made.

However, *Fargo Forum* editor Lloyd Sveen had attended the convention and the story that appeared in his paper's Monday edition was quite different. He wrote that "endorsement was 25 1/2 to 23 1/2 for Knutson, a clear-cut victory for Mrs Knutson." Sveen explained that a two-year undercover struggle had erupted at the convention, and when the six-hour battle of ballots was over, Congresswoman Knutson emerged with a full slate of officers pledged to her support. So intense was the fight, Sveen wrote, that delegates quarreled over procedure, rules and even over taking a coffee break. The coffee break lost, and the convention ran from 2:15 p.m. to 8:15 p.m.

When Myrtle McKenzie learned that she had not been told the truth, the newspaper ran a correction in which DFLers were blamed for giving false information. The *Crookston Times* claimed that not only convention chairman Harvey Wilder but also state Senator Louis Murray of East Grand Forks had told them that delegates to the coming state convention would attend it with no instruction regarding the congresswoman's support. Moreover, the *Crookston Times* reported that no delegate interviewed by them had indicated that the convention had been "anything but a harmonious affair."[9]

Myrtle McKenzie was upset. The *Crookston Times* was deluged with calls from news services all over the U.S., and she still did not have the correct story. She was especially angry with Spot Reierson, who had told her "in words that were partially unprintable" not to run the story about DFL dissension within the district.[10]

Other newspapers picked up the correct information. The *Fergus Falls Daily Journal* reported that the division cut through loyalties of liberal-conservative elements in the party. Conflict within county organizations was evident, the *Journal* said: Clay county (Moorhead) had cast three votes for Evenson and one vote for Michels, even though Marvin Evenson was endorsed by the county. A Clay delegate complained of Coya's people that "they treated us pretty rough. Several incumbent legislators said they were warned they should support Coya Knutson, or they might be embarrassed in their re-election campaign."[11]

Once the sensational Coya, Come Home story exploded in the press, Republican newspapers in the district no longer ignored the district convention fight. "Demand That Coya Fire Her Secretary Brings Bitter Fight Inside Party to Light", a *Fergus Falls Journal* headline announced. The article reported that *Fargo Forum* editor Lloyd Sveen had spent the weekend in St. Paul with a number of DFL politicians, and he contended that while the DFL put on a bold front in public, their private conversations showed that they were very much worried. "While the big headlines have tended to obscure the division in the Ninth District revealed by last week's bitter convention fight, party leaders here haven't forgotten it." The *Journal* reported that "they considered it a 'family fight' which must be settled in the district and were hopeful that neither faction would involve the state DFL in the fracas."[12]

The Coya, Come Home press releases made newspaper headlines all over the nation. A *New York Daily News* headline announced, "Demands Wife Quit Congress: Resents Her Right Hand Man." The

Washington News proclaimed, "Public Statement: Husband of Rep. Knutson Urges She Stay Home, Not Run Again." Across the Atlantic, the *London Daily Express* made it a front page story.[13]

Coya, her staff, and district spokesmen were asked to comment on Andy's letters, but reporters were given no more than the original press statement. "'Personal Matter' Declares Coya," said an Associated Press headline. "An office aide of Mrs Knutson said today the congresswoman had telephoned from Minnesota to say that her personal relationship with her husband is a personal matter and she does not care to discuss it with the press."[14]

Andy had his telephone service disconnected and reporters could not reach him. Omer Sundrud, the editor of the *Oklee Herald*, complained in print that he had been roused from deep slumber at 1:30 a.m. by a Minneapolis wire service. When Sundrud subsequently interviewed him at the hotel, Andy proudly displayed a stack of some fifty letters he had received from fans around the nation and commented, "I meant what I said."[15] The calls to the Oklee editor continued with little interruption for a week after Andy's letter had been released to the press.

Mrs Arthur Edwards of Johnstown, Pennsylvania wrote to the *Oklee Herald* that if Coya loved her husband and son she should quit and stay at home "as God meant." "If a woman is married, she should quit working—there should be a law," she wrote. St. Paul's Mother of the Year declared that "any woman's place is in the home. Home is the first duty." The president of the Minnesota department of the American Legion Auxiliary said, "At the moment, perhaps, she ought to give up politics and go back home."[16]

In support of Coya, a Daytona, Florida newspaper editorial stated that "if Mr Knutson really wanted to see his wife more often he might consider that the distance is no more from Oklee to Washington than it is from Washington to Oklee. Marital obligations and airplanes work both ways." Ruth Montgomery wrote in the *San Francisco Examiner* that sympathy for Rep. Coya Knutson's complaining husband was as hard to find on Capitol Hill as votes to abolish Mother's Day.

Doris Fleeson commented in the Washington, D.C. *Evening Star* about the political double standard that plagued Coya. Fleeson said that the congresswoman's colleagues in Washington lauded her as a hard worker and that many in Washington, not all of them women, felt that Coya was marked down as "fair game" simply because she was a woman: "There are many better stories here than *l'affaire* Knutson and they are about much more prominent people, but it is not considered cricket to use them as a political weapon. The lesson is that, as a practical matter, women are held to a far higher standard of accountability in politics than men are. Women clearly cannot count on the club spirit for protection."[17]

When the terrible week was finally over and she had performed her ceremonial duties for the centennial celebration, Coya sat alone in the Minneapolis-St. Paul airport waiting for the night flight to Washington. She reflected on her life with Andy and the events of the past week. Nothing remained of her marriage when she and her son had left in haste for Washington D.C. four years ago, but at that time only she and Terry knew it. Now, because of Andy's letters, the world knew it, too. There was nothing she could do to change these events, but there was plenty she had to do in Washington, D.C., while there was still time. Her bills on cystic fibrosis and college loans were coming up, and this session would be her busiest yet. If it proved to be her last session in Congress, then she had better "make hay while the sun is still shining."

When she arrived at her desk the following morning, the in-tray was piled high with letters. She glanced at several of them and then opened a desk drawer to take out another letter she had placed there the day she had left for the district convention. She read:

Oklee, Minn.
April 29, 1958
My dear wife,
Coya I want you to tell the people of the 9th Dist. Sun. May 4, 1958, that you are true [sic] in politics. That you want to go home & make a home for your son & husband. As your husband, I compel you to do this. I'm tired of being apart from my family. I'm sick and tired having you run around with other men all the time, & not you [sic] husband.
I love you honey.
Your husband
Andy Knutson [18]

Coya studied the sheet of lined paper a long time. She had scarcely glanced at the letter when it had arrived. She had been in a great hurry that day, and she remembered she had been relieved that

Andy's letter had not been another plea for money—whenever she saw his familiar handwriting on an envelope, she had come to expect that. It would have been a lot closer to the truth had he said, "I love your money."

Her thoughts were dark but she did not want to let them dwell long on bitter memories. She pushed the pain out of her mind and shoved Andy's letter under her desk blotter. She needed to get back to work. Blessed work.

It was music that helped restore her spirits. That week she played "Happy Days Are Here Again" on her accordion for a Democratic National Committee fund-raising event at the Sheraton Park Hotel in Washington, D.C.[19] She had also composed lyrics supporting Alaska's statehood and sang them to the tune of "Rudolph the Red-nosed Reindeer:"

Welcome Alaska statehood
She'll be number forty-nine
One of the U.S. family
Hope you'll think that we are fine.
All of us join to cheer you
Make your path to liberty
To hasten the U.S. Senate
A shining star you'll surely be.[20]

On June 30, 1958 the U.S. Senate approved statehood for Alaska and that summer Coya had many opportunities to sing her song at Washington gatherings. She also worked to secure approval by the Civil Aeronautics Board for Northwest Airlines as the carrier between Minneapolis and Anchorage.

Coya needed her equanimity to face the reactions of colleagues to Andy's press releases. DFLers outside her support group did not come to her defense. East Grand Forks state senator Louis Murray, who had been a friend of Coya's in the Minnesota legislature, announced he would seek Coya's seat if she quit.[21] Coya was not surprised—she knew that other DFLers wanted her job.

Former Ambassador Eugenie Anderson, who had been promised endorsement for the U. S. Senate by Minnesota DFL leaders, was asked whether Coya Knutson should seek a third term. Anderson would make no comment.[22] It seemed the press was always trying to foment a feud between Eugenie and Coya, but they would not succeed. According to Coya, there was tacit agreement between the women that "I would keep my mouth shut and Anderson would keep still."

The reactions of Coya's colleagues on Capitol Hill were mixed. Some had little sympathy for Andy. Representative Harold D. Cooley, chairman of the House Agriculture Committee, sniffed disdainfully at Coya's husband's plea and said, "She's a faithful and diligent member of my committee. In fact, she's a devoted and dedicated public servant who is intensely interested in the welfare of the farmer. What's the matter with her husband, anyway?" Republican Congressman Richard M. Simpson, a fellow Agriculture Committee member, grinned when asked about Coya's plight, and joked that "I'm for the ladies. After all, they cast more votes than the men, and Coya Knutson is a nice looking Swedish blonde." Another Agriculture Committee member, in a back-handed compliment, admitted that she worked at her job, which "was a pleasant surprise, because she is a cheerful blonde, addicted to rather bright costume jewelry, and I had thought she might trade on her personality." [23]

Indeed, not only some of her colleagues but also many reporters were inclined to emphasize her appearance: "A blonde with a positive manner," a "blonde, blue-eyed wife," "a plump blonde who always seems excited," "the honey-blonde congresswoman," and "a chubby blonde with twinkling blue eyes."[24] Describing Coya as a "trim, brown-eyed Democrat," Virginia Keating reported in Albany's *Times Union* that the "blonde congresswoman" gave the major address to a thousand women at a district meeting of the Lutheran Women's Missionary League.[25]

Other married congresswomen had the spotlight turned on them now that the question of "home or politics" had been raised. When *U.S.News and World Report* interviewed congresswomen for an article titled, "Women's Dilemma, Home or Politics," their answers indicated that the question should be phrased, "How can home and politics be combined?"

Former Congresswoman Clare Boothe Luce suggested that a congresswoman's home should be within commuting distance of the Capital—Minnesota was too far away from Washington. "A congresswoman's choice, in case her home is not within commuting distance, is to move her home to where her job is, or she won't have a home. If she has growing children, she plainly can't do a job as a mother if she is separated from them for long periods of time."[26]

Luce's home was in Connecticut, which was within commuting distance, and her husband, *Time-Life* publisher Henry Luce, often went to Washington, D.C. on business. They had no children to raise. Besides, the Luces' marital situation was so different from Coya's that they could hardly be compared. Luce alluded to this when she explained, "I think it is easier for a man who is successful himself to adjust to a successful wife than for a man who is a failure."

U. S. News and World Report compared the other married congresswomen's home lives and their lifestyles with Coya's. Martha Griffiths and her husband, attorney Hicks G. Griffiths, spent weekends together either in their Washington apartment or their Detroit home. Martha complained that she was apt to buy more food than if she just maintained one home because they often had to change their plans at the last minute.

Erwin and Iris Blitch bought a home in Virginia and their son, a student at George Washington University law school, resided there with his mother. Erwin maintained the family home at Homerville, Georgia where he ran a timber business. The Blitches spent weekends and holidays together, with one or the other commuting. When Congress adjourned, Iris made a "beeline for home," she said, and she was proud to report that her husband had suggested that she run for office.

Frost R. and Cecil Harden, who lived in a Washington hotel when Congress was in session, wrestled for four years with the problem of each working in different parts of the country. When Frost retired the year Cecil began her third term, he began to spend most of his time in Washington with only occasional trips to Indiana to look after business interests. They had a son, 43, who was a physician. Frost remarked that a husband had nothing to lose by having his wife in politics. "If he accepts it as I have, it is all for the gain."

When Gracie Pfost was elected to Congress from Idaho in 1952, John Walter Pfost resigned his job as chief engineer for a milk company and moved to the Capital to be with his wife. They had no children. They spent eight months in Washington and vacationed at their ranch in Idaho. "My husband has never been on my payroll," said Congresswoman Pfost, "but he has done everything he could to help me. He campaigns with me and sits in my office, both in Washington and Idaho, where he is available to turn to and talk over problems with at all times." John Pfost said that he could not "see much difference in a woman's holding an elective office and in her holding a job in business."

Joseph and Florence Dwyer were just arriving at a solution. Since she had been elected to Congress in 1956, Florence had been living in a hotel in Washington and commuting to New Jersey on weekends. In 1958 Dwyer retired from his public relations job to work full time with his wife as her adviser. "I never took one step in civic affairs and in politics without consulting my husband," said Congresswoman Dywer. "As my son grew up, he joined in the family decision making. I doubt if I would have done it without their enthusiastic support."

All but Coya and Edith Green of Oregon commuted weekly or had husbands who moved to Washington. Although Green was rounding out her fourth year in Congress, *U. S. News and World Report* recorded that the couple had not yet found a solution to their 3,000-mile separation. Their 16-year-old son, Richard, lived with his mother in Washington and their second son was married. "What keeps Mrs Green and me going would separate others," said Arthur Green. "We will have been married 25 years in August. We have our family. We think an awful lot of our sons and are working in their interest."

While great readjustments had had to be made, most of these couples had resolved the dilemma by combining home and politics. Of the congresswomen interviewed, *U.S.News and World Report* referred to six as "Mrs," followed by by their husbands' names; only Coya Knutson and Clare Boothe Luce were identified by their first names.

Washington *Evening Star* columnist Doris Fleeson pinpointed the double standard that existed for women politicians when she wrote that many of the wives of the 515 male members of Congress were unhappy in exactly the same way as Mr Knutson, and those wives mentioned that fact freely. While that was a hardy staple of political conversation, wives' complaints never seemed to be news. If a congresswoman had an unhappy husband back home, his criticisms could make headlines. If, on the other hand, a congressman's wife complained, little attention would be given. Sometimes, Fleeson wrote, a departing statesman would mention that he was bowing to his homesick wife's wishes, but that fact would be recorded unobtrusively in the story because that would rarely be believed to be the real reason for his departure.

Fleeson added that "more is expected of women than of men, in ability, character and conservative behavior. Women never get to run for office unless their personal affairs are in perfect order, which is not true of the other sex. They are not perhaps watched more closely than their male colleagues because they are women, but because there are so few of them."[27]

Jack Anderson, writing for syndicated columnist Drew Pearson, described the Knutsons in romantic terms: Coya as "golden-haired," Andy as "big, brooding. Through it all he swore his undying love for her." He sided with Coya as he told of her marital problems: "For years, Andy blew his wife's money on costly drinking sprees and sponged off her between binges. She paid for most of his living expenses, bought him a 1955 Plymouth and kept him in cigar money—he smokes twenty a day. For the sake of his pride, she painted her husband's name—'Andy's Hotel'—on a small, two story frame hotel she owns. Several months ago her patience ran out. Oklee merchants received a letter from her, warning that she could no longer make good her husband's debts. Andy threatened to sell out unless she released the purse strings."[28]

The aspect of Andy's letter that columnists did not write about was his jealousy of William O. (Bill) Kjeldahl. When Andy identified William O. (Bill) Kjeldahl by name, he loaded the issue with speculation and gossip about a love triangle. Although not mentioned in news commentary and not alluded to in print, the suspicion of sexual impropriety lingered and severely damaged Coya's reputation. Coya held fast to the statement agreed on by her political advisers that family problems were personal and that she would not discuss them in the press, but she knew that by saying nothing she was also lending credence to the speculation about her and William O. (Bill) Kjeldahl. It was bitter medicine. She had gotten along fine in politics for eight years without her husband's help or active support, and now his public statements were destroying her career.

References to the Coya, Come Home story were in the news throughout the six months preceding the election. When Coya would not say anything about her husband, reporters sought out Andy, thus keeping alive the embers of speculation and innuendo.

Coya's public answer to the dilemma of career versus home was clear and concise. She said that marriage and career can be combined, and that millions of women were doing that. "Women don't want to stay inside their kitchen walls anymore. They want to keep abreast of the times to prepare their children better for life and living—and also to see they're well provided for," she said in a speech in Albany, New York in June 1958.[29]

Coya knew she could not let the support she was finding in the nation's press lull her into thinking that all was well. Her future depended on how people in the Ninth District regarded a woman's career outside the home. She read some of the articles sent to her from newspapers around the country, but she focused her attention on the clippings and letters she received from her district. The weekly and daily papers of villages and towns in the Ninth District offered a range of differing viewpoints.

B. L. Benshoof, the editor of Detroit Lakes' *Becker County Record*, wrote, "It is rather hard to conceive of a personal letter published all over the country as being an effective way for a husband to induce his wife to return and resume her normal duties about the house."

J. H. Ulven, editor of the *Park Region Echo* in Alexandria, asked "Does the DFL Party Feel Too Cocky? To leave Washington just to make a home for Andy is so senseless and absurd that only a few troublemakers and weak-minded persons will heed the wail." Ulven commented that he thought Coya "made the mistake of her life when she married Andrew Knutson, but for some to bring cheap domestic affairs against a congresswoman of the ability and courage of the Ninth District lawmaker just about hits the bottom."

The *Badger Enterprise* attacked her administrative assistant, commenting that "ridding herself of William O. (Bill) Kjeldahl could help smooth ruffled feelings" and that "strong arm tactics of her supporters at the convention did not endear her to people."[30]

Republican papers promoted sympathy for a neglected husband: "Will It Ever Be The Same?" asked the *Fergus Falls Daily Journal* in an editorial reprinted from the *Fairmont Sentinel*: "Washington, the nation and the world will probably manage to get along, should Coya decide to come home, but for Andrew—if she doesn't—the world would probably never be quite the same. Those of us who are ruled by the finest in human emotions join with Andrew in the hope that Coya will come home, and that they will live happily ever after." But for all the rhetoric that espoused being "ruled by the finest in human emotions," the editor's conclusion—in boldface print—was strictly political: "Republicans and Independents in the Ninth District have a golden opportunity to render yeoman service in the cause of humanity. Let them make hay."[31]

Republicans referred to State Representative Odin E. Langen of Kennedy, who was expected to oppose Coya in the general election, as a gentleman who would not think of commenting on a lady's personal situation. According to a news article in the *Fergus Falls Journal*, Langen "literally hid from the press" while in Fergus Falls for the centennial celebration. 'I don't know anything about it [the letter] and I don't want to comment on it,' Langen said."[32]

Perhaps the most emotional story was a front-page interview with fifty-year-old Andy, under the by-line of Donald H. McKenzie, Republican publisher of the *Crookston Daily Times* and the husband of editor Myrtle McKenzie: "He's a lonely man, this Andy Knutson. The loneliness is written all over his thin, somewhat careworn face. It is betrayed by the slight stoop of his shoulders. It is evident in the somehow desperate way he clinches an ever-present cigar between his teeth. It is brought out most of all by the way he doesn't want to talk about his troubles, but when he does start the words pour out as though they have been too long damned up within him. 'The only thing I want is that Coya should come back and make our home as happy as it used to be,' Andy said as the sun shone on his eyeglasses and brought the sharply-etched wrinkles of his face into prominence. 'I wouldn't have said anything about this if we hadn't had such a happy life before.' He spoke with deep affection of their son, who had recently graduated from a Virginia military school, and was presently in college. With obvious pride, Andy exhibited a picture of his family. Taken ten or so years before, the photo showed a far heavier-appearing man than the Andy of today. 'We were all happy together then,' Andy reminisced with a touch of wistfulness in his pleasant voice. We thanked Andy, leaving him standing on the sidewalk of Oklee's tidy main street. As we drove away, Andy remained standing, cigar in mouth. As the evening shadows lengthened, the shadows in Andy's face seemed to deepen too."[33]

"Poor old Andy, he sure got stuck with a terrible wife," Coya thought as she read McKenzie's maudlin interview. She could imagine the smug and self-satisfied reaction of readers who saw Andy as a patient, long-suffering martyr to Coya's ruthless quest for political power at the expense of marital fidelity and duty. Coya knew how damaging this article would be to the public's perception of her. She could not defend herself against this sort of damning portrait in which she was painted as a vengeful, coldhearted woman who had abandoned her husband and child. How could she counter McKenzie's portrayal of the "lonely," "desperate," "wistful" husband who only wanted his wife to come back?

Would anyone care that Andy is losing weight because he replaces food with alcohol, she wondered. Coya reflected that little could be said in her defense that would erase this ugly image of her. No wonder Langen did not have to comment. After Andy released his letters to the press, whenever Coya made public appearances, newspaper reports would make reference to her troubled homelife.

Press coverage dominated even minor events in her career—those which normally would have gone unnoticed. When Coya was one of thirty teachers nominated for a Maria Sanford civic-leadership award from the General Federated Women's Club, she, rather than the winner Mae Barsness, got the headline in the *Minneapolis Tribune*: "Coya in State; Will Visit Oklee 'If She Has Time.'" The article reported that "a laughing Representative Coya Knutson" went to the honors dinner in Minneapolis, "leaving her well-publicized domestic squabble outside."[34]

The Federated Women's Clubs also sponsored a Maria Sanford essay contest for high school students, and the award was to be presented by Coya. Marge Michels, Ninth District DFL Secretary, recalls that the Coya, Come Home letter had a tremendous influence on the club women who attended the banquet. Many of them would not speak to Coya. "The women stood around in little groups, gossiping and eyeing Coya, but not talking to her. I was furious, and I decided that Coya was the most maligned woman in Minnesota."[35]

However, other women's groups saw her as a staunch ally and she enjoyed celebrity status as a guest speaker. She was invited to give the major address to the thousand women attending a district meeting of the Lutheran Women's Missionary League in Albany, New York, and told them she still thought of herself as a country girl: "I was green as a cabbage when I ran for the legislature, but I felt I could be of more service to people if I went into government work. I'd have a larger orchestra and a bigger repertoire."[36]

At another gathering, Coya reflected on her choice of a political career: "It's no easy decision for a man to make—to embark on a legislative career. That decision is doubly difficult for a woman." She warned distaff office seekers that a woman in political work has many strikes against her because she is vulnerable to criticism not aimed at men. "Don't enter into personality or faction fights," she cautioned. "The less said, the better—bite your tongue but don't fight back. Stay above it".[37]

She quoted the British Statesman Edmund Burke, who in 1774 said "It is a representative's duty to sacrifice his repose, his pleasure, and his satisfaction to his constituents, and above all to prefer their interests to his own. " Coya said that she had made Burke's precepts her own.

Coya's legislative work in Washington remained her top priority. The 85th Congress was a busy session and she was conscientious about being available for floor votes. Coya was absent for only one of the 93 roll call votes.

In its coverage of her re-election campaign, the press began to shift its focus from Andy and Coya's marital problems to DFL dissatisfaction with Bill William O. (Bill) Kjeldahl. An "unnamed DFL official" who had known William O. (Bill) Kjeldahl for more than eight years interpreted the situation for the *Fergus Falls Journal*: "Bill seems to be one of those people whose personality just seems to rub me the wrong way—and not just me, but many others. Ever since I've known him he's been hanging around fringe outfits in the party." The anonymous DFLer said that William O. (Bill) Kjeldahl had made Senator Humphrey cool his heels waiting to see Coya and had kept her away from the district chairman, which was "part of the reason" the fuss was stirred up in the Ninth District."

The extent of William O. (Bill) Kjeldahl's influence over Coya was a prime issue among her detractors. The *Crookston Times* reported that "Andy's distaste for the 'talented' youth is shared by a good many others. Andy's request she return to Oklee to take up again her role of wife and mother is not really the important issue. Voters should instead decide if they are voting for power behind the throne: an ambitious, would-be anonymous nonentity."[38] A similar editorial in the Bemidji State College student newspaper claimed that "William O. (Bill) Kjeldahl and his minions had put on a 'puppet show' at the District convention. We'd like Coya without William O. (Bill) Kjeldahl and Gerner."[39] The *Minneapolis Star* reported that "Citizens of Oklee were generally unanimous in giving William O. (Bill) Kjeldahl much credit for organizing Coya's successful political campaigns. Most were also of the opinion that Representative Knutson had the right to do what she pleased. They said their congressional representative had 'done a mighty fine job for us.'"[40]

William O. (Bill) Kjeldahl's name came up repeatedly in press coverage of Coya and that helped fuel the flames of gossip. Linking the congresswoman and her young assistant romantically was the real political dynamite. The talk was that they were having an affair. Coya tried to set the record straight, but her attempts to do so misfired. She defended William O. (Bill) Kjeldahl and many read that as proof that the rumors of romance between them were true. In "Coya's Capital Chat," she wrote that "there is no member of Congress with greater fortune in securing an assistant with the widespread qualities, imagination, foresight and integrity. He [William O. (Bill) Kjeldahl] has accomplished *every job* I have delegated him to do and that really frightens my foes."[41]

She said that William O. (Bill) Kjeldahl, with help from Congressman John Blatnik, had been responsible for organizing her office. She reminded readers that she had sent William O. (Bill) Kjeldahl to Minnesota to be campaign director for Senator Kefauver, and could still hear the thunderous roar that that produced. They had planned the campaign and won the primary which "made it possible for either Senator Humphrey or Senator Kefauver to become Vice President." She then sent William O. (Bill) Kjeldahl back to Minnesota to help dislodge the opposition to her among the district officers. Spot Reierson had laid the groundwork for her, but when he had to return to hospital with a bleeding ulcer the night before the district convention, Bill organized the delegates that Spot had lined up. She mentioned William O. (Bill) Kjeldahl's high school achievements and Korean War record, concluding: "Thank God I had the wisdom to recognize and secure such talent to help elect me to Congress."

When Hubert Humphrey read this column, he was not pleased. He wrote to Ray Hemenway: "I urged her not to make Bill William O. (Bill) Kjeldahl the issue. This newsletter will undoubtedly make headlines in Minnesota. It is most indiscreet and could cause her a great deal of trouble. What she had to say about Bill William O. (Bill) Kjeldahl and his work in 1955-56 and 1958 could be the subject of an investigation by General Accounting Office, and indeed, a very hot political issue in the hands of any clever Republican. I have advised Coya to get her campaign on high ground at once—to talk issues and not personalities. If she doesn't, there will be plenty of trouble."[42]

Humphrey's fears of an investigation were not realized.

State legislator Harvey Wilder, who was up for re-election, wrote Coya a letter echoing Humphrey's words. He was the district convention chairman who had not allowed Andy to read his letter to the assembly. "Let's face it: That while I personally have a great deal of admiration for Bill and respect for his ability, yet he don't cotton too well with many real liberals. Keep him on your payroll but keep him out of the District in this coming campaign." He concluded: "Well Coya, my idea of a real friend is one who will tenderly admonish another of their faults. If these are the facts, then I hope that you do something to correct them."[43]

Before he sent this letter to Coya, Wilder sent a copy to Spot Reierson with a note. "Let me know, Spot, if this meets with your approval." Spot replied, "Cut this out— *'Keep him on your payroll but,'*—and leaving in— *'Keep him out of the District.'*"[44]

William O. (Bill) Kjeldahl continued to be under attack as the Svengali who dominated the housewife from Oklee. Similar accusations were hurled at the young male adviser of Republican Senator Margaret Chase Smith of Maine. Coya says that "people at that time did not believe that a woman was capable of doing all that legislative work." While there was support for, as well as criticism of both Coya and Andy after the letter, no one other than Coya supported Bill.

As Bill became the villain in the drama, Andy began to rehabilitate his public image and defend himself against earlier charges. Andy refuted Jack Anderson's claim that he was in arrears in Oklee. "I pay my bills—just ask anyone in Oklee," he told a reporter, and added that he was not sorry for the plea to Coya. He also stated that he had paid someone in Oklee to type the letter.[45]

However, Jack Anderson's charges had been correct. An Oklee banker remembers that Coya circulated a notice to local businessmen that disclaimed responsibility for any debts that her husband might incur.[46] Coya also published a disclaimer for her husband's debts in the *Oklee Herald.*

Taking this drastic action had been a difficult decision for Coya to make, but Andy's demands for money had become unreasonable. He had insisted that she deposit her congressional salary in their joint account in Oklee where he could manage it. In cutting Andy off from her earnings, she had not left him destitute; he still had some income from the hotel and could supplement it by working at odd jobs.

Gunhild also contributed to household expenses out of her monthly income from the sale of the farm. But Coya knew that her public disclosure would be humiliating to him. For Andy it was the last straw. She had not only taken away his spending money, but she had diminished him in the eyes of the community. Andy was mortified by the publication of Coya's disclaimer for his debts and the subsequent comments on that action by Jack Anderson.

After Jack Anderson's column was published, a group of seventeen men calling themselves "Friends of Andy Knutson Committee" signed a public notice in the *Oklee Herald* stating that Andy was neither alcoholic nor paranoid, and that he was a man of responsibility who paid his debts.

This ad further polarized townspeople, with some citizens openly lining up behind Coya or Andy. Others were left in the middle: they liked Coya and thought she was doing a fine job for them in Congress, and they liked Andy and did not want to reject him.

Political supporters who knew the true situation begged her to tell the press that Andy was an alcoholic and to explain the circumstances of her married life. Coya wanted to adhere strictly to her initial press release: no comment on her personal life. She felt that revealing her personal story to the public could not help her campaign and would distract attention from the political issues she did want to discuss.

Although Coya did not talk publicly about her problems at home, she did take action to set the record straight in Oklee. A tersely worded letter authorized removal of the office sign at Andy's Hotel: "The bearer of this letter has the authority to remove from Andy's Hotel the painted sign entitled 'Office of Coya Knutson.' This is government property and it will be removed to the District Office at Crookston, Minnesota."[47]

Four weeks after Andy's press statements, the story was still news. Coya had five months to campaign for re-election. As she prepared to leave Washington for the DFL convention in Minnesota, Coya hoped that the negative publicity would soon run its course and that her constituents would focus their attention on her record in Congress.

Coya quoted a couplet in "Chat:" *Two people looked out from prison bars; One saw the MUD the other the STARS.*[48] Coya thought she could ignore the mud.

Chapter 14

OUTSIDE THE
LOCKER ROOM

What about those free love books in our state library? I tell you ladies it is the duty of every one of us mothers to go to the polls on March sixteen 1920 and vote against this man.

"Red Flame Denounces Townleyism"
Red Flame (IVA): January 3, 1920

Upon their arrival in Minneapolis for the state convention, Coya and Bill Kjeldahl were summoned to a meeting called by L. J. Lee and Marvin Evenson to discuss their dissatisfaction with Kjeldahl as Coya's administrative assistant. Spot Reierson and John Michels also attended. Lee and Evenson contended that Kjeldahl's influence on Coya was dictatorial and that he was preventing them from communicating with her. They insisted that she dismiss Kjeldahl.

Coya was adamant: Kjeldahl would remain on her staff. Bill did his work reliably and well, and no one else was as conversant with the district as he was. Besides, if she did fire him or if Bill quit, people would suspect that "where there is smoke there is fire."

Neither side listened to the other and the meeting ended in a shouting match. Evenson thought the situation was made worse by the confrontation.[1] He felt that once more Coya was getting her way—she would not replace Kjeldahl. As a result of Coya's intransigence, district DFL leaders resolved to turn her out of office. Only Spot remained on Coya's side.

Kjeldahl hated being under fire, but he would not alter his style to accommodate anyone. Although he had been thrust into the glare of publicity by Andy's press release Kjeldahl chose not to make a public statement, believing that there was nothing he could say in his defense that would alter public opinion.[2] George Farr, a DFLer from Moorhead who was running for Minnesota State Auditor at the time, claims that severe criticism of Stevenson for being divorced lingered on from the Kefauver-Stevenson race. "Morality was the quiet issue here," he says.

Kjeldahl was not a ladies' man. The slim, darkly handsome young man may have provoked jealousy in Andy, but there was no indication of any romantic attraction between Kjeldahl and Coya. DFLers regarded him as an intensely ambitious, ruthless and power-hungry congressional aid who was using Coya as a steppingstone to further his own political career. They felt that he had overplayed his hand and had assumed too much control and influence over Coya. She was the elected official, not Bill Kjeldahl. The truth was that Kjeldahl was shy and so quiet that staff members nicknamed him "The Thinker." Rae Arliss Murray, who had a summer job with Coya as an office assistant, recalls that Kjeldahl was fiercely protective of his boss and tried to act as a buffer between Coya and everyone else, particularly journalists.[3]

However much Coya depended on him, Bill was a political liability. A newspaper article reported that in assessing the damage of the Coya, Come Home letter to Knutson's political career, a DFL party official had described the problem as centering not around Coya's marriage but around Bill Kjeldahl's treatment of congressmen and the district chairman.[4] According to Marge Michels, "Lee, Evenson and Hemenway hated Bill Kjeldahl because he restricted their access to Coya. Bill was young and had not developed the hard crust needed for politics. Kjeldahl did not know how to stand up to tough politicians like Lee and Evenson, and he tried to ignore them rather than deal with them. They interpreted his behavior as a power play. They thought he isolated her so that he could manipulate her. From the outside, the ousted party leaders could not see that Coya was in charge."

Lee and Evenson wasted no time in taking action. The day after the meeting, they announced to the press that an organization had been formed to oppose Representative Knutson in the Ninth District. A news release stated that "unless an alternative is offered the people of the Ninth District, the voters will turn to the Republican party for relief."

In a session closed to the press, twenty people in the newly-formed organization formulated a resolution requesting that the Minnesota DFL Convention refrain from endorsing Coya for Congress. A second resolution called for the formation of an organization to "foster and promote the principles of the DFL Party and the National Democratic party and to elect a person to the office of Congressman who can and will command the respect and confidence of the voters."

Five reasons for opposing Coya Knutson were given:

1) The DFL party has been distorted to serve the personal interest of a group not interested in the true welfare of Ninth District people.

2) The congresswoman arrogantly refused to give support to Senator Hubert Humphrey in 1956 for vice-president.

3) She has absented herself from Congress for long periods.

4) Her staff has usurped political power and dictated to and threatened party workers and officials.

5) Because the GOP will attempt to capitalize on the congresswoman's difficulties with her husband and that may create sufficient dissension to lose the congressional seat.[5]

These were strong words, but the DFL leadership felt they were necessary to justify opposing the incumbent congresswoman who was in control of district offices.

The list of nine names proposed as possible opponents to Coya in the primary election included L. J. Lee and Marvin Evenson, both former chairmen of the Ninth District. State Representatives Ben Wichterman of Plummer and Louis Murray of East Grand Forks were also proposed as suitable candidates. Some of the officers of this newly-formed organization were former supporters of Coya—including Millie Melby, a friend and campaign companion from Oklee and Harding C. Noblitt, the professor who had invited Coya to speak at Concordia College in 1954.

While final preparations for the DFL state convention were being made, media attention focused on Ambassador Eugenie Anderson, another woman who was fighting for political survival. She and Congressman Eugene McCarthy were vying for the DFL nomination for U. S. Senator. The *Fargo Forum* reported that a high-ranking party official claimed that if Anderson were to win the nomination over McCarthy, she would "undoubtedly be hurt by the Coya affair."[6]

When Coya was asked which of the senatorial candidates she favored, she chose McCarthy because she felt that his experience as a congressman had prepared him for the job. Although Anderson had worked in the DFL party since its birth and had been the nation's first woman ambassador, she had not had legislative experience. Both candidates predicted they would win on the second ballot, but McCarthy easily captured the nomination.

At the convention, Ninth District party members expressed strong resentment against Coya. Anti-Coya delegates from Oklee, referring to themselves as the "duly elected and acknowledged DFL organization in the 9th Congressional District," tried to prevent the state endorsement of Coya by sending a telegram to the convention that stated: "We will endeavor to deal with the insurgent group which has arisen in 9th district and divert them from their present destructive practices... [The insurgent group] was organized to further the political careers of a few self important individuals they are blatantly attempting to ignore local sentiment, party philosophy and the high ideals of good government. They are constantly attempting to destroy DFL strongholds which do not conform to their dictates. Their recent action clearly demonstrates they have no intention of letting democracy rule the 9th District."[7] The telegram was signed by W.W. Turgeon, DFL chairman of Red Lake County, and seventeen Oklee residents.

On the second day of the convention, delegates had to deal with the "Coya problem." The endorsement committee brought a motion to the floor endorsing all DFL congressmen seeking re-election. However, this motion did not stand because the rules committee recommended that the state convention not endorse any congressional candidates, and the convention voted to accept this recommendation. But Coya's campaign chairman would not accept the decision and a fight over endorsement of Coya broke out among delegates.

Gus Landrum, who had helped draft her press release in the wake of the Coya, Come Home letter, urged endorsement because "lack of it would be a slap at Coya." After much discussion the convention reversed its decision and endorsed the four incumbent congressmen and Congresswoman Knutson.[8] She tried to smooth over hard feelings by delivering a speech to the convention in which she pledged her support of the entire DFL ticket. Coya had again won the bout, but the main event was still ahead.

Coya wrote to Spot Reierson to tell him that he, more than anyone else, was responsible for her survival at the convention. "I personally still have a little more work to do in contacting a few more people, but I feel that you beyond everyone else showed the greatest understanding in trying to work out a solution."[9]

The relative calm after the convention lasted only a short time. Marvin Evenson announced to the press his candidacy for the congressional seat held by Coya. "It has become very evident," he said, "that deep concern is being expressed in all areas of the ninth over dictatorial and arrogant performance of the district congresswoman and her newly-elected district officers." He asserted that citizens were "expressing doubt that Knutson's record contributes to the House and the prestige of the district."[10]

Marvin Evenson, like Coya, was also a native of North Dakota. Married and the father of four children, Evenson traveled throughout the Ninth District as an air-conditioning and heating-equipment salesman. He felt he knew what the voters wanted, and he was very unhappy about being ousted as district chairman.

Coya decided that the best way to combat Evenson's opposition was to get back to Washington, D.C. She was ready to work harder than ever on impending legislation, sensing that her achievements in Congress would be the most effective challenge to Evenson's campaign.

Meanwhile Coya's supporters in Minnesota, convinced that the DFL network of campaigners would not be available to her, organized "Coya's Continuous Volunteers." Their mission was to "promote the re-election of Coya Knutson or whomever members shall designate." Membership was open to "all men and women who believe in the principles and program advocated by Congresswoman Knutson." Contributions of not less than one dollar per month were required from members who would each receive a card bearing the congresswoman's signature.[11] Listed as members of the executive committee of the Continuous Volunteers were Spot Reierson; Cliff Bouvette, editor of the *Kittson County Enterprise*; Gus Landrum, chairman of the Coya for Congress Volunteer Committee; and John Michels, the district chairman.

Coya's Continuous Volunteers did not live up to their name. In fact, little was done by this group beyond creating the document specifying its aims. Coya has no recollection of the organization. Marge Michels, one of its members, explains that "we were not going to be pushed off the edge of the earth by L. J. Lee and Marv Evenson. Coya's Continuous Volunteers was Spot Reierson's brainchild and we all agreed to it because we wanted to form an organization to oppose the DFL's splinter group. It's very difficult to get something of that nature going, and it turned out to be a kind of conversational agreement, a pledge of loyalty from those who had invested a great deal of effort and time in Coya's cause." Michels claims that of this group only Spot could deal with the Minnesota DFL people. "He would look an official right in the eye and say, 'Tell me what is going on here.'"[12]

Coya's opposition regarded this newly formed organization as a threat to the unity of the DFL. They did not want to have supporters of the Farmer-Labor group split off from the DFL and resurrect the old third party. Thirty years later, L.J. Lee referred to the constitution of Coya's Continuous Volunteers to defend his role in challenging Coya.

The gap widened between the two factions of the DFL. Polarization, with influential people on each side, confused many DFL members who wanted to remain loyal to their party as well as to their congresswoman.

Coya would not be able to concentrate on her legislation after all. The anti-Coya faction had decided on its candidate and she would have to campaign in a primary. After a third term in office—and with an official party endorsement—Coya's seat in Congress should have been relatively secure. However, a recent district chairman was her challenger and, in light of recent events, Kjeldahl told her that she was extremely vulnerable.

The summer campaign was a hard and bitter contest, with many heartaches for Coya. Andy supported Coya's opponent. "I still want Coya to come home. But she's not going to do it," he told a reporter for *U. S. News and World Report*.[13]

Evenson's campaign literature implied that the state DFL endorsed him. Although Coya was the convention-endorsed DFL candidate, a "sample DFL ballot" distributed in the Ninth District was presented as "A Memo from Hubert H. Humphrey" and listed Marvin Evenson for

Congress alongside DFL candidates for the top offices. This "ballot" was divided into three sections: the first promoted Orville F. Freeman for Governor and Karl F. Rolvaag for Lieutenant Governor; the second endorsed Eugene McCarthy for a "Strong U.S. Senator;" and the third stated that "For Full Time Representation Vote for Marvin A. Evenson. A Family Man. For Congress—Ninth District." Evenson's qualifications for office included being a businessman, having four children, owning a home, and growing up on a farm.

When Coya saw this brochure, she had a House page deliver a copy of it—marked "personal"—to Humphrey. [14] There is no record of Humphrey's response—nor is it known whether Humphrey supported Evenson and had authorized the use of his name. Evenson's attack had Coya on the run "constantly putting out brush fires."

She was confident that Evenson could not challenge her record in Congress because she had consistently voted with the Democrats. Of the thirty-four key votes—those considered most important and most controversial by the *Congressional Almanac*—Coya had voted with her party thirty times. [15] Her voting participation in the first session of the 85th Congress was 94% of roll call votes, an excellent record for a Representative on a major committee. However, Evenson attacked Coya on her attendance record. "I am running so the Ninth District will no longer be deprived of representation," Evenson said as the campaign heated up. He accused Knutson of absenting herself when Congress was debating farm bills. [16] The charges were not true, but Coya was vulnerable to the suspicions that were planted. Voters were left to wonder—if not in Congress and not at home, just where was she? With Kjeldahl?

Newspaper editors in the district did not choose to clarify the attendance question. "Now what are the facts?" asked William Dahlquist, editor of the *Thief River Falls Times*. He pointed out that Coya Knutson said many nice things about herself, taking "clear pride" in her "above average attendance record." Dahlquist pointed out that her DFL opponent placed emphasis on her below average voting record, accusing her of absenteeism and neglect of her voting responsibilities. He concluded that it was up to the voters to decide the truth.

Her committee did not make it clear that her attendance record was good. They ran an ad that stated she had never missed any session where farm legislation had been discussed or voted on, but they did not use statistics. The ad was a reprint of an editorial written by Cliff Bouvette for the *Kittson County Enterprise* in which he claimed that Mrs Knutson had a perfect right to urge her constituents to vote for Kefauver. He cited the Kefauver victory as an example of a quarrel where those who believed in dictatorship were injured because they had not had their way.

L. J. Lee responded in an ad stating that it was ridiculous to think that he was against Coya because she opposed his choice of Stevenson. Lee claimed that he chose to work against her because he opposed the "Bouvette-Kjeldahl-Knutson machine" in their attempt to start a new party, which "was one reason Mrs Knutson was away from congress. She is not the same woman I helped elect to the House for two terms." He said a representative should be one who commands the respect and admiration of people in both parties and gives dignity to the position. He concluded by comparing her work in Congress to Nero's fiddling while Rome burned, claiming that she was playing her accordion and writing songs while Benson's farm bill passed through the agriculture committee.[17]

Few voters had the patience to read either of the long-winded ads to discover what was being said. Missing were the customary campaign promotions with portraits and lists of the candidate's qualifications. Before each election a DFL Sample Ballot was printed in district newspapers; in this election it was signed by Ray Hemenway and listed nine candidates. Ordinarily, a congressional candidate's name was listed third, after senatorial and gubernatorial candidates. However, Coya's name appeared in ninth place—at the end of the ballot. Even more unusual was that the box next to Coya Knutson's name was the only one with no "X" marked in it.[18]

Evenson did not overtly refer to Coya's marital problems, but he left-handedly spotlighted them by placing his own family at the center of his campaign. A series of television commercials included his wife and children. *U. S. News and World Report* pointed out that although Evenson did not talk about Coya's family, he "put his attractive wife and his handsome children into a station wagon and drove about the district—a picture of family united."[19]

Although Coya commuted between Washington and Minnesota every weekend, she made far fewer appearances in the district than Evenson. While working on Capitol Hill during the week, she relied on Kjeldahl to keep her informed of the campaign. However, to meet the demands on their time, Kjeldahl was writing and signing his own name on letters to Coya's constituents. Kjeldahl used Coya's letterhead in writing to a Crookston farmer, asking her to organize and head a campaign committee of sugar-beetgrowers and enclosing a draft of a letter to send to five hundred other farmers.[20] The farmer took no action. Letters in a similar vein—instructing supporters to form a "Family Farm for Coya Committee" were also ignored by the recipients. While administrative assistants often corresponded on behalf of their congressmen, Bill Kjeldahl was not accepted in this role. The opposition had labled him "power-hungry" and it stuck.

Coya did not let the fracas get her down. During the campaign she composed several new songs including "General Ike He Had a Farm" and "Koya's Khorus," the latter sung to the tune of "America the Beautiful."

In a lighthearted vein, because her volunteer committee had called Oklee a tiny hamlet, newspaper editor Omer Sundrud defended the town in the *Oklee Herald*, saying that he had had a good deal of resentment against the kind of attitude taken toward the small rural village by newsmen and politicians in Chicago, New York, Washington, D.C. "and other metropolitan areas like Detroit Lakes (population 5,500)."

He complained that Coya's re-election campaign chairman, Gus Landrum of Detroit Lakes, had released a statement that "it is ridiculous to think that Mrs Knutson should give up her seat in congress to return to the menial job of chambermaid in the five-room hotel in Oklee which isn't even a modern hotel." The editor said he was offended—Andy's Hotel was "neat and clean, had two bathrooms, hot water, automatic laundry, automatic dishwasher, clean linen, no cockroaches and no drunken conventions." He concluded by telling those "over-taxed, over-paid and over-fed friends from the big cities that in Oklee people are so friendly that when we get a wrong number on the telephone we chat a while anyway."[21]

Sundrud's humorous defense of Oklee came at a time when Coya was leaving small town life behind. Aside from personal belongings, Coya had taken only some bed linens and sheet music when she moved to Washington in 1954. During the campaign in the summer of 1958 Coya returned to Oklee to retrieve her hope chest and gather a few other items she wanted to take with her. Andy followed her around the hotel, complaining and begging, and she could not stand it. They talked about divorce, and Andy said he wanted alimony. "Not on your life," Coya said. "You have gotten enough." He refused to let her take her hope chest and would not let her have anything else. She managed to take her parents' silverware and a few more sheets of music from the attic. Later she heard he had sold her piano.

The Comstock Hotel remained her campaign headquarters, but she preferred to live at Ray Gesell's home outside Moorhead. Coya was conscious of appearances. Although there was nothing to the gossip about an affair with Bill, Coya prudently refused to stay in the hotel suite. The Gesell family provided a bed on the front porch of their farmhouse, and that summer Coya could come in late at night, park next to the door, and not disturb the family. When she was farther afield in the district, she would stay with other friends.

One of Coya's biggest problems was shuttling between Washington, D.C. and Minnesota to campaign and to appear at various centennial events. She was exhausted, losing two nights of sleep a week on the red-eye flights, and began losing weight.

The 1958 legislative climate of Congress was unusual. While in 1957 there had been a cry for economy, in 1958 the recession as well as the shock of Russia's demonstrated technological capability changed the legislative atmosphere. On November 2, 1957, a month after the Soviet Union had launched Sputnik I—the first artificial earth satellite—they sent Sputnik II into orbit. The second Russian satellite was ten times as heavy as the first, and it carried a dog into space.

In contrast, the U. S. satellite, Vanguard I, exploded. On January 31, 1958 the U. S. successfully launched a very small satellite called Explorer I. It was apparent that the U.S.S.R. had usurped the longstanding technical superiority of the U.S., and control of space became a major issue. The funding of education programs to restore the balance emerged as a national goal.

Coya wrote in "Capital Chat" that "practically every noted authority maintains that not only are we behind Russia but also that we will remain behind Russia until 1962. If we do nothing now, we will remain behind Russia until the hereafter. In the interests of our country—possibly its very existence—I have decided to vote the largest possible appropriation for education."[22]

Speaking on the floor of the House, Coya introduced her "Dollars for Scholars" plan. "Even though education is a right in a Democracy," she said, "we have seen destitute students go by unnoticed. The opportunity for capable students to go to college is the latest horizon to be faced." In previous generations, only the wealthy and privileged could afford a college education, but the GI Bill—which paid for tuition and basic expenses at college for returning World War II veterans—treated everyone alike and opened the doors to subsidized higher education. In 1958, thirteen years after the end of the war, the GI Bill was no longer in effect.

Coya told Congress: "If we are to have an informed electorate, a substantial portion of the population must also know enough to decide intelligently our country's domestic and foreign policies... As a public high school teacher for many years, I was distraught whenever any one of my students had the will but not the funds to go to college. They were capable students... These students were lost to the technical benefit of our country... We cannot disregard any longer the need of these talents when we measure the future of the U.S. industrial potential, world position, and the American place in the space age of our future... We must recognize this tremendous natural resource—the fountain of our future. Title II provides for long-term, low- interest loans to undergraduate and graduate students to enable them to continue their higher education."[23]

Times were right for allocating federal money to education. The college-loan bill, incorporated within Title II of the National Defense Education Act of 1958, passed in the House without a dissenting vote (H. R. 5479) and was signed into law by President Eisenhower.

Coya was standing in the rear of the House chambers when the Speaker announced that the President had signed the bill. "I jumped sky-high, I was so happy," she remembers.

Millions of students would benefit from its provisions in the coming years. Although Coya did not emphasize it, the student loan fund for the first time opened doors of colleges to women who otherwise could not afford it. Under the old GI Bill, women who had served in the nurse corps, women's army corps (WACS), or in the women's navy corps (WAVES) had indeed been eligible for financial aid, but they had been very few in number. Now all women, as well as all men, were eligible for college loans if they needed help.

That summer Coya also spoke for an omnibus education bill that would provide one-fourth of defense costs to bring the educational system up to date. It was a comprehensive bill, including aid for first grade through the senior year in high school. Its long-range purpose was to serve as an alternative to defense spending because "education is a means of defending the nation."[24]

Coya named the bill after Paul Bunyan, the mythical giant lumberjack who could accomplish great things. The printed bill itself was literally big—more than an inch thick. The Paul Bunyan bill was stalled until two years later when Congresswoman Edith Green picked it up. A modified version was eventually passed during the Kennedy administration, and became the first large-scale federal aid to education.

Another bill that Coya introduced was the check-off on tax returns to fund presidential elections, an idea suggested to her by Barney Allen. Taxpayers would be given an option to check a box on their federal return setting aside a one-dollar contribution to fund presidential campaigns. As was the case with the Paul Bunyan bill, it was not passed during Coya's term of office. The bill languished in the Library of Congress archives for several years, until it was rediscovered and passed into law.

Coya requested a million-dollar appropriation to fund cystic fibrosis research, then the third-ranking fatal disease among children (H.R. 12331, May 5, 1958). The bill passed, and the University of Minnesota was awarded a major portion of the research funds. This was the first federal money provided for the battle against cystic fibrosis, and Coya was honored for her work by the Minneapolis-St. Paul chapter of the Cystic Fibrosis Foundation. When Coya flew to Minneapolis for the testimonial dinner that summer, she was met at the airport by a group that included Nancy Sjobeck, a little girl with cystic fibrosis who presented her with a bouquet of roses. Coya's eyes flooded with tears as she hugged the child. Terry, who was among the welcoming party, saw a tenderness and vulnerability that he had not before seen in his mother.

Although Coya had successfully launched education and health bills that passed, she was unable to initiate successful farm legislation. A bill that would have given farmers 90% of parity was vetoed by the Eisenhower administration. She contributed long hours and hard work to the development of the 1958 Omnibus Farm Bill, a major effort to protect and benefit the family farm. That bill was voted down, but set a pattern for family farm legislation that was passed later.

Of the 61 bills Coya introduced during her four-year tenure, 24 related to farming. She initiated legislation that permitted Otter Tail and Polk counties to retain two soil-conservation committees. She introduced a bill providing loans for fur farmers, payments for acreage reserve, a wheat marketing quota amendment, potato grade labeling, auxiliary credit sources for family-type farms, and supplemental direct assistance to extremely low-income family farms. Her criticisms of the "big-business farm policies" of GOP Secretary of Agriculture Ezra Taft Benson filled many pages in the *Congressional Record.*[25]

When she was asked how she could accomplish so much in a short time, she responded that the conflict in her life fueled her. "I am sitting on a powder keg, and working my fool head off." Besides that, she felt like an outsider and had to work all the harder to prove herself. She had never been summoned to Sam Rayburn's "red room" in the basement of the Capitol building where congressmen "in the know" discussed impending bills—but she wanted to be invited. During the 1958 session when the House paused in its work to pay tribute to Rayburn, who had been Speaker longer than any other man in American history, Coya composed a song for him to the tune of "The Yellow Rose of Texas."[26]

Aside from the stress of the campaign and the political dissension within her district, Coya felt good about herself because she was getting much of her legislation through Congress. Yet in Minnesota some constituents were not happy with her record, and her campaign was not going well.

Even though the Sugar Beet Bill that Coya had introduced and followed through passage had added 3,600 acres of sugar beets in her district, one beet farmer was unhappy about the Agriculture Committee's—and Coya's—trip to the Dominican Republic in 1956. The farmer saw the agreement made there as a threat to crop prices, and wrote that local sugar beet acreage had been reduced from 64.8 in 1955 to 63.9 in 1956 "because she and a party of congressmen extended them a glad hand so they could import more sugar cane into the U.S."[27]

Coya's campaign committee complained that they were unable to make any headway in some counties. One of her supporters wrote that he needed plenty of campaign material at the Clearwater county fair: "This is very important because the DFL committee here in this county is not going to do anything for her." Little campaign literature for Coya is available, the committee continued, and "while Mr Evenson and his pals are busy campaigning, all Coya's people can do is distribute a few Doris Fleeson and Drew Pearson stories."[28]

It was a relief for Coya when Congress adjourned in August and she and her office staff could move to Minnesota to campaign full time. One afternoon, Bill and several workers began stuffing 10,000 envelopes with letters to district households. They started work at 3 p.m. and continued through the evening. After midnight, the workers left one by one to go home and sleep. Only Bill continued, working through the night until 9 a. m. when all the letters were ready to be mailed.[29]

Although Bill had a steady girlfriend, campaign work consumed his time. Coya and Bill had decided not to travel together during the campaign. Bill stayed in the background, and he and Coya were not seen together. In earlier campaigns, both Bill and Coya called the Comstock Hotel headquarters "home," but Marge Michels makes it clear that Coya and Bill always stayed in separate rooms. "I could tell you if there was anything between them. There was not. Coya was passionate about only one thing—her job."[30]

At this point in her life, Coya could concentrate fully on her career. Terry, at age nineteen, was taking responsibility for himself. That summer, after his first year at college, Terry had taken a summer job with North Central Airlines in Brainerd, Minnesota rather than continuing his job in Washington, D.C. He wanted to be free to join his mother wherever she happened to be for her campaign. He helped pass out literature, placed flyers under windshield wipers and put posters in store windows, just as he had in other campaigns; but his main contribution was providing Coya with moral support. Terry thought Coya drew crowds on this campaign because she had become a curiosity.

The one DFLer who did campaign with Coya was Representative Eugene McCarthy, who was after Edward J. Thye's U.S. Senate seat. Coya had supported McCarthy's Senate race from the outset and was glad to have him in the district to campaign with her. McCarthy and his wife Abigail were both good campaigners and related well to farmers. Although McCarthy was—like Stevenson—an intellectual, he could talk in language farmers liked and understood because he had grown up on a Minnesota farm.

Coya and McCarthy both chose to ignore the fact that Hjalmer Peterson, who was challenging McCarthy in the primary, had been co-chairman with Coya of the Minnesota Kefauver race. Hubert Humphrey thought that Hjalmer Peterson's race in the Senate primary election would hurt Coya. He wrote, "Hjalmer can hardly press his right to challenge the party's endorsement [of Eugene McCarthy] without supporting those against Coya Knutson's endorsement."[31]

As election day approached, Andy, not Coya, again made front page news in Minnesota. A welcome-home rally for Coya was held in Oklee two days before the election, and drew an exceptionally large audience—more than three times the population of Oklee. The *Minneapolis Tribune* reported that while the congresswoman spoke to the 1,200 constituents, her husband sat alone in their hotel "waiting for her to come and see him." Before the speech, Andy had been asked if he would go to the schoolhouse to see his wife. "She said she was coming home, didn't she?" he asked. Indicating the hotel, he said "This is her home, isn't it? I'm going to sit here and see what she does."

The *Minneapolis Tribune* went on to say that after her address, Mrs Knutson had coffee and cookies with acquaintances. Then she drove out of town. "I'm too busy working to come back and fight a few personal battles," she explained.[32]

But Andy had made the election battle personal—he was publicly backing Marvin Evenson.[33] Andy had appeared at several meetings with Evenson and the two had been photographed shaking hands. Many observers believed Coya would beat Evenson but that in November, she would face a stiff challenge.[34]

Coya says, "I did feel sorry for Andy. He made such a jackass out of himself. But being on the front pages made him feel important."

The day of the primary election, the Associated Press reported that of all the contests, the Knutson congressional bid had captured most of the voter interest because Coya had disregarded the written request of her husband to give up politics and restore their home life.

In the 1958 Minnesota primary election, Coya did it again. On September 9, 1958, she won by a margin of 4,158 votes over former party chairman Evenson. Banner headlines three inches high in the *Grand Forks Herald* hailed her victory: "Coya Nips Come Home Bid." She had gained the majority in 12 of the 15 counties. Only Evenson's home county, Clay, plus the counties of Wilkin and Mahnomen did not give her a majority. Three times as many DFL ballots as Republican had been cast. "The Republican Party suffered a tragic loss," Coya claimed, knowing that crossover votes in Republican counties such as Otter Tail were partly responsible for her victory.[35]

When he conceded victory, Marvin Evenson did not say he would support Coya in the coming election: "The majority gave approval to the candidacy of the incumbent and I respect their decision. I have always been a Democrat and I will be supportive of all DFL candidates to whom people of our district can look with respect and who are a credit to the cause of good government."[36]

Coya carefully pointed out that her home town had voted for her, not Evenson. She wanted everyone to know that the majority of voters in Oklee understood her situation and wanted her to ignore Andy's demand.

Coya had outmaneuvered party leaders, managed to have a supporter elected district chairman and won endorsement by the state convention. She had beaten the DFL leaders' candidate in the 1958 primary just as she had in 1954.

Still, this had been a lonely campaign for Coya. She had alienated her team and now she was outside the locker room with no chance of getting assistance from the coaches. She would be alone on the playing field and facing a tough opponent.

Chapter 15

APPLE PIE
OR POLITICS?

*What shall it be, recipes for apple pie, or discussion of
what women can do in public affairs, or a little of both?
Write us.*

Nonpartisan Leader: January 12, 1920.

After she won the primary election, Coya received a letter from Ray
Hemenway, chairman of the Minnesota DFL Central Committee, who
told her it was necessary that she appear on television with Andy,
Terry, and Andy's brother, Torkel, and that she mention them in press
releases. According to Hemenway, it was a mistake that she had not
stopped at the hotel to say hello to Andy.

Coya ignored Hemenway's command to present her family to the
public. The idea of appearing with Andy at this point was ridiculous.
Hemenway also told her it was imperative that she make peace
overtures to the Lee and Evenson groups, "without bragging."
Coya was aghast. "Heavenly days, why should I do what they say?
They never helped elect me. They did not even help me with money.
Why should I crawl to them? I was glad they got taken to the
cleaners."

Hemenway's next point was the "absolute necessity" of removing Bill Kjeldahl from the payroll. "Your primary fight was won not because of Bill but in spite of him; dumping of the unnecessary loads is a necessity," Hemenway warned. "You will have my wholehearted support up to the time that Kjeldahl re-enters the Ninth District."[1]

There was nothing new here; L.J. Lee had made similar demands two years earlier. Again, Coya ignored state DFL leaders, and Bill Kjeldahl continued to be her office manager. The only concession she made was the continuing agreement with Kjeldahl that he stay out of sight. They would not be seen in public together.

After the Coya, Come Home letter, a few other congresswomen quietly fired their male assistants and replaced them with females. Coya thought it was a mistake. In her opinion, everything functioned more smoothly when men and women worked together. She was convinced that the chemistry of the male-female combination worked to everyone's advantage in problem-solving and creative output. She did not want to have an all-woman staff to satisfy propriety at the expense of good talent and a productive working atmosphere. Besides, it was discriminatory—both to her and to male employees—to avoid hiring men. She had come to depend on Kjeldahl's managerial skills and, whatever rancor there was toward Bill among the DFL leadership, her office staff worked well together.

Coya's relationship with Bill was of quite a different nature than the one portrayed by the DFL leadership. Bill and Coya drew strength from the interplay of their personalities: he was fascinated by her charisma and intelligence; she appreciated his youthful vigor and intellect. The strongest connection between them was a mutual admiration of limitless energy and unquenchable thirst for work. Their intimacy grew out of the long hours and lengthy conversations they shared on the road and in the office. They trusted each other and enjoyed being together.

Kjeldahl looked much younger than his 29 years. Congressman Roy A. Wier (DFL) used to ask him, "Are you 16 yet?" Coya, at 46, thought Bill looked like a kid and it amused her when people meeting him for the first time asked if he were her son. Despite the difference in their ages, Coya and Bill met on common ground: both were well educated and shared social and political ideals.

Coya and Bill focused their attention on the Republican opposition, 45-year-old Odin Langen, who was serving his fourth term in the

Minnesota House and had been elected minority leader in the recent session. Langen owned and operated a successful farm near Kennedy in the far northwestern corner of the district, thirty miles from the Canadian border and six miles from the North Dakota border. Odin (named for the chief god of Norse mythology) attended Dunwoody Institute, a Minneapolis trade school, for two years after high school graduation. In his community he had served on the Kennedy school board, chaired the Kittson County Production Credit Association—a government farm-lending institution—and was a member of the Swedish Lutheran Church.

Langen employed a college student, David Stenseth, 21, as his campaign manager. Like Kjeldahl, Stenseth had analyzed northwestern Minnesota elections and had identified swing precincts in the district, particularly in Otter Tail and Clay counties. Langen had met the young man in early spring while Stenseth, a Crookston native, was working as a student intern at the state capitol . When Langen saw Stenseth's statistics and analysis late that summer, he hired him immediately. After Stenseth graduated from St. Olaf College in June he worked full time for Langen.

Langen's wife Lillian, a tall, dignified woman, was a superb campaigner who "grew on the job," according to Stenseth. She occasionally accompanied Langen and at other times represented her husband at events that were once Coya's turf, such as Ladies Aid meetings. With the gossip about Coya and Kjeldahl lingering, Lillian rather than Coya frequently got the invitations to address women's meetings. The Langen staff also wanted husband and wife to be seen together often, presenting an image of a devoted couple.

Another dedicated worker was Audrey Hagen, the widow of defeated Congressman Harold C. Hagen. Audrey Hagen managed Langen's headquarters in Moorhead and was an astute, experienced politician herself. Determined that Coya should lose, Hagen enlisted her husband's old friends to campaign for Langen.[2]

Coya had four full time staff members: Kjeldahl; Margery Sieber, her Washington, D.C. secretary; Arliss Rae Murray and Terry. Terry had attended classes for a few weeks at Concordia College, but he withdrew because he preferred to campaign full time. Coya was unhappy that Terry was not in college that fall. She had wanted him to go back for his sophomore year.

Langen spoke in general terms on issues of the day. In a foreign policy statement, he asked for peace throughout the world and backed President Eisenhower's strategy in the Middle East. Coya advocated use of the United Nations as an open forum to "talk out" rather than "shoot out" the antagonisms. She said the recent Middle East resolution emphasized armament without showing adequate concern for the people of the Middle East.[3] Although international affairs entered into the campaign, farm prices were again the main concern in Minnesota.

More than issues, people remember Langen's campaign slogan: "A big man for a man-sized job." He was six-feet tall and well built. Stenseth says he "went to the wall" to prevent the use of this slogan, but Langen liked it. It was coined by Flint Advertising of Fargo, the agency that also designed and produced Langen's ads for television and radio. Coya did not use an ad agency.

Langen's campaign was almost a rerun of Coya's 1954 campaign. Like Coya, he would visit a dairy barn at 6 a.m. to ask a farmer for his vote. With his campaign headquarters in the trunk of his car, he would spend a Wednesday in Roseau County and on Thursday drive 200 miles to Otter Tail County to make it seem he was everywhere, campaigning 24 hours a day. He, too, had a loudspeaker on top of his car. While he worked Main Street chatting with locals and seeking out voters in restaurants and shops, his staff would filter into the residential sections inviting people to come into town to meet the candidate. Stenseth says, "Langen was one hell of a campaigner."[4]

Langen, too, had a special song but, unlike Coya, he did not sing it himself. Marvin Lundin, a young newspaperman in Warren, Minnesota, wrote the ballad "Odin Langen, Pride of the Great Northwest," to be sung to the tune of " Davy Crockett". The *Minneapolis Tribune* printed the ballad on its front page, with the headline "Muse is Loose in Ninth District." "No one is more noted on Capitol Hill for her iambic pentameter and poetic feet than Mrs Coya Knutson, the Bard of Oklee. Now the other side has released a poem by Marvin Lundin, city editor of the *Warren Sheaf.*

ODE to ODIN
A man with a purpose
A man with a goal
A man large in body
And larger in soul
A man who will labor

Not grow sleek and fat
On taxpayer's money
and Capital Chat.[5]

"This was the first of twelve verses which laud the tall candidate and hint, we fear, at supposed shortcomings of his woman opponent."

Langen went after women's votes, but Coya thought that he conveyed the feeling that they were nuisances and that only men should hold public office. He spoke to a Crookston women's club on "Your Responsibility and Mine" saying that "it is up to us to see we have men placed in our government that are God-fearing men, that these men see we not only have freedom under law, but to see we have freedom from political tyranny, freedom from overbearing economic burdens and freedom from ravages of war."[6]

Langen did not make overt reference to the problems between Coya and Andy, surmising that his opponent's own party had generated sufficient talk about it during the primary. Both DFLers and Republicans saw Coya as rebellious, a characteristic Langen feared would endear her as the underdog. He and his staff knew that no Republican could easily beat Coya and that Langen needed to win votes from Norwegian Lutherans who were still loyal to Coya but wary of her personal entanglements.

They hoped to appeal to voters by portraying Coya as the local girl who had gone off to the Big City and changed her life style—"farm girl to hot dog girl." There were whispers that Coya had dyed her hair and bought lots of clothes. Stenseth, however, claims that he believes Langen ran a clean, conservative campaign and was concerned about saying anything that might be misinterpreted. He did not want to see Coya reap the benefits of a backlash.

Langen's Volunteer Committee chairman, attorney Maurice Nelson of Fosston, charged in newspaper articles and political ads that Coya had part-time workers on full-time wages. He accused her of shortchanging the Ninth District's taxpayers and padding her payroll. Coya refuted the charges.[7]

Nelson needed to do little research of his own—he simply referred to the primary campaign literature of her defeated DFL opponent, Marvin Evenson. "These issues of payroll padding and absenteeism are so fundamental to good representation of the 9th District that party lines are swept aside," Nelson said. "These are facts people of the 9th district should know."[8] Republicans, like DFLers in the primary campaign, did not acknowledge her actual record of 88% attendance.

Nevertheless, Langen's ads were headlined "Vote for Full-Time Representation," and again attacked the "disturbing and alarming record of absenteeism when full-time representation is so important."[9] According to Stenseth the issue of absenteeism was hit hard because it reminded voters of the suspicions first aroused during the primary: if she wasn't at home and she wasn't in Congress, where was she?

The image of a honey-haired, high-stepping congresswoman who had a handsome and boyish younger male aide had been projected earlier by Evenson's committee and now Langen capitalized on it without having to make direct references. The Come Home letter's image of a lonely, languishing husband whose pleas for togetherness had been spurned while the congresswoman led a fancy life in Washington had been firmly fixed in the public's consciousness. Those images combined to create an effect that was dynamite.

Her insistence that Bill remain on her staff was seen as proof of a romantic involvement. Two weeks before the election Langen's ads reminded voters that "Mrs Knutson publicly defied DFL leaders in her weekly newspaper column and announced she was loaning Kjeldahl to be campaign director for Senator Kefauver in the Minnesota presidential primary."[10] Langen reminded voters that in January 1956 "Mrs Knutson's own party asked her to fire Bill Kjeldahl." Another ad pointed out that DFL leaders were disturbed because Kjeldahl had spent three months in Norway while he continued to draw a $1,010 monthly salary. Langen also charged that Coya's office continued to pay Kjeldahl's salary while he took courses at the University of Minnesota.

Coya could easily refute everything except gossip; she claimed that she was becoming resigned to allegations of an affair with Kjeldahl as being "part of the territory, something that goes with public life." However, to counter the whispering campaign, she could only ask why she was not confronted with specific allegations publicly if her opponents had "so much dirt" about her private life. There was only innuendo, she insisted. She particularly resented comments that Kjeldahl was the "brains" behind Coya—"as if a woman could not be accomplishing so much."

In September, Evenson and his supporters said that they would "sit on their hands" if Coya were nominated. A few DFLers who had supported Evenson, such as Harding Noblitt, did work for her after the primary. Some of the others who needed votes in northwestern Minnesota went on the campaign trail with Coya, but most of them waited out the election. There was little help from the state DFL organization.

Among those who supported her were Governor Freeman and Congressman Eugene McCarthy, who toured with her throughout the Ninth District. Coya, who had always supported McCarthy, was upset by rumors in her district that she was not expected to campaign for him because he was Catholic. Coya saw it as another barrier to break; a Catholic candidate had not been elected to the Senate in Minnesota's hundred year history. "People are people no matter what their label, and a candidate's religion should not determine a voter's decision," she said.

On October 27th, Estes Kefauver campaigned with Coya on a twelve stop, 500 mile swing through the Ninth District. Robert Short accompanied them.

When she was asked by reporters whether the Coya, Come Home letters would be a factor in her re-election campaign, she replied that she had not given the matter much thought. "A person who worries takes a lot of steam out of his own initiative," she explained.[11]

But Coya's banner was drooping. Not only had the gossip campaign accelerated, but the fall of 1958 was cold and rainy. Crowds did not gather on street corners. When she did have an audience, she tried to talk about her record, but clearly she was speaking from a defensive position. The waves of support and enthusiasm she usually felt when speaking to voters was missing. During the chilly, drizzly first days of November, Coya took a final swing through the district, speaking and shaking hands with her constituents.

The schedule was full, the days seemed very long. She got up early every morning, bathed, dressed, and was ready for the campaign trail, "looking neat, not fancy," as Coya was fond of saying. A quick cup of coffee at the kitchen table and she was off. Even though people did not flock to her as they had in earlier campaigns, she managed to keep her enthusiasm. She wanted to take it all in, to experience everything. She loved people and, if she needed adrenaline, she would seek out voters to talk to and that would fuel her energy. But she needed more than people's good will and the euphoria she felt talking with them to keep her going this time.

Nothing prepared her for the "dirty tricks" she encountered. One night when she left her car in front of the hotel in Moorhead, someone put sugar in the gas tank. It ruined the engine, and the expense of replacing the car was beyond her means. Coya had to rely on cars borrowed from supporters until she could afford to buy another one.

Coya was told that a woman impersonating her, wearing a blonde wig, was visiting various bars in the Moorhead area. The Coya look-alike would slap the fellows at the bar on the back and say, "Set 'em up. I am Coya Knutson." It was a humorous tale that traveled fast and, whether or not the story was apocryphal, it captured the public's fancy. People were willing to believe the worst. There are those in the district who still recall Coya's "shameful behavior in the bars" as though they had witnessed it firsthand. Coya, who rarely drank alcohol, never campaigned in a bar. In social situations where alcohol was served, she drank ginger ale. The two alcoholics in her immediate family—her father and her husband—had left Coya with a strong aversion to hard liquor.

However, during this campaign she tried smoking cigarettes and liked it. Cigarettes relieved tension and kept her weight down. But, knowing that a rural woman who smoked was looked upon as "fast," she did not smoke in public.

U. S. News and World Report described the Coya who went to Washington in 1954 as "a fairly typical Midwestern farm woman," but added that in 1958 "her hair is brighter, her dress is modish. Her figure is trimmer."[12] This did not sit well with many of her constituents. Some were unhappy that the four years in Washington had changed Coya's appearance; they liked her the way she used to be. Several Ninth District residents complained that "Coya's looks changed while she was in Washington."

Earl Strinden, a Republican resident of Thief River Falls, thought she looked very little like the housewife she had been four years earlier. When she spoke at a rally at Lincoln High School, he perceived her as loud, even brash—a woman who came on strong. She was not the '50s stereotype of a quiet, unassuming homemaker. She wore make-up, and it gave her a "somewhat flashy appearance" to people not accustomed to seeing women wearing cosmetics. To Strinden, and to others, she seemed out of character for the rural district she represented. Above all, according to Strinden, she was not the person they remembered sending to Washington, and her appearance gave credence to the gossip about her. [13]

Ann Hamre, a former Oklee neighbor, recalls that in 1958 "people talked about her because she had changed so. If she had stayed as she was and let her hair go grey, people would not have talked so much." [14] Coya was irked by these comments on her appearance. She saw herself as "a plain Jane and dumpy."

Coya's self-confidence was bolstered by former President Harry S. Truman, whose appearance at a DFL bean feed in Minneapolis attracted 11,000 supporters. Hubert Humphrey warmed up the crowd by telling them that the "GOP alone is responsible for Ezra Taft Benson as Agriculture Secretary—Benson didn't get there by divine edict, although he may think he did." President Truman told the gathering that Republicans had to answer for the drop in farm parity and advocated 100% parity. He added that the farmers' best customers were well paid laboring men in industrial centers, not the millionaire processer. [15]

After Truman's speech, Coya talked with him and said, "That was a good farm speech, Mr President."

"I should think so," Truman replied. "It is all your speech." He had incorporated much of her 1956 Kansas City speech that he had liked so much. Coya could not have been more pleased.

The opposing view was published in a lengthy *Minneapolis Tribune* article printed the same day that Truman spoke: "Benson may Win Crown as Biggest Farm Spender." A billion dollars had been expended during the Truman administration, but by 1957, the Eisenhower administration had spent $4,800,000,000 on farmers. [16]

Financing the 1958 campaign was a problem. Television had become an important and expensive campaign tool; the Republicans were using it very effectively. The best television reception in the district was close to the WDAY transmitter in Fargo, and that well populated area also included swing precincts. Coya needed more money than in past campaigns, but she could not get help from either the state or national Democratic party. She wrote to House Majority Leader John McCormack asking for assistance. He replied, "I am in receipt of your recent letter. I agree with you. I have urged for some years the appointment of a committee of friends outside the House to raise money for House members of our Party. The Senate does this with great success. However, we have not been successful...I called some friends of mine in recent weeks and they have donated several thousands of dollars. I am of the impression that is how you? [sic] and some 39 other members received #250 [sic]."[17] The question mark must have meant that even the knowledgeable McCormack was not sure whether Coya was among the chosen 39 members.

In the letter he was referring to the Congressional Campaign Committee established and headed by Senator Lyndon B. Johnson in 1940. Johnson funneled thousands of dollars from individuals and lobby groups to selected Democratic congressmen.[18] McCormack promised that he would write to Mike Kirwan and to Jim McDivitt of the Political Action Committee of the AFL-CIO. He closed the letter "with kind regards, I am Sincerely, John." Apparently he enclosed money of his own, for on a separate memo he wrote, "No need of mailing a record or return on this if you do put it in the name of some friend of yours. J."

McCormack's requests to the Congressional Campaign Committee for money for Coya Knutson were denied. Nine days later he wrote to her a second time: "Dear Coya: I am sending the within to you from myself. It will help you out. I know you will win. Good Luck, Kind regards. Sincerely, John."[19] McCormack evidently sent Coya a second contribution of his own.

McCormack knew that the head of the Minnesota delegation would only have to say the word in order to use money from the special fund, since Humphrey had been vice-chairman of the Democratic Campaign Committee raising funds for the 1958 campaign. Senator Lyndon Baines Johnson had written Humphrey the year before: "1956 was one of the most successful years that the Senate Democratic Campaign Committee ever had. That success can be attributed primarily to the splendid job that you and George Smathers did for the Party."

Coya did not know that Humphrey was the fund-raiser, but she did see that Johnson used money like a whip. Besides the fact that the Democrats did not help her, she was not good at raising money herself. She sees it now as "silly on my part, but I did not know what to do, and in Washington I was so busy with legislation, that work, not fund-raising, was uppermost in my mind."

It seemed a very long time from May to November, Coya recalls. Marge Michels agrees: "It was the most drawn-out election I have ever been a part of. But the most difficult thing was that people who had been friendly with each other six months before would not speak to one another."[20]

The Sunday before the election, area newspapers assured voters that the "big drawing card for Northwest Minnesota voters is the show between Coya Knutson and Odin Langen."[21]

Election day was quiet. Coya had already voted by absentee ballot in Oklee. When she arrived at Ray Gesell's farm, she found Terry and Gesell heatedly discussing a segment they had watched that morning on NBC's "Today" show. During an interview Dave Garroway had asked, "Do you think a certain congresswoman will be elected today?" They were angry that Garroway had mentioned Coya's race while the polls were open on election day.

Coya spent election night quietly with supporters at her campaign headquarters in Moorhead awaiting returns. She felt numb. She was so drained and exhausted that she could barely talk. She slept a few hours during the night, knowing that returns from some rural areas would not be in until mid-morning of the following day.

Coya lost the election, 47,863 to 46,473.

Banner headlines in the *Minneapolis Star* proclaimed "McCarthy Elected; Coya Trailing. Democrats Pile Up National Gains."[22] The *Minneapolis Tribune* described Langen as "a towering Kennedy farmer" who campaigned with the slogan, "a big man for a big job." The *Grand Forks Herald* said that the "45 year old former school marm lost to Odin Langen, also 45, a six-foot-five farmer-legislator."[23] The *Minneapolis Sunday Tribune* commented, "Langen, a candidate of considerable legislative and physical stature—he is six feet, five inches tall—campaigned hard and fairly on the issues to win a narrow victory over the blonde incumbent."[24]

While reporting Langen's victory in terms of the candidate's physical stature, the *Minneapolis Tribune* conceded that the race had been won on a personal, not issue-oriented basis. "Langen wisely decided to steer clear of his opponent's domestic difficulties but these were widely advertised anyway in the DFL primary. And it was obvious that not a few Democrats sat on their hands during the campaign. Privately, more than one DFL leader heaved a sigh of relief at Mrs Knutson's defeat. While they would not oppose her publicly in the 1958 primary, it is no secret that they wouldn't support her again."

In "Who Won, Who Lost Around the Nation," *U.S. News and World Report* described her defeat: "Matrimonial disharmony contributed to the only loss of a House seat sustained by a Democrat to a Republican."[25].

It was not a victory for those who believed that voters in the rural Midwest thought a woman's place was in the home. The majority of voters in the ten counties west and north of Oklee continued to vote for her in spite of the letter, in spite of gossip. They wanted her in Congress. A resident of an adjacent county wrote, "The village of Oklee and all surrounding townships went overwhelmingly for Coya. These are the people who are best acquainted with Coya, and more to the point, with her husband, Andy. He will not be awarded the prize for chivalry."[26]

Despite overwhelming support in her home county, there were enough voters who did believe that a "woman's place is in the home—a boy needs his mother most at that age," and "a woman shouldn't be running around."[27] A letter from a woman in Fargo chastised Coya and quoted five different Bible verses including *I Corinthians 7:10*: "Lo, let not the wife depart from her husband," and *Ephesians 5: 22*: "Wives submit yourselves unto your own husbands as unto the Lord."[28]

The votes that had cost her dearly had come from the more populous, urban, Republican-leaning counties in the southern part of the district—Wilkin, Becker, Clay and Otter Tail. Republicans' attitude toward the choice between apple pie or politics were summed up in the December 12, 1958 issue of *U. S. News and World Report* in an interview with Clare B. Williams, assistant chairman and director of women's activities for the Republican National Committee. Williams said that Coya's problem was one reason why a woman who became active on the Washington scene usually was, as she [Williams] was, a widow, or unmarried. Few had husbands. She said that no married woman could go into anything on a more or less full-time basis—whether it was Girl Scouting or politics or becoming president of the General Federation of Women's Clubs—unless her husband was generous in his support and understanding. It had to be that way, Williams said, "because, of course, to any woman a husband is the most important aspect in her life."

Democrats tried to overlook the congressional loss—there was no mention of the Knutson-Langen race in the "Special Election Issue" of the Democratic Digest, November-December 1958, which reported the Democrats' victory in glowing terms. Hubert Humphrey's portrait appeared on the cover of *Time* in an issue that touted the Democratic congressional sweep of 1958. However, the newsmagazine did not mention that the single Democratic congressional loss in the U. S. that year had been in Humphrey's state.

Coya was hurt and humiliated, but she tried not to show it. When a reporter from the *Fargo Forum* asked her about her loss, Coya replied "That's politics," and the reporter observed that she "said it with the air of one who knows how to lose as well as to win." Coya dressed in a rose-colored housecoat and slippers for the interview in her two-room hotel suite. The reporter said that while they talked, Coya smoked cigarettes and fended off the steady clatter of three telephones.

The phones never stopped ringing as reporters called from a nation desperate for comment or interviews from "the blonde, forty-five year old woman who seems hemmed in by trouble." Yet, the reporter pointed out, "those who know her well say it would not be in character for Coya not to fight back." Coya made only one cryptic statement and she would not elaborate: "It's not over yet."[29]

In a 14-paragraph letter to the *Minneapolis Tribune*, Brenda Ueland, a controversial figure in the progressive artistic and intellectual life of Minneapolis, defended Coya. Ueland's letter described Coya as "an intelligent, friendly, daring, warm-hearted, responsive, sensible congresswoman" and pointed out that no newspaper in the United States would think there was news if a wife demanded her husband give up his political work. And no big newspaper would think there was even a "sigh of news in a wife's jealous caterwauls against a man's secretary. Why, it is utterly inconceivable! A joke, a scream! It made us laugh—though wryly."

Ueland also said that she regretted that this episode had shown what animosity there is "against women struggling gamely into public life. We need, as George Bernard Shaw said, intelligent, kindhearted women who transcend, at least once in a while, the idiocy of war and money."

But Ueland best summed up Coya's own feelings when she declared that it was "an excruciatingly painful experience to have everybody in the country believe something vulgar, utterly horrifying about you that is entirely untrue."[30]

Among letters from people outside Minnesota was one from Boston written in a spidery hand: "I am sure it was husbands like yours that made a lot of women of my generation militant suffragettes. I do not think an intelligent, mature man would have entertained the nation with this domestic comedy. Nor do I think he would have humiliated you if he had loved you. I know what I would do with a weak-kneed jackass like that."[31]

Women in Coya's district also had an extended view of what women's roles should be. One of her constituents, a Republican, wrote: "Why must a woman be twice as capable and twice as 'everything' to compete in this so-called 'man's world?' If a man had campaigned as well, he would have been 'in' a-la-Langen. To say I am sorry you lost is saying it mildly. I am especially irate at people who do not consider results of good work done by a candidate in office, [people] who think in horse and buggy style—a woman's place is in the home, no matter what the circumstances in that home may be. My husband joins in the same wish."[32]

Coya had little time to read the deluge of letters that poured in following the election. As usual, she avoided letting the hurt sink in deeply by immersing herself in work. She was angry, and that spurred her to action. As soon as the election was over, she returned to Washington, D.C. determined to clear her name. Indeed, she had been planning her next move when she had told the *Fargo Forum* reporter "It's not over yet."

Chapter 16

IT'S NOT OVER YET

*By 2007 "women's rights" will have passed out of mind.
They'll have to look it up in an encyclopedia to find its
meaning, as we do Shay's Rebellion. Or will the thing
that modern women want pass away like a fad and
leave nothing but a motto and a queer feeling of "Why
did they want that anyhow?"*

*"Knitting or Women's Rights?"
Nonpartisan Leader: October 4, 1917*

Within days of the election, Coya was again front page news. A
friend called to tell her that Andy had filed a $200,000 suit against
Kjeldahl for alienation of affection. Coya could read all about it in the
Minneapolis Tribune.

"The wretched, distraught, distressed husband of Coya Knutson
charged that William Kjeldahl ruthlessly snatched from him Coya's
love. Claiming that boyish-looking Kjeldahl, 30, added insult to injury
by calling him an 'impotent old alcoholic whose departure from the
farm to the nation's capital would shock society.' Knutson said he was
filing suit because Mrs Knutson, the beneficiary of my long silence,
has stood the test of public opinion.'[1]

"Knutson complained that after Coya met Kjeldahl, she no longer had any love or affection for him nor had she any desire or wish for his companionship, love or assistance. He added, "I've got nothing against her. I love her and I want her back.'"

But the text of his complaint was full of innuendoes as well as accusations against his wife: "The defendant (Kjeldahl) moved into the plaintiff's (Knutson's) home in Oklee and occupied a bed therein, and following his ejection from the aforesaid bed, by the plaintiff, he (Kjeldahl) went off with the plaintiff's wife to other towns in Minnesota and other areas, crossing state lines and entering the District of Columbia together in open disregard for the rights of our plaintiff."[2]

Knutson also asked the General Accounting Office to help him *recover* (italics the *Tribune's*) $3,000 which, he claimed, Coya had been reimbursed by the federal government for office space in the Oklee hotel. Knutson complained that the checks, allegedly issued from January 1955 through December 1957, were not co-signed by him. He put in a claim against the United States for $5,000 for improperly honoring those checks.

These suits had been drawn up by Knutson's attorney, Benedict Fitzgerald of Washington, D. C. Fitzgerald's comment to the press was that Andy was neither old (he was 50) nor an alcoholic; the attorney claimed that he had affidavits from Oklee citizens attesting to the latter.[3] The *Tribune* quoted Fitzgerald as acknowledging that during the time Andy had led the Coya, Come Home campaign in her primary, and during the more recent general election when Knutson had apparently had a sudden change of heart—announcing he would vote for Coya to "make her feel better"—Andy had been preparing this suit.

Family members intervened. His brother Torkel, who was so disgusted by DFL infighting that he joined the Republican Party, made Andy realize that he was being used. Although Torkel had publicly supported Coya, he remained on good terms with Andy and visited him regularly. Terry, who had remained in Minnesota after the election to work for North Central Airlines, traveled to Oklee and helped persuade his father to drop the case.[4]

Andy, with Terry's help, composed a letter to Fitzgerald: *"I am firing you as my lawyer because you did not drop the case against Kjeldahl like I told you to do almost two weeks ago. I want you to know that you do not represent me in any way any more and I want you to send back to me all the papers and letters you got from me. The main thing is that you understand that I don't owe you a red cent more than I already paid you. I told you that I didn't have any money when you said you could prove the two counts against Kjeldahl. I told you I didn't have any evidence but you went ahead on your own. A lot of innocent people got hurt, including me. A lot of people said they were trying to help me but they really just wanted to get Coya defeated.*[2]

Andy also wrote to Kjeldahl to tell him he had dropped the case and that he had nothing against him. Andy wrote another letter to the District of Columbia District Court stating that he no longer wanted to sue Kjeldahl, and that it had not been his idea in the first place. He claimed his new lawyer, Maurice Nelson, had told him he could get out of the suit by writing this letter.[3]

Coya had held her counsel throughout the long campaign, never wavering from the statement that she would not discuss personal problems in the press. Now that the election was over, she was ready to break her silence. Convinced that she had lost because of the Come Home letter, she initiated a congressional investigation.

One week after Andy dropped his suit, Coya again made headlines when she disclosed that she was asking the House Elections Committee to investigate the Ninth District election. She refused to answer any questions, saying that the Committee investigation was already underway and would bring out what was pertinent.

Odin E. Langen had received his certificate of election and was scheduled to take his seat in Congress on January 7, 1959. When he heard of Coya's action, he said, "'That's interesting. We conducted a clean campaign.'" He declined further comment.[4]

Coya had a short respite when she went to Philadelphia to accept the Honor Award of the Year from the National Cystic Fibrosis Research Foundation. About 400 people attended the banquet.

With no money to spend on an apartment in Washington, Coya gratefully accepted an invitation from her secretary, Margery Sieber, to be a houseguest. Coya needed her husband to testify at the hearings and borrowed $500 from Ray Gesell's aunt to pay for plane tickets to the Capitol for Andy and Terry.

Terry helped his father pack his best clothes. When they arrived at the Minneapolis airport after an all-night train trip, Terry discovered that Andy was—as Terry had been on his first flight—too terrified to step onto the airplane. Eventually persuaded to board, Andy remained frightened throughout the arduous journey. The Northwest Stratocruiser landed in Chicago, where they transferred to a TWA Constellation for the flight to Washington's National Airport.

Coya and Andy met in a Virginia motel room and, according to Terry, behaved like two strangers. She had grown strong and independent; Andy had become dependent on others. Andy was remorseful but behaved like a little boy who did not know what it was he had done wrong. He said he was sorry if he had had any part in Coya's defeat and hoped that the hearings would go her way.

The reunion was uneasy and unproductive. The usually articulate Coya, still numb from the arduous campaign, was mute. Andy became tearful. Terry was angry. The recent events were so painful that none of the three could face being together to prepare for the hearing that would take place the following week.

The next day her secretary's husband, Harold Seiber, helped Andy write an affidavit that explained his part in the Coya, Come Home letter. Andy had to place a call to Jim Turgeon in Oklee for help in untangling the threads of recent events.

Coya eagerly anticipated the hearings. She wanted to "get the facts out in public." The Special House Committee to Investigate Campaign Expenditures began on December 15, 1958 with Tennessee Democratic Congressmen Clifford Davis as chairman.

Coya's attorney was Walter S. Surrey and his assistant was Monroe Karasik. Ready to testify were a handwriting expert, Charles Andrew Appel, Jr., that Coya had hired; Coya; and Andy Knutson.

Coya charged that press releases and letters had been used in a malicious conspiracy to defeat her. Since she was the only one of the 222 Democratic incumbents in Congress who had been defeated, she believed that the stories related to the Coya, Come Home letters had unfairly prejudiced voters against her. The purpose of the investigation was to discover whether the letters had been part of a campaign of fraud and conspiracy against the congresswoman's re-election.

The letters, actually three in number, were introduced: the *"Come Home"* letter, the *"Command,"* and the *"Press Release."* The Come Home letter had been given to newspapers immediately after the 1958 Ninth District DFL convention. It was handwritten. The Command, another hand-written letter, was mailed to Coya in Washington a week before the Come Home letter was made public. The Command letter had not been made public up to the time of the hearing. A third letter, the Press Release, was typed, but signed by Andy, as a follow-up to the Come Home letter and sent out two days after the release of the Come Home letter.

Testimony from Andy revealed that on April 27, 1958, a week before the Ninth District DFL convention, a meeting had been held at the Walter Turgeon farm home near Oklee. Present were former Ninth District chairman L.J. Lee; the DFL Red Lake County chairman, Walter Turgeon; Walter's son, Jimmy Turgeon, the secretary of the county DFL; and Andy Knutson. Andy was asked the purpose of this meeting.

Mr Knutson: Well, they wanted me to write Coya a letter first for her to come home and then they wanted me to write a letter—they wrote it, and I was supposed to give it to the Ninth District Chairman at the meeting.[5]

Mr Surrey [Coya's attorney]: When you say "they wrote it," who is "they?"

Mr Knutson: It was handed to me by Mr L. J. Lee. I was supposed to give it to the Ninth District chairman Sunday to be read at the convention.

Mr. Surrey: Was it handed to you at this meeting at the Turgeon farmhouse?

Mr Knutson: Yes, I rewrote the letter and he tore it up.

Mr Surrey: And he was given the job of writing this letter?

Mr Knutson: Yes.

Mr Surrey: But did he write it at the farmhouse then or did he give it to you later?

Mr Knutson: He wrote it right at the farmhouse there at the dinner table.

Mr Surrey: Now, was this a letter to your wife?

Mr Knutson: No, this was a letter I was supposed to hand to the Ninth District Chairman.

Mr Surrey: And this letter was written by them—Jimmy Turgeon?

Mr Knutson: And L. J. Lee.

Mr Surrey: And copied by you, and then he tore up the original from which you had copied?

Mr Knutson: That is correct.

Mr Surrey: And it said: *I have as of this date, May 4, informed my wife, Coya Knutson, the 9th Dist. Rep. in Congress that I do not want her to file for re-election to Congress. I expect her to comply with this request. Therefore, because of my interest in the D. F. L. party and as a party member, I believe it should be the business of this convention to discuss a candidate or candidates to file in the primary so that my wife's position will again be filled by a D.F.L. member."*

Andrew Knutson
(crossed out) May 3 (crossed out) 4
Oklee, Minn.

Mr Surrey: That you were to give to the committee chairman?

Mr Knutson: That is right.

Later in the testimony several congressmen questioned Andy:

Congressman Kenneth B. Keating: And that letter is in Mr Lee's handwriting?

Mr Knutson: He tore up the original.

Congressman Thomas P (Tip) O'Neil: When you sat at the farmhouse of the two brothers, whose idea was it? Where did the idea stem from to write this letter?

Mr Knutson: Coya Come Home?

Congressman O'Neil: Yes.

Mr Knutson: Lee was the one who said we had to write a letter like that.

Congressman O'Neil: Whose idea was it after you had written the letter to release it to the press?

Mr Knutson: I am sure it was Lee's idea but we all talked about it, that I should release it to the press that Sunday.

Congressman Keating: These two Turgeon boys, are they Democrats? Is L.J. Lee a Democrat?

Mr Knutson: Supposed to be.

Andy testified that he was also told to write a letter (the Command) to his wife telling her what he proposed to do and how he felt about her coming home. This letter, addressed to "My Dear Wife" and dated April 29 had not previously been made public. It was read:

Coya, I want you to tell the people of the Ninth District, Sunday, May 4, 1958, that you are true [sic] in politics. That you want to go home and make a home for your son and husband. As your husband, I compel you to do this. I am tired of being apart from my family, I am sick and tired of having you run around with other men all the time and not your husband. I love you honey. Your husband.
Andy Knutson

Mr Surrey: That is signed by you?

Mr Knutson: Correct.

Mr Surrey: Did you write that letter?

Mr Knutson: Yes, I wrote that letter myself.

Mr Surrey: When did you write that, after the meeting?

Mr Knutson: That was after the meeting up at Walter Turgeon's.

Congressman Keating: Did you compose that letter yourself?

Mr Knutson: Well, he told me what to write and I wrote it myself at home.

Congressman Keating: Lee told you what to say?

Mr Knutson: Certain things.

The third document signed by Andy, the Press Release, was read into the record:

"I have requested to my wife that she withdraw from the congressional campaign in the Ninth District. I have several reasons why I have taken this action and why I expect her to comply with my request. The first and most important is that since her election four years ago our home life has deteriorated to the extent that it is practically non-existent. I want to have the happy home that we enjoyed for many years prior to her election. Coya hasn't been home for Christmas for 2 years and for Easter the past 3. I have seen our son but a few times and only for brief visits. Another reason for my request is her executive secretary, Bill Cheldahl [sic] who by his actions and dictatorial influence on my wife has taken away the close relationship and affection we enjoyed before. Finally I believe that it is usless [sic] for her to be elected as the decisions that are made are not hers but Cheldahls, an individual who assumes no responsibility, yet dictates the policy of her office.

Press Release from Andy Knutson: Crookston, Minn.

Oklee, Minn. May 4, 1958

Andy said that the handwriting in the copy was not his own, but he had signed his name to the typed copies of the Press Release. Coya's attorney questioned him.

Mr Surrey: And that is not your language, either, is it Mr Knutson?

Mr Knutson: No. It is not.

Referring to the typed copy of the press release, Congressman Keating asked, "Did you read that before you signed?"

Mr Knutson: That is right.

Congressman Keating: Did you understand what you read in there?

Mr Knutson: No, I don't think I really understood what it meant.

Congressman Keating: What time of day did you sign it?

Mr Knutson: I can't remember exactly. I think it was in the daytime. I can't remember when.

Congressman Keating: You do read, don't you?

Mr Knutson: Yes.

Congressman Keating: You mean you didn't understand what it said?

Mr Knutson: Well, I got the hang of what the letter meant.

Congressman Keating: It was not a letter but a press release?

Mr Knutson: A press release.

Congressman Keating: Did you understand it was being given to the press?

Mr Knutson: Yes, that is what they told me, to give it to the press.

Congressman Keating: And the contents of it were clear to you at the time, were they not?

Mr Knutson: There were certain words in there I didn't quite know the meaning of.

Congressman Keating: Did you raise any question about the words that you did not know the meaning of?

Mr Knutson: No, I didn't.

Congressman Keating: Where were you when you signed it?

Mr Knutson: In the hotel near home.

Congressman Keating: In your own hotel?

Mr Knutson: That is right.

Congressman Keating: In what room of the hotel?

Mr Knutson: I was in the kitchen.

Congressman Keating: Was it in the daytime?

Mr Knutson: Yes.

Congresssman Keating: There was nothing about the situation there at that time that would cause you not to understand what you were reading, is there?

Mr Knutson: Pardon?

Congressman Keating: Was there anything in connection with your condition or condition of the premises which would cause you not to understand what you were reading?

Mr Knutson: I don't think so.

Congressman Clifford Davis: Pardon me; he wants to know if you were sober, I think.

Mr Knutson: I get it now; thank you. Yes, I was sober.

Mr Davis: Pardon me, Senator.

Congressman David S. Dennison asked Andy if he had ever asked his wife whether or not the allegations about Mr Kjeldahl were true. Andy said he had not asked his wife.

When questioned why he signed the press release, Andy explained that he had signed it because people in Oklee had told him that Coya and Kjeldahl were "running around" and that Kjeldahl was "dictating to her what she should do."

Although Andy was never shown any evidence that these allegations were true, he claimed he was told that a Republican in the state attorney general's office did have "all kinds of evidence." Andy was told he was the one who was going to do all the dirty work. He was angry about that and upset because "quite a few" people in Oklee were talking about Kjeldahl and Coya. He said he believed the stories because "people kept repeating them and repeating them."

Surrey pointed out that the Press Release discussed Mr Kjeldahl's dictatorial influence, saying that Coya's decisions were not her own, and that these ideas were not in the first letter. Before it was typed, the press release had been handwritten. Andy said that the handwritten copy of the press release was shown to him on Friday or Saturday before the district convention by Jimmy Turgeon. Surrey said that although Andy had assumed that Turgeon had written it, experts had compared the handwritten copy of the press release with writing samples of several people and had come to a different conclusion.

Handwriting expert Charles Appel Jr. gave lengthy testimony comparing the handwriting of Maurice Nelson, Langen's Volunteer Campaign chairman, and the handwritten press release. Appel, a former special agent of the FBI, had testified in espionage, murder, extortion and forgery cases in courts throughout the U.S., most notably in the notorious case of Bruno Hauptmann, convicted kidnapper of Charles Lindbergh's son. Appel gave detailed analysis of the style and design of handwriting in the handwritten copy of the press release. He concluded that it had been written not by Jimmy Turgeon but by someone who had entirely different writing habits. He decided that the design, slant and spacing were similar to the handwriting of Maurice Nelson.

Appel's analysis contradicted Andy's earlier testimony. Andy then gave additional information. He testified that when he had called Jimmy Turgeon from his motel room in Virginia to tell him that people in Washington were raising questions about who really wrote the letter, and that the FBI had the letter, Jimmy Turgeon "got kind of surprised. He said once, I think he said that he wrote the letter, and he said that he would take the blame for it; he wrote it...He said, 'I wrote the letter,' at last."

Turgeon then asked Andy if there was anything he could do to help him. Andy explained that he answered Turgeon: "Well, I told him that I was broke. I told him, you know, my wife don't give me any money."

Mr Surrey. Did he ask you whether there was anything that he could do to help you?

Mr Knutson: That is right.

Mr Surrey. And did he indicate he would send you money?

Mr Knutson: That is the feeling I had.

Mr Surrey. Did anything happen out of that conversation?

Mr Knutson: He said he would have to go see a couple of guys and he would wire me the money.

Andy testified that later that night Turgeon left a message at the desk for Andy to call Benedict Fitzgerald at the National Press Club. But Andy did not call because of his tangled relationship with Fitzgerald.

Andy related that in late September, just after the Minnesota primary, he had received a letter on National Press Club stationery from a Gervaise Trevalion in Washington that told about "that rat, Kjeldahl." The Washington informer suggested he contact Benedict Fitzgerald, a Washington lawyer, who in turn told Andy by telephone that he had "plenty on Kjeldahl." Andy went to Maurice Nelson, his lawyer in nearby Fosston, to seek advice about suing Kjeldahl. Attorney Nelson advised Andy that he could not represent him, and that no one in the district would take the case.

Desperate, Andy engaged Fitzgerald, whose office also happened to be in the Washington Press Club building, to represent him. Fitzgerald filed the suit for $200,000 against Kjeldahl, plus the claim against the United States for improperly honoring checks for office rental. With Fitzgerald's help, Knutson also sued columnist Drew Pearson for $200,000 for slander. Andy said he did not hear from the informant, Trevalion, again, nor could anyone ever find such a person.

Mr Surrey asked Andy what he would say if Mr Nelson actually had written the press release that Jimmy Turgeon had handed to him.

Andy replied that when he asked Nelson's advice, he had not known that Nelson had an official position in the campaign of his wife's opponent.

Coya's attorney repeatedly brought Maurice Nelson back into the picture:

Mr Surrey: If it develops to be that way—that Mr Nelson had really drafted the handwritten copy of the press release Coya Come Home, if you had known that the Democrats who opposed your wife were working with the Republicans in this campaign against your wife, if you had known that Mr Nelson was a voluntary campaign chairman for your wife's opponent, would you have signed that press release that was prepared for you by someone else?

Mr Knutson: No, I would not.

Andy submitted an affidavit, a confession filled with contrition. This time he said he did not know who wrote the letters: *"There were some people that I thought were my friends and who said they were trying to help me but all they really wanted to do was to get Coya defeated. I should have smelled a rat a long time ago but I guess I was too mixed up from all the stories they told to me. They said all over the place in all the newspapers that I wrote the Coya, Come Home letter. I will swear on a stack of Bibles that I don't know who wrote the original letter but I know I didn't write it. It was handed to me by someone already written and the next thing I knew things were moving so fast that I did not have time to stop and think. They kept after me.*

"My lawyer in Fosston never told me that he was volunteer campaign chairman for the Republicans. It's hard for me to trust anyone now. This trick seems to have hurt everybody except the Republicans. I have been a Democrat all my life and I voted for Coya but the Coya, Come Home letter which was written for me has hurt an awful lot of people I didn't mean to hurt. Our boy who has been going to college has been hurt. Coya got hurt. A lot of stories and lies came out of this and most of all the good things Coya worked so hard for got hurt. Not to mention me. It may be too late for a lot of things but it isn't too late to get the truth out into the open. All the good people in Oklee and

*Fosston and Crookston and all the other towns should know that it's
no use having elections if you can't keep them clean. In all my fifty
years I have never seen a campaign like this one."*

*"Coya told the newspapers that she would not talk about her
personal life and I was real proud of her. I wish that it would not
have taken me all these months to tell her and everybody that I am
sorry. It's a terrible feeling for a man to think that he might have had
something to do with defeating one of the the best people in Congress."*

Coya took the stand with a 15-page document of statistics on the
campaign. She claimed the stories and allegations had "absolutely"
been the chief cause of her defeat. She charged that a conspiracy had
defrauded the voters of the Ninth District and she accused Odin
Langen of knowing about and having connection with campaign
tactics used against her. In particular, she cited a television program
detrimental to her campaign that aired on October 29; the television
station would not let her have a copy to use in evidence and she
requested a subpoena.

The committee ruled that exploitation of the Knutsons' family life
was indeed a contributing factor in her defeat; however, no matter
how distasteful the interjection of the family life of a candidate into a
campaign might be, it was something that must be left to the "good
taste of the electorate for correction."

The special committee also concluded that if there was unethical
conduct on the part of her husband's lawyers, it was not within the
jurisdiction of that committee. No further action was warranted, they
ruled.

The day the hearings concluded, Coya, Terry and staff members
returned to the office to pack up everything. They worked as fast as
they could so that they could put the ordeal behind them. There was
additional pressure for Coya because with each day the motel bill
mounted.

While Coya and Terry were working at the office, Andy waited at
the motel for his son to return. Andy was so fearful of the city that he
did not venture out of the motel to eat lunch unless Terry went with
him. Andy stayed sober the entire week he was in Washington,
spending most of his time at the motel reading detective stories. He
was anxious to return to Oklee, but he was too frightened to make
the journey by himself.

Terry, now 19 years old, felt "real sad and lonely." His family was truly breaking up and his parents each had to cope with the heart-breaking aftermath of the Come Home letter. He would have to make his own way in the world.

Even on that last day of packing up her office, Coya worked so feverishly that for the most part she managed to avoid feeling the pain and emptiness. By concentrating on the work at hand, she could numb herself with physical and mental fatigue. Nevertheless, memories and stray thoughts she would rather forget kept intruding.

Toward the end of the day, as workmen sealed the last of the crates, Coya could take no more of the grim reminders of her defeat. She hurried away from the near-empty office, and stood on the Capitol steps gazing past the Potomac River. She wondered whether it was really over. She felt healthy and able-bodied. She loved working and knew she would eventually find a job she liked doing. But politics had put her in the mainstream of life and she wanted to stay there. There was nothing more exhilarating and nothing had consumed her more than politics had. Maybe she would run for office again.

It would be almost two years before another election. Meanwhile she had to eat and find a place to live. Like Harold Hagen, the man she had defeated in 1954, Coya had not had the time, nor the inclination, to think about finding another job.

Coya had met clairvoyant Jeane Dixon two years earlier at a Washington, D.C. party that Senator Kefauver had given for his supporters. The two women had become friends and Dixon knew Coya needed a job. She hired Coya to help set up an office in New York City to start production of "Mike the Magic Cat," a television program. The job in New York City was short-lived and the television show was never aired. Coya was then unemployed for nearly two years.

She knew that the DFL party would prefer that voters forget about Coya Knutson as soon as possible. But Coya was determined to run for political office again. She established residence in Minnesota and again challenged her party in the 1960 election. Both the Ninth District DFL and the state DFL endorsed Roy W. Wiseth, a Goodridge farmer and state senator, for the U.S. Congress. Coya was accompanied on her campaign tour by Bill Kjeldahl, who had recently married and was working for a radio station.

Back on the familiar campaign trail, Coya bucked her party and again strutted her stuff in her own inimitable style. Senator Eugene McCarthy recalls campaigning in the Ninth District with Wiseth. Both were guests of honor for a parade and were comfortably seated in the reviewing stand watching it pass down the main street of town. Just as Wiseth mentioned to McCarthy that earlier that day his supporters had been removing and destroying Coya's campaign signs, a float decorated in sunflowers came down the street—with Coya standing amidst the sunflowers, smiling and waving.

"Looks to me like Coya has joined the parade," McCarthy told Wiseth.

Wiseth could only nod miserably. He was seated where few could see him.[6]

Two weeks before the election, a political column in the *Minneapolis Star* claimed: "DFL Hard at Work to Keep Coya Home." In an attempt to "douse the flickering flames of Mrs Coya Knutson's political hopes," the article reported, Senator Humphrey, Governor Freeman, Lt. Governor Rolvaag, and Democratic National Committeeman Ray Hemenway were all campaigning in the 9th district for Wiseth. The reporter called Coya a "headache to the DFL brass for four years" and a tireless campaigner, while describing Wiseth as a hard plugger but "no fireball campaigner."

Coya did it again. She embarrassed the DFL by whipping their endorsed candidate. She won the district primary, 14,249 to 11,484. In her three primary campaigns for Congress, she had fought her own party each time and had emerged victorious in all three elections.